D0869129

ZAGAT

Westchester
Hudson Valley
Restaurants
2012/13

Plus Nearby
Connecticut and
the Berkshires

LOCAL EDITORS
John Bruno Turiano, Julia Sexton, Lynn Hazlewood and
Elizabeth Keyser

STAFF EDITOR
Michelle Golden

Published and distributed by
Zagat Survey, LLC
76 Ninth Avenue
New York, NY 10011
: 212.977.6000
westhud@zagat.com
w.zagat.com

KNOWLEDGMENTS

e thank Kathleen Cei, Frank Cohen, Janet
rawshaw, Liz Daleske, Jan Greenberg, Carrie
Haddad, Lora Pelton, Dale Salm, James Sexton,
Alex Silberman and Jenn Smith, as well as the
following members of our staff: Danielle
Borovoy (editor), Brian Albert, Sean Beachell,
Maryanne Bertollo, Reni Chin, Larry Cohn,
Nicole Diaz, Jeff Freier, Alison Gainor, Matthew
Hamm, Marc Henson, Ryutaro Ishikane,
Aynsley Karps, Cynthia Kilian, Natalie Lebert,
Mike Liao, Vivian Ma, Polina Paley, Josh Rogers,
Alice Urmey, Yoji Yamaguchi, Sharon Yates,
Anna Zappia and Kyle Zolner.

The reviews in this guide are based on public
opinion surveys. The ratings reflect the average
scores given by the survey participants who
voted on each establishment. The text is based
on quotes from, or paraphrasings of, the
surveyors' comments. Phone numbers,
addresses and other factual data were correct
to the best of our knowledge when published
in this guide.

Contents

Ratings & Symbols	4	Singles Scenes	224
About This Survey	5	Sleepers	225
What's New	6	Trendy	225
Most Popular	7	Views	226
Key Newcomers	9	Winning Wine Lists	227

Top Ratings:

Food 10

Decor 14

Service 15

Best Buys 16

Connecticut/Berkshires 18

WESTCHESTER/ HUDSON VALLEY/CT DIRECTORY

Names, Locations, Contact
Info, Ratings & Reviews 19

WESTCHESTER/ HUDSON VALLEY/CT INDEXES

Cuisines 180

Locations 193

Special Features:

Additions 206

Breakfast 206

Brunch 207

Buffet 207

Business Dining 208

BYO 208

Catering 210

Child-Friendly 210

Dancing 211

Delivery 211

Early-Bird Menus 212

Entertainment 212

Fireplaces 212

Green/Local/Organic 213

Historic Places 214

Hotel Dining 216

Late Dining 217

Meet for a Drink 217

Offbeat 219

Outdoor Dining 219

People-Watching 220

Power Scenes 221

Private Rooms 222

Prix Fixe Menus 222

Romantic Places 222

Senior Appeal 223

BERKSHIRES DIRECTORY

Names, Locations, Contact
Info, Ratings & Reviews 229

BERKSHIRES INDEXES

Cuisines 244

Locations 246

Special Features 248

Wine Chart 252

Ratings & Symbols

Zagat Top Spot	Name	Symbols	Cuisine	Zagat Ratings			
				FOOD	DECOR	SERVICE	COST

Area, Address & Contact

Z Tim & Nina's ◗ *Eclectic* ▽ 23 | 9 | 13 | $15

Yonkers | Dockside Rd. (Harm's Way) | 914-555-1234 | www.zagat.com

Review, surveyor comments in quotes

A chef "passionate about local cuisine" sets the mood at this "unrestored 1920 warehouse" on the banks of the Hudson; a low-budget menu featuring "fresh" produce, including lots of leaves, leaves most diners particularly pleased, but some find it "more than a bit much" to be asked to "pick veggies" from the adjacent "manure-covered" garden by staffers who "do a great job imitating Rip Van Winkle."

Ratings

Food, Decor & **Service** are rated on a 30-point scale.

0 – 9	poor to fair
10 – 15	fair to good
16 – 19	good to very good
20 – 25	very good to excellent
26 – 30	extraordinary to perfection
▽	low response	less reliable

Cost

The price of dinner with a drink and tip; lunch is usually 25% to 30% less. For unrated **newcomers** or **write-ins,** the price range is as follows:

I	$25 and below	E	$41 to $65
M	$26 to $40	VE	$66 or above

Symbols

Z	highest ratings, popularity and importance
◗	serves after 11 PM
Z M	closed on Sunday or Monday
⊄	no credit cards accepted

About This Survey

This **2012/13 Westchester/Hudson V...**
Restaurants Survey is an update reflecting signif...
developments since our last Survey was published...
covers 988 restaurants in Southern New York (plu...
nearby Connecticut and the Berkshires), including 84
important additions. We've also indicated new addresses, phone numbers and other major changes. Like all our guides, this one is based on input from avid local diners – 5,143 all told. Our editors have synopsized this feedback, including representative comments (in quotation marks within each review). To read full surveyor comments – and share your own opinions – visit **zagat.com,** where you will also find the latest restaurant news, special events, deals, reservations, menus, photos and lots more, **all for free.**

ABOUT ZAGAT: In 1979, we started asking friends to rate and review restaurants purely for fun. The term "user-generated content" had yet to be coined. That hobby grew into Zagat Survey; 33 years later, we have over 375,000 surveyors and cover everything from airlines to shopping in over 100 countries. Along the way, we evolved from being a print publisher to a digital content provider, e.g. **zagat.com** and Zagat mobile apps (for Android, iPad, iPhone, BlackBerry, Windows Phone 7 and Palm webOS). We also produce marketing tools for a wide range of blue-chip corporate clients. And you can find us on Google+ and just about any other social media network.

UNDERLYING PREMISES: Three simple ideas underlie our ratings and reviews. First, we believe that the collective opinions of large numbers of consumers are more accurate than those of any single person. (Consider that our surveyors bring some 715,000 annual meals' worth of experience to this survey, visiting restaurants regularly year-round, anonymously – and on their own dime.) Second, food quality is only part of the equation when choosing a restaurant, thus we ask our surveyors to rate food, decor and service separately and then estimate the cost of a meal. Third, since people need reliable information in an easy-to-digest format, we strive to be concise and we offer our content on every platform – print, online and mobile.

THANKS: We're grateful to our local editors, John Bruno Turiano, managing editor of *Westchester Magazine*; Julia Sexton, restaurant critic, food writer and CRMA Award–winning blogger; Lynn Hazlewood, freelance journalist and former editor-in-chief of *Hudson Valley* magazine; and Elizabeth Keyser, food journalist and restaurant critic. We also sincerely thank the thousands of people who participated in this survey – this guide is really "theirs."

JOIN IN: To improve our guides, we solicit your comments – positive or negative; it's vital that we hear your opinions. Just contact us at **nina-tim@zagat.com.** We also invite you to join our surveys at **zagat.com.** Do so and you'll receive a choice of rewards in exchange.

...w York, NY
...30, 2012   Nina and Tim Zagat

t's New

...Manhattan to Cuba to Greece, Westchester is drawing inspira-
...rom all over the map this year, but sourcing ingredients close to
...me. That's in step with the many surveyors who tell us that it's im-
...ortant that the food they eat be locally grown or raised.

HOT SPOTS: As has been the trend in recent years, many of the county's most-anticipated debuts are coming from NYC-trained chefs. Scott Riesenberger, recently of **Corton** in TriBeCa, unveiled **Hudson,** bringing farm-to-table fare to the Haymount House mansion in Briarcliff Manor. Michael Psilakis, who made his name at Manhattan's **Anthos, Kefi** and on the Food Network, is readying **MP Taverna,** which will serve updated Greek fare in Irvington. And Jean-Georges Vongerichten, a weekend resident of Waccabuc, is set to open a Pound Ridge restaurant in late 2012 with a modern locavore menu similar to that of his **ABC Kitchen.**

HOPS HAPPY: Westchester is poised to become a beer aficio-nado's mecca with the arrival of **Craftsman Ale House** in Harrison, **Growlers Beer Bistro** in Tuckahoe and **Thornwood Ale House.** Even **Polpettina** in Eastchester and **Club Car** in Mamaroneck make beer a bragging point with pairing dinners and rotating craft beer on tap, respectively. Microbrews and small bites are also the focus of **MTK Tavern,** opening this spring in Mt. Kisco.

IT'S ALL GREEK (AND LATIN): Greek food reigned su-preme with both casual entries like **Ionian Grill** in New Rochelle and **Mythos** in Thornwood as well as the more stylish **Nemea Greek Taverna** in Mamaroneck. We also saw our ethnic options diversify with a spate of Latin American newcomers, from Rafael Palomino's **Bistro Latino** in Tuckahoe (Latin fusion) to **Sofrito** and **Siete Ocho Siete** in White Plains and New Rochelle (Puerto Rican), respectively, to **Salsa Fresca** in Bedford Hills (Mexican) and **La Bella Havana** in Yonkers (Cuban).

HUDSON VALLEY HIGHLIGHTS: The Valley saw an influx of international flair via **A Tavola,** serving farm-fresh Italian in New Paltz; **Panzur,** dispensing nose-to-tail Spanish specialties in Tivoli; **Ramiro's,** offering Nuevo Latino in Mahopac; and **Cinnamon,** bringing regional Indian and Sri Lankan cuisine to Rhinebeck. On the French front came a flurry of new bistros, notably **Alain's** in Nyack, **Cafe Le Perche** in Hudson and the snazzy **Brasserie 292** in Poughkeepsie. Taverns are on the uptick too, providing an easygoing welcome for rea-sonably priced American eats. In Rhinebeck, the folks behind **Arielle** launched **Liberty Public House** in the atmospheric Starr Building. New Paltz's **Rock and Rye Tavern** blends a bygone vibe and pre-Prohibition cocktails with a modern menu, while the **Bangall Whaling Company** brings upscale pub grub to the boonies of Dutchess County. Expect fancier New American fare at **Swift,** the restaurant in The Roundhouse at Beacon Falls hotel and **Crimson Sparrow,** a stylish launch from alumni of Manhattan's famed **wd-50,** both opening this spring.

Southern New York
May 30, 2012

John Bruno Turia...
Lynn Hazlev...

Vote at za...

Most Popular

This list is plotted on the map at the back of this book.

1. X2O Xaviars | *American*
2. Blue Hill/Stone Barns | *American*
3. Tarry Lodge | *Italian*
4. Xaviars/Piermont | *American*
5. Harvest/Hudson | *Ital./Med.*
6. Red Hat on River | *American*
7. Rest. X/Bully Boy | *American*
8. Crabtree's Kittle Hse. | *American*
9. La Panetière | *French*
10. Buffet de la Gare | *French*
11. Cookery | *Italian*
12. Iron Horse Grill | *American*
13. Freelance Cafe | *American*
14. BLT Steak | *Steak*
15. Haiku | *Asian*
16. Lefteris Gyro | *Greek*
17. Cheesecake Factory | *American*
18. Lusardi's | *Italian*
19. Eastchester Fish | *Seafood*
20. La Crémaillère | *French*
21. City Limits | *Diner*
22. Equus | *American/French*
23. American Bounty | *American*
24. Moderne Barn | *American*
25. Mulino's | *Italian*
26. Ocean Hse. | *Seafood*
27. Sonora | *Nuevo Latino*
28. Terrapin | *American*
29. Gigi Tratt. | *Italian/Med.*
30. Aroma Osteria | *Italian*
31. An American Bistro | *American*
32. Serevan | *Mediterranean*
33. Sushi Mike's | *Japanese*
34. Rosie's Bistro | *Italian*
35. 121 Rest. | *American*
36. Wasabi/Grill* | *Japanese*
37. Escoffier | *French*
38. Frank Pepe Pizzeria | *Pizza*
39. Le Château | *French*
40. Le Provençal* | *French*
41. Ruth's Chris | *Steak*
42. Caterina de Medici | *Italian*
43. Hudson Hse. Nyack | *American*
44. Il Cenàcolo | *Italian*
45. Artist's Palate | *American*
46. Aberdeen | *Chinese*
47. Zephs' | *American/Eclectic*
48. Bedford Post/Farm | *American*
49. Le Petit Bistro | *French*
50. Il Barilotto | *Italian*

Many of the above restaurants are among the Westchester/Hudson Valley area's most expensive, but if popularity were calibrated to price, a number of other restaurants would surely join their ranks. To illustrate this, we have added two pages of Best Buys on pages 16–17.

Key Newcomers

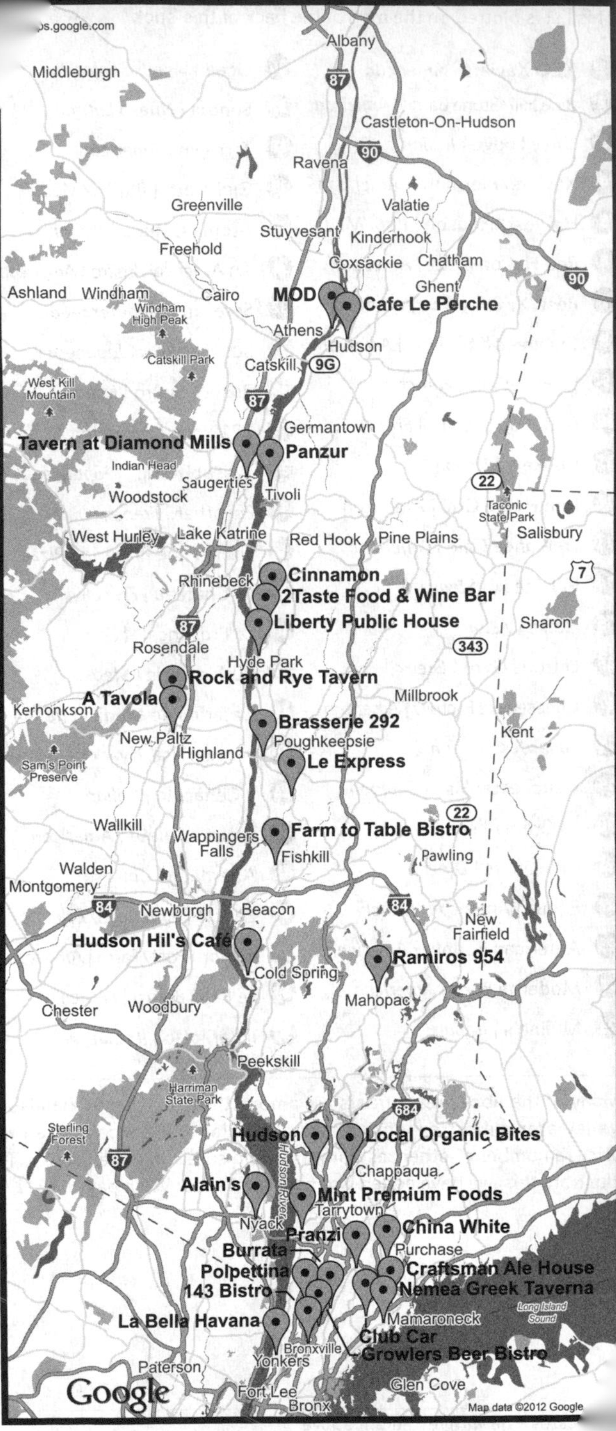

Key Newcomers

Our editors' picks among this year's arrivals. See full list at p. 206.

Alain's | *French* | Bistro fare in Nyack

A Tavola | *Italian* | New Paltz arrival with NYC pedigree

Brasserie 292 | *French* | Chic entry on Poughkeepsie's Main Street

Burrata | *Pizza* | Neapolitan pies in Eastchester

Cafe Le Perche | *French* | Hudson patisserie and bistro

China White | *Chinese* | Modern Asian in Purchase

Cinnamon | *Indian* | Regional eats spice up Rhinebeck

Club Car | *American* | Elegant dining in Mamaroneck's landmark train station

Craftsman Ale House | *American* | Beer lover's haven in Harrison

Farm to Table Bistro | *American* | Local and seasonal eats in Fishkill

Growlers Beer Bistro | *American* | Craft brews and small plates in Tuckahoe

Hudson | *American* | Farm-to-table fare in a Briarcliff mansion

Hudson Hil's Café | *American* | Cheerful Cold Spring locavore

La Bella Havana | *Cuban* | Bit of Havana in Yonkers

Le Express | *French* | Convivial Poughkeepsie bistro

Liberty Public House | *American* | Set in Rhinebeck's historic Starr building

Local Organic Bites | *American* | Sweets and snacks in Chappaqua

Mint Premium Foods | *Med* | Tarrytown cafe and market in expanded digs

MOD | *American* | Homey Hudson newcomer

Nemea Greek Taverna | *Greek* | Updated classics in Mamaroneck

Panzur | *Spanish* | Tapas in Tivoli

Park 143 Bistro | *American* | Swank stop in Bronxville

Polpettina | *Italian* | Pizza and locavore eats in Eastchester

Pranzi | *Italian* | Contempo Italian in White Plains' Trump Tower

Ramiro's 954 | *Nuevo Latino* | Lively Mahopac arrival

Rock and Rye Tavern | *American* | Cocktails and seasonal fare in New Paltz

Tavern at Diamond Mills | *American* | Upscale hotel dining in Saugerties

Taste Food & Wine Bar | *American* | French-inflected cuisine in Hyde Park

p Food

Sushi Nanase | *Japanese*

28 Xaviars/Piermont | *American*
Il Cenàcolo | *Italian*
Freelance Cafe | *American*
Buffet de la Gare | *French*
Blue Hill/Stone Barns | *Amer.*

27 Escoffier | *French*
La Crémaillère | *French*
Caterina de Medici | *Italian*
La Panetière | *French*
Rest. X/Bully Boy | *American*
X2O Xaviars | *American*
Ocean Hse. | *Seafood*
Arch | *Eclectic*
Iron Horse Grill | *American*
Serevan | *Mediterranean*
Il Barilotto | *Italian*
No. 9 | *American*

26 Big W's Roadside | *BBQ*
Aroma Osteria | *Italian*

Rraci | *Italian*
Apple Pie | *Bakery/Sandwiches*
Cookery | *Italian*
American Bounty | *American*
Marcello's | *Italian*
Sapore | *Steak*
Wasabi/Grill | *Japanese*
Back Yard | *American*
Restaurant North | *American*
Ship Lantern | *Amer./Cont.*
Sushi Mike's | *Japanese*
Artist's Palate | *American*
Spadaro | *Italian*

25 Zephs' | *American/Eclectic*
Hajime | *Japanese*
McKinney & Doyle | *American*
St. Andrew's | *American*
Coromandel | *Indian*
Mima Vinoteca | *Italian*
Eastchester Fish | *Seafood*

BY CUISINE

AMERICAN (NEW)

28 Xaviars/Piermont
Freelance Cafe
Blue Hill/Stone Barns
27 Rest. X/Bully Boy Bar
X2O Xaviars

AMERICAN (TRAD.)

25 Village TeaRoom
24 Sweet Sue's
Birdsall House
Peekamoose
23 Catherine's

BURGERS

23 Flatiron
22 Piper's Kilt
Candlelight Inn
Blazer Pub
Pony Express

CHINESE

23 Aberdeen
22 Golden House
21 China Rose
20 Bao's Chinese
Empire Hunan

CONTINENTAL

26 Ship Lantern
23 Jennifer's
Canterbury Brook
22 Sammy's Downtown
21 Swiss Hütte

ECLECTIC

27 Arch
25 Zephs'
Calico
Nina
22 Crew

FRENCH

28 Buffet de la Gare
27 Escoffier
La Crémaillère
La Panetière
25 Equus

FRENCH BISTRO

25 Le Petit Bistro
24 Café Les Baux
Chiboust
23 Encore Bistro
Le Provençal

Excludes places with low votes, unless otherwise indicated

Vote at zap

INDIAN

- 25 Coromandel
- Tanjore
- Mughal Palace
- 24 Orissa
- 23 Jaipore Indian

ITALIAN

- 28 Il Cenàcolo
- 27 Caterina de Medici
- Il Barilotto
- 26 Aroma Osteria
- Rraci

JAPANESE

- 29 Sushi Nanase
- 26 Wasabi/Wasabi Grill
- Sushi Mike's
- 25 Hajime
- Azuma Sushi

MEDITERRANEAN

- 27 Serevan
- 24 Gigi Tratt.
- Il Sogno
- Chiboust
- 23 Moscato

MEXICAN

- 23 Que Chula es Puebla
- Coyote Flaco
- La Puerta Azul

- 22 Santa Fe (Tivoli)
- Cafe Maya/Maya Car
- Tomatillo

PIZZA

- 25 Johnny's
- 24 Frank Pepe Pizzeria
- Baba Louie's
- 23 Sal's Pizza
- 22 Anthony's Pizza

PUB FOOD

- 22 Piper's Kilt
- Bridge View Tavern
- Candlelight Inn
- Blazer Pub
- 21 Raccoon Saloon

SEAFOOD

- 27 Ocean Hse.
- 25 Eastchester Fish
- 23 Ruby's Oyster
- Aquario
- 22 Conte's Fishmkt.

STEAKHOUSES

- 26 Sapore
- 25 Ruth's Chris
- 24 Frankie & Johnnie's
- Morton's
- Willett House

BY SPECIAL FEATURE

BREAKFAST

- 26 Apple Pie Bakery
- 25 Village TeaRoom
- Equus
- 24 Sweet Sue's
- 21 Le Jardin du Roi

BRUNCH

- 27 X2O Xaviars
- Arch
- 25 McKinney & Doyle
- Crabtree's Kittle House
- 23 Bedford Post/Barn

BUSINESS DINING

- 27 La Panetière
- 24 Mulino's
- Benjamin Steak
- 23 BLT Steak
- 22 42

CHILD-FRIENDLY

- 26 Sushi Mike's
- 24 Bear Cafe
- 23 Blue Dolphin
- 21 Wobble Café
- 19 City Limits

HOTEL DINING

- 27 No. 9 (Simmons' Way Inn)
- 25 Ruth's Chris (Marriott)
- Crabtree's Kittle House
- Bedford Post/Farm
- 24 Glenmere

LATE DINING

- 24 Mulino's
- 23 Don Coqui
- 22 Piper's Kilt
- Candlelight Inn
- 21 Le Jardin du Roi

FOR A DRINK

- lue Hill/Stone Barns
- Rest. X/Bully Boy Bar
- Restaurant North
- Armadillo B&G
- 4 Mulino's

SINGLES SCENES

- 24 Frankie & Johnnie's
- 23 Hudson Hse. Nyack
- Zuppa
- 22 121 Rest.
- 19 Porter House

TRENDY PLACES

- 26 Cookery
- Restaurant North
- 24 Birdsall House
- Tarry Lodge
- 22 Moderne Barn

WINNING WINE LISTS

- 28 Xaviars/Piermont
- Il Cenàcolo
- Buffet de la Gare
- Blue Hill/Stone Barns
- 27 La Crémaillère

BY LOCATION

WESTCHESTER

ARMONK

- 26 Restaurant North
- 23 Kira
- 22 Moderne Barn
- 21 Made In Asia
- Beehive

BRIARCLIFF MANOR

- 24 Yama Fuji
- 22 Flames Steak
- 19 Terra Rustica
- Amalfi
- Squires

BRONXVILLE

- 24 Japan Inn
- 23 Elia Taverna
- Rosie's Bistro
- 22 Sammy's Downtown
- Haiku

DOBBS FERRY

- 26 Cookery
- Sushi Mike's
- 24 Orissa
- 23 Scaramella's
- 22 Tomatillo

HARRISON

- 25 Hajime
- Tratt. Vivolo
- Emilio Ristorante
- 21 Gus's Franklin Pk.
- 20 Halstead Ave. Bistro

HARTSDALE

- 25 Azuma Sushi
- 23 Tsuru

- 22 Masala Kraft Café
- Caffé Azzurri
- 21 Frankie & Fanucci's

IRVINGTON

- 25 Mima Vinoteca
- 23 Chutney Masala
- Red Hat on River
- 21 Il Sorriso
- 19 River City Grille

LARCHMONT

- 25 Plates
- 24 Lusardi's
- La Villetta
- 23 Encore Bistro
- Pascal's

MAMARONECK

- 24 Il Castello
- 23 Le Provençal
- Sal's Pizza
- Rani Mahal
- Turkish Meze

MT. KISCO

- 23 Neo World Bistro
- La Camelia
- Via Vanti!
- 22 Passage to India
- Conte's Fishmkt.

NEW ROCHELLE

- 26 Spadaro
- 25 Coromandel
- 23 Don Coqui
- Coyote Flaco
- 22 Modern Rest./Pizza

PLEASANTVILLE

27	Iron Horse Grill
24	Haven
22	Pony Express
20	A' Mangiare
	Mediterraneo

PORT CHESTER

24	Sonora
	Il Sogno
	Tarry Lodge
	Piero's
	Willett House

RYE

27	La Panetière
24	Frankie & Johnnie's
23	Ruby's Oyster
	Koo
	Watermoon

SCARSDALE

25	Eastchester Fish
23	Moscato

	Meritage
22	808 Bistro
	Tengda

TARRYTOWN

25	Ruth's Chris
	Equus
24	Chiboust
22	Caravela
21	Lefteris Gyro

WHITE PLAINS

29	Sushi Nanase
24	Mulino's
	Morton's
	Benjamin Steak
23	Seasons Japanese

YONKERS

27	X2O Xaviars
24	Frank Pepe Pizzeria
	Valentino's
23	Tombolino's
	Zuppa

HUDSON VALLEY
(NORTH OF WESTCHESTER)

COLUMBIA COUNTY

24	Swoon Kitchenbar
	Baba Louie's
23	Local 111
22	Ca'Mea
21	Swiss Hütte

DUTCHESS COUNTY

27	Escoffier
	Caterina de Medici
	Serevan
	Il Barilotto
26	Big W's Roadside

ORANGE COUNTY

28	Il Cenàcolo
26	Back Yard
25	Il Tesoro
	Nina
24	Glenmere

PUTNAM COUNTY

27	Arch
26	Rraci
24	Riverview
23	Jaipore Indian
	Cathryn's

ROCKLAND COUNTY

28	Xaviars/Piermont
	Freelance Cafe
27	Rest. X/Bully Boy Bar
26	Marcello's
	Wasabi/Wasabi Grill

ULSTER COUNTY

25	Village TeaRoom
	Armadillo B&G
	Main Course
	Cucina
	Cafe Tamayo

p Decor

2 Glenmere	Charlotte's
28 Blue Hill/Stone Barns	Arch
Equus	**24** Two Spear Street
X2O Xaviars	American Bounty
27 La Panetière	Il Cenàcolo
Caterina de Medici	Rest. X/Bully Boy Bar
Harvest/Hudson	Half Moon
42	Bedford Post/Barn
Le Château	Thyme
26 La Crémaillère	Red Devon
Moderne Barn	Bird & Bottle Inn
Red Hat on River	Sapore
Bull & Buddha	**23** BLT Steak
Bedford Post/Farm	Il Barilotto
25 Aroma Osteria	Shadows on Hudson
Escoffier	Cena 2000
Crabtree's Kittle House	Iron Forge Inn
Tavern at Beekman	Serevan
Xaviars/Piermont	Buffet de la Gare
Plumbush Inn	Terrapin

OUTDOORS

Bartaco	Karma Lounge
Cena 2000	Red Hat on River
Dolphin	Tarry Lodge
Glenmere	Tavern/Diamond Mills
Half Moon	Vox
Harvest/Hudson	Would

ROMANCE

Bedford Post/Farm	Equus
Bird & Bottle Inn	La Crémaillère
Blue Hill/Stone Barns	La Panetière
Buffet de la Gare	No. 9
Crabtree's Kittle House	Xaviars/Piermont

ROOMS

Blue Hill/Stone Barns	Glenmere
Chateau Hathorn	Hudson
Equus	La Panetière
Escoffier	Moderne Barn
42	X2O Xaviars

VIEWS

Cena 2000	Red Hat on River
42	Shadows on Hudson
Half Moon	Striped Bass
Harvest/Hudson	Tavern/Gunk
Mohonk Mtn. House	X2O Xaviars

Vote at zaga

Top Service

28 Blue Hill/Stone Barns

27 Xaviars/Piermont
La Panetière
Arch

26 Freelance Cafe
La Crémaillère
X2O Xaviars
Buffet de la Gare
Il Cenàcolo
Ship Lantern
Iron Horse Grill
Rest. X/Bully Boy Bar
Escoffier

25 Glenmere
Aroma Osteria
Equus
Rraci
Zephs'
Café Barcel
No. 9*

Serevan*
Il Barilotto
Caterina de Medici
Crabtree's Kittle House
Le Château
Tratt. Vivolo*
Flatiron
Emilio Ristorante
La Fontanella
Il Castello
Julianna's
Restaurant North

24 Iron Forge Inn
Tombolino's
St. Andrew's
American Bounty
Mulino's
Marcello's
Ruth's Chris
Back Yard

Best Buys

Everyone loves a bargain, and the Westchester/Hudson Valley area offers plenty of them. All-you-can-eat options are mostly for lunch and/or brunch. For prix fixe menus, call ahead for availability.

ALL YOU CAN EAT

25 Coromandel
Tanjore
Mughal Palace
23 Jaipore Indian
Rani Mahal
22 Bukhara Bistro
Q Restaurant
21 Malabar Hill
Copacabana
Swaddee Hse.
Tandoori Taste
20 Bollywood
19 Abis

BYO

27 Ocean Hse.
26 Big W's Roadside
22 Masala Kraft Café
21 Thai Angels
Wobble Café
Red Hook Curry Hse.
Turkish Cuisine
20 Shiraz
16 Temptations Cafe

EARLY-BIRD

26 Ship Lantern
25 Eastchester Fish
Plates
24 Orissa
23 Le Canard Enchaîné
20 Enzo's
19 Grande Centrale
Zitoune
Pas-Tina's
18 Mt. Ivy Cafe
Pasta Cucina

FAMILY-STYLE

26 Marcello's
Spadaro
25 Coromandel
24 Valentino's
21 China Rose
Frank Guido's Little Italy
Il Forno
20 Piatto Grill

OFFBEAT

24 Birdsall House
23 Neo World Bistro
22 Conte's Fishmkt.
Cafe Mirage
Bridge View Tavern
New World
Would
21 Gusano Loco
Max's Memphis BBQ
Yobo
19 Painter's

PRIX FIXE LUNCH

27 La Panetière ($32)
Rest. X/Bully Boy Bar ($25)
X2O Xaviars ($25)
26 Cookery ($21)
23 Le Canard Enchaîné ($15)
Turkish Meze ($10)
21 Quinta Steak ($10)
La Riserva ($12)
La Stazione ($25)
Posto 22 ($11)

PRIX FIXE DINNER

25 Village TeaRoom ($22)
24 Bear Cafe ($20)
23 Canterbury Brook ($18)
Tombolino's ($31)
22 Harvest/Hudson ($28)
Jackie's Bistro ($27)
20 Halstead Ave. Bistro ($22)
Wild Ginger ($19)
Mamma Assunta ($25)

QUICK BITE

26 Apple Pie Bakery
25 Johnny's
24 Poppy's ▽
22 Masala Kraft Café
Another Fork/Road
Pony Express
21 Turkish Cuisine
20 Blue Plate
Eveready Diner
AJ's Burgers
18 Red Rooster
Chat

BEST BUYS: BANG FOR THE BUCK

In order of Bang for the Buck rating.

1. Soul Dog
2. Walter's
3. Bagels & More
4. Red Rooster
5. Apple Pie Bakery
6. Bread Alone
7. AJ's Burgers
8. Harney & Sons
9. Big W's Roadside
10. Portofino Pizza
11. Sal's Pizza
12. Irving Farm Coffee
13. Eveready Diner
14. Pony Express
15. Lange's Deli
16. Anthony's Pizza
17. Sweet Sue's
18. Così
19. Frank Pepe Pizzeria
20. Daily Planet
21. Frankie & Fanucci's
22. Baba Louie's
23. Masala Kraft Café
24. Egg's Nest
25. Blazer Pub
26. Johnny's
27. Aversano's
28. Rue des Crêpes
29. Main Course
30. Another Fork/Road
31. Sukhothai
32. Tomatillo
33. Golden House
34. Amedeos Pizzeria
35. Red Hook Curry Hse.
36. Piper's Kilt
37. Wobble Café
38. Lefteris Gyro
39. Bao's Chinese
40. Aroi Thai

BEST BUYS: OTHER GOOD VALUES

Abatino's
Babycakes Cafe
Bartaco
Bellizzi
Boitson's
Cafe Mozart
Caffé Macchiato
City Limits
Coyote Flaco
Don Juan
D Thai Kitchen
Earth Foods
Friends & Family
Gaby's Cafe
Gunk Haus
Homespun Foods
Ionian
Karamba Café
'isco Kosher
'ibela

La Manda's
Larchmont Tavern
Little Kabab Station
Little Mexican Cafe
Niko's Greek
On the Way Café
Oriole 9
Poppy's
Q Restaurant
Red Lotus
Rye Roadhouse
Seasons Japanese
Taiim Falafel Shack
Tandoori Taste
Thai Angels
Turkish Cuisine
Twisted Soul
Ümami Café
Westchester Burger
ZaZa

Thomas Henkelmann | *French*
Jean-Louis | *French*

Cafe Silvium | *Italian*

27) Harvest Supper | *American*
Bernard's | *French*
Tawa | *Indian*
Schoolhse./Cannondale | *Amer.*

25) Capital Grille | *Steak*
Valbella | *Italian*
Adrienne | *American*
Coromandel | *Indian*
Meli-Melo | *French*
Columbus Park | *Italian*
Bistro Bonne Nuit | *French*
Chef Luis | *American*
Brasitas | *Pan-Latin*
Colony Grill | *Pizza*

26) Luca Ristorante | *Italian*
Rebeccas | *American*
Ondine | *French*

BY LOCATION

DANBURY

26) Ondine
23) Koo
22) Café on the Green
21) Sesame Seed
18) Chuck's Steak

DARIEN

25) Coromandel
24) Ching's/Wild Ginger
Aux Délices/Ponzek
23) Little Thai
22) Burgers/Shakes

GREENWICH

28) Thomas Henkelmann
Jean-Louis
26) Rebeccas
25) Meli-Melo
24) Elm St. Oyster

NEW CANAAN

27) Harvest Supper
25) Bistro Bonne Nuit
Chef Luis
24) Ching's/Wild Ginger
Thali

RIDGEFIELD

27) Bernard's
26) Thali
24) Luc's Café
23) Sagi
Little Pub

STAMFORD

27) Tawa
26) Cafe Silvium
25) Capital Grille
Coromandel
Columbus Park

THE BERKSHIRES' TOP FOOD

27) Old Inn/Green | *American*
Blantyre | *American/French*
25) Wheatleigh | *American/French*

Nudel | *American*
Tratt. Rustica* | *Italian*

WESTCHESTER/ HUDSON VALLEY WITH NEARBY CONNECTICUT TOWNS RESTAURANT DIRECTORY

FOOD | DECOR | SERVICE | COST

Abatino's *Italian*

20 | 14 | 18 | $27

North White Plains | Super Stop & Shop Ctr. | 670 N. Broadway (bet. Central Westchester Pkwy. & Cloverdale Ave.) | 914-686-0380 | www.abatinosrestaurant.com

Every neighborhood needs a "local haunt" and this "likable" Italian in North White Plains fits the bill with "better-than-average" "home-style" fare, "solid" pizzas and a "friendly" vibe; true, the decor is on the "spartan" side, but the pricing's "economical" and it's a "low-stress" stop for takeout.

Aberdeen *Chinese*

23 | 12 | 19 | $31

White Plains | Marriott Residence Inn | 3 Barker Ave. (Cottage Pl.) | 914-288-0188 | www.aberdeenwhiteplains.com

"When you can't make it to Flushing", try this "authentic" Chinese in the White Plains Marriott Residence Inn, a "classic" famed for its "wonderful", "fresh" dim sum and "excellent" Cantonese seafood straight "from the tanks"; although the "dreary", "run-down" looks are "not up to the quality of the food", tabs are modest and service "personal" (ask for recommendations), so there's a reason it's a "mob scene" on weekends.

Abis *Japanese*

19 | 16 | 19 | $36

Thornwood | 14 Marble Ave. (B'way) | 914-741-5100
Greenwich | 381 Greenwich Ave. (Grigg St.), CT | 203-862-9100 | www.abisjapanese.com

"Kids love" this "popular" Japanese duo in Greenwich and Thornwood, a "solid standby" for "tween birthdays" thanks to its "entertaining" hibachi show (it's "a hoot") and "reliable" sushi dinners; "good-value" pricing and "welcoming" service overcome the "hectic" vibe and "dated", "no-frills" decor that's certainly "not the place for a romantic dinner."

Abruzzi Trattoria *Italian*

▽ 21 | 20 | 20 | $35

Patterson | 3191 Rte. 22 (Danby Ln.) | 845-878-6800 | www.abruzzitrattoria.com

"Solid" red-sauce Italian deemed "very good for the price" plus "cheerful" hospitality make this "friendly" Patterson spot a local "favorite", whether "to grab a bite" at lunch or linger on "date night"; the "comfortable" room is "often crowded" and loud, but an "energetic" staff willing to "go that extra mile" makes up for it.

Adrienne Ⓜ *American*

25 | 21 | 23 | $53

New Milford | 218 Kent Rd. (Rocky River Rd.), CT | 860-354-6001 | www.adriennerestaurant.com

Ordering from the "seasonal American menu" is a "delightful task" at Adrienne Sussman's "cozy" New Milford eatery, where the "talented" toque "caters to each customer with special care" while creating "ingenious, fresh" fare at "reasonable prices", and the rest of the staff is "friendly" as well; the circa-1746 Colonial is "quaint, but not luxurious", with a fireplace and an outdoor patio that's a "true joy" in the warmer months; P.S. the "cooking classes are also fun."

	FOOD	DECOR	SERVICE	COST

Agriturismo Ⓜ *Italian*   ▽ 23 | 19 | 21 | $46

Pine Plains | 2938 Church St./Rte. 199 (bet. Main St. & Poplar Ave.) | 518-398-1000 | www.agriturismorestaurant.com

"Acclaimed chef Mark Strausman" (of NYC's Fred's at Barneys and the now-shuttered Campagna) combines "city-caliber" Italian cooking with "abundant local produce" at his "sophisticated" Pine Plains eatery set in a "cute, bistro-like space"; it's "a bit pricey", the fare can be "uneven" and the staff "overextended", but it "holds promise"; P.S. hours are limited, so call ahead.

AJ's Burgers ⊘ *American*   20 | 13 | 18 | $17

New Rochelle | 542 North Ave. (Hamilton Ave.) | 914-235-3009 | www.ajsburgers.com

They "make a mean burger", "killer milkshakes" and a range of "hearty" American eats "served in a skillet" at this "reliable" New Rochelle eatery; the "diner atmosphere" doesn't faze the "Iona college crowd" or "locals with small children" who think the "obliging" staff and "incredible value" are "way cool."

🆕 Alain's French Bistro *French*   - | - | - | E

Nyack | 9 Ingall's St. (Rte. 59) | 845-535-3315 | www.alainsbistro.com

A petite patch of France in a ho-hum strip mall, this upmarket Nyack newcomer from chef-owner Alain Eigenmann (ex Sidewalk Bistro in Piermont) serves all the bistro classics – bouillabaisse, moules, rabbit in mustard sauce – along with hearty dishes that reflect his Alsatian heritage; vins to match, plus buttery walls, wood trim and a cozy vibe in the low-lit, spacious setting evoke a rustique farmhouse feel that completes the illusion.

Alba's Ⓢ *Italian*   23 | 20 | 21 | $54

Port Chester | 400 N. Main St. (Wilkins Ave.) | 914-937-2236 | www.albasrestaurant.com

"Old-fashioned Italian done well" sums up this Port Chester "standard" offering "first-rate" Northern-style cuisine and "wonderful wines" in an "attractive" recently expanded space equipped with a working fireplace; its "attentive", "service-oriented" staff appeals to the "older crowd" that doesn't flinch at the "pricey" tabs.

Alvin & Friends Ⓜ *Caribbean/Southern*   ▽ 26 | 26 | 26 | $45

New Rochelle | 49 Lawton St. (bet. Huguenot & Main Sts.) | 914-654-6549 | www.alvinandfriendsrestaurant.com

Early reports on this "exciting" entry in Downtown New Rochelle laud the "interesting flavors" of its "spectacular" modern Caribbean-Southern cooking (think jerk duck, fried chicken), the "gracious" service and "beautiful setting" spiced up with "welcoming host" Alvin Clayton's "evocative paintings"; a few find they still "have to work out a few kinks", but the majority maintains they'll "definitely be back."

Amalfi Restaurant *Italian*   19 | 16 | 19 | $41

Briarcliff Manor | 1112 Pleasantville Rd. (Dunn Ln.) | 914-762-9200

"Convenience" is key at this "casual, neighborhood" Italian in Briarcliff Manor, a "comfortable" place to "relax" over "ample" portions of "standard family fare" dished out in an "attentive" fashion; service strikes some as "slow", while the "not-so-elegant" "strip-mall" setting can make prices seem "higher than you might expect."

A' Mangiare *Italian*   20 | 13 | 17 | $28

Bronxville | 26 Palmer Ave. (bet. Paxton Ave. & Pondfield Rd.) | 914-793-9224
Elmsford | 121 E. Main St. (bet. French & Perkins Aves.) | 914-592-8800
Pleasantville | 152 Bedford Rd. (B'way) | 914-747-2611
www.amangiare.com

Amici insist this "dependable" trio "hits the spot" for a "casual meal" of thin-crust pizza or "respectable" Southern Italian dishes, "cooked well" if "without flair", at "fair" prices; service is "decent", though occasionally "slow", and the digs range from "somewhat tired" to "blah", leading some to think of these as "perfect for takeout."

Amedeos Brick Oven Pizzeria *Pizza*   21 | 22 | 21 | $29

LaGrangeville | 476 Lauer Rd. (County Rd. 47) | 845-454-4563 | www.amedeosbrickovenpizzeria.com

A "pizza parlor morphed into a beautiful", "Tuscanesque" eatery describes this "nicely designed" LaGrangeville "gem" dispensing "delish", wood-fired, brick-oven Neapolitan pies that are "a cut or two above", plus "ample salads" and a "small menu" of pastas and panini; owner Patrick Amedeo sets a "friendly" tone, so the only gripe is that it's a little on the "costly" side.

☒ American Bounty Restaurant ☒ Ⓜ *American*   26 | 24 | 24 | $55

Hyde Park | Culinary Institute of America | 1946 Campus Dr. (Rte. 9) | 845-471-6608 | www.ciarestaurants.com

This "standout" eatery at Hyde Park's "big kahuna" culinary school presents "delicious" New American fare based on "market-fresh", "wonderful regional" ingredients capped by "out-of-this-world desserts" that suggest "there must be one heckuva pastry class"; most forgive sometimes "bumbling" service from "nervous" "students learning their craft" and focus on the "beautiful" surroundings, "magnificent view" and "affordable" rates for such a "treat."

American Pie Company *American*   22 | 16 | 21 | $21

Sherman | 29 Rte. 37 Center (Old Greenwoods Rd.), CT | 860-350-0662 | www.americanpiecompany.com

The bakery counter selling "amazing pies" and "divine" cookies makes you "want to eat dessert first" at this "affordable" Sherman Traditional American, the "epitome of a cute country restaurant", which offers "hearty country-style breakfasts, lunches and dinners" in a "cozy" setting; the staff is "welcoming", but it's so popular the "wait can be unbearable."

☒ An American Bistro *American*   23 | 17 | 22 | $41

Tuckahoe | 296 Columbus Ave. (bet. Fisher & Lincoln Aves.) | 914-793-0807 | www.anamericanbistro.com

A "steady" performer, this Tuckahoe New American is "always a pleasure" for its "older" clientele thanks to its "excellent" "comfort" eats and "solicitous" service; diners divide on whether the atmosphere is "homespun" or "dated", but most agree that while it "hasn't changed" in years, it still "never gets old"; P.S. the weekday prix fixe "is one of the best bangs for your buck" in town.

Angelina's *Italian*

21 | 16 | 19 | $37

Tuckahoe | 97 Lake Ave. (Elm St.) | 914-779-7944 |
www.angelinasoftuckahoe.com

Whether you're in the pizzeria or the more "formal" dining room done up in a "kitschy" angel motif, this Tuckahoe hybrid is "always packed with regulars" munching on *"bella"*, "homestyle" Italian cooking; a "pleasant" staff makes it "a solid choice" for families, and it's a "good buy for the money" too.

Anna Maria's ☑ *Italian*

21 | 18 | 22 | $43

Larchmont | 18 Chatsworth Ave. (bet. Addison St. & Boston Post Rd.) |
914-833-0555 | www.annamariasrestaurant.com

"Eat like Giuliani without the stress of New York politics" at this "comfortable", "old-world" Larchmont Italian helmed by former Gracie Mansion chef Anna Maria Santorelli who turns out "family-style" fare "that doesn't stray far from tradition"; though the atmosphere's "warm", prices relatively moderate and service "aims to please", a few find the "pedestrian" fare's "not up to what you'd expect."

Another Fork in the Road *American*

22 | 15 | 19 | $25

Milan | 1215 Rte. 199 (bet. Milan Hill Rd. & Morehouse Ln.) |
845-758-6676 | www.anotherforkintheroadmilan.wordpress.com

"Locavores love" this "laid-back", "little" Milan American, a "culinary find" where "fresh, local ingredients" are "whipped up" into "inventive" "diner food with a twist"; the "informal" black-and-white space exudes an "unassuming", "neighborhoody" feel, while "low prices" and a "lovely staff" add to the appeal; P.S. open for breakfast, lunch and dinner Thursday–Monday.

Anthony's Coal-Oven Fired Pizza *Pizza*

22 | 16 | 19 | $22

White Plains | 264 Main St. (bet. B'way & E.J. Conroy Dr.) |
914-358-9702 | www.anthonyscoalfiredpizza.com

"Sports-bar" ambiance teams up with "crispy, paper-thin" pizza "with just enough chew" and chicken wings that "will knock your socks off" at this large and loungey White Plains outpost of a Florida chain; "friendly" service, a "nice full bar" and "lots of flat-screen TVs" also make it a good place to "go with a group" and "catch a game."

Antoine McGuire's *French/Irish*

▽ 24 | 19 | 20 | $41

Haverstraw | 19 Main St. (Wayne St.) | 845-429-4121 |
www.antoinemcguire.com

French bistro meets Irish pub "with flair" at this "wonderful" Haverstraw restaurant serving a menu ranging from "tasty hamburgers" to "awesome" Gallic-Celtic hybrids like Le Shepherd's Pie, along with "great fresh oysters and clams" at the raw bar; a "welcoming" staff serves in the "appealing" dining room, while a "happening" bar, "fun wines", craft beers and "good prices" help make it a "go-to spot" for locals.

☑ Apple Pie Bakery
Café ☒ *Bakery/Sandwiches*

26 | 20 | 19 | $19

Hyde Park | Culinary Institute of America | 1946 Campus Dr. (Rte. 9) | 845-905-4500 | www.ciarestaurants.com

"Bodacious breakfasts", "lovely lunch fare", "irresistible" pastries and "incredible desserts" are the lure at this "informal" student-run eatery in the Hyde Park cooking school, where everything is so "glorious" it almost "guarantees a five-pound weight gain"; "diner prices" are a plus, while the "cheerful" "culinary stars of tomorrow" manning the cafe compensate for "waits", leaving one drawback: it's not open on weekends, or after 5 PM.

Aquario *Brazilian/Portuguese*

23 | 18 | 21 | $46

West Harrison | 141 E. Lake St. (bet. Columbus Ave. & Grant St.) | 914-287-0220 | www.aquariony.com

"Old-world charm" is alive and well at this West Harrison Portuguese-Brazilian specializing in the "freshest seafood", "properly prepared" and served by an "immensely gracious" staff; the interior is "pleasant" and tables are "are well spaced so you're not eating off of someone's plate", although "expensive" prices are a sticking point for some.

☑ The Arch ☒ *Eclectic*

27 | 25 | 27 | $71

Brewster | 1292 Rte. 22 (end of I-684) | 845-279-5011 | www.archrestaurant.com

"A golden oldie that never loses its luster", this "delightful" Brewster Eclectic "changes just enough to keep up with the times", offering "exceptional", "refined" "classics" and "amazing soufflés" in a "pretty" stone house where "fireplaces, well-spaced tables" and "charming", "never-stuffy" service make "romantic evenings a natural"; of course, it's "not cheap" (although "Sunday brunch is a relative bargain"), but "worth every penny" for something "special"; P.S. jackets suggested at dinner.

Arielle *Mediterranean*

22 | 22 | 19 | $48

Rhinebeck | 51 E. Market St. (bet. Center & Montgomery Sts.) | 845-876-5666 | www.ariellerhinebeck.com

You "feel transported" to the "countryside of France" at this "charming" Rhinebeck sibling of nearby Belvedere Mansion, thanks to the "rich, smartly executed" French-accented Mediterranean fare and "quaint" space, "tastefully decorated" in a "provincial" motif with "tufted seats covered in toile"; "cozy" and "intimate" translates to "seating a little tight" for some, but the "helpful staff" "is there to please" and overall it's "a pleasure."

Armadillo Bar & Grill ☒ *Southwestern*

25 | 19 | 23 | $32

Kingston | 97 Abeel St. (bet. Hone & Wurts Sts.) | 845-339-1550 | www.armadillos.net

"It feels like a party" at this "fabulously funky" Kingston cantina serving "exceptional" Southwestern eats with "lots of veggie choices" that are "robust but not too spicy, even for kids"; "enthusiastic service" and "fantastic margaritas" fuel the "camaraderie" in digs as "colorful" as the "wonderful owner, Merle", and the patio is "dog-friendly" – no wonder it's "been around for two-dozen years."

Aroi Thai *Thai*   22 | 17 | 20 | $28

Rhinebeck | 55 E. Market St. (bet. Center & Montgomery Sts.) | 845-876-1114 | www.aroirestaurant.com

Rhinebeck residents "yearning for Thai" head here for "tasty", "home-cooked" dishes "gently" spiced and served by a "lovely" staff at "reasonable" rates (the "prix fixe lunch is a bargain"); "minimal" decor in the "historic", "converted house" makes for a "gracious, calming" setting, as does the "lovely garden" with its fountain in summer months.

⊠ Aroma Osteria Ⓜ *Italian*   26 | 25 | 25 | $49

Wappingers Falls | 114 Old Post Rd. (Rte. 9) | 845-298-6790 | www.aromaosteriarestaurant.com

"Bountiful servings" of *molto delizioso* Southern Italian fare and a "spectacular wine list" earn "high marks" for Eduardo Lauria's Wappingers Falls "gem", where the "polite", "well-trained staff" serves in a "sensual", "pretty" space done up like "a Tuscan villa"; one "turnoff for romantics": it's "acoustically challenged, so be prepared to talk with your hands", or eat "outside in the grape arbor" in summer.

Aroma Thyme Bistro *American/Health Food*   23 | 19 | 20 | $45

Ellenville | 165 Canal St. (bet. Hermance St. & Maiden Ln.) | 845-647-3000 | www.aromathymebistro.com

"Everyone from carnivores to vegans" can "indulge" at this "enjoyable" Ellenville New American "organic" "oasis" where "inspired" chef Marcus Guiliano's "diverse", "mouthwatering dishes" prove that "healthy food can be fabulous"; the "pleasant" space, jazzed up with harlequin-stenciled walls, plus "good prices" and a "fantastic beer and wine selection" help the "lively crowd" that gathers to overlook sometimes "spotty service."

Arrivederci Trattoria Ⓜ *Italian*   - | - | - | E

Sherman | 1 Rte. 37 E. (Gaylordsville Rd.), CT | 860-210-1266 | www.arrivedercitrattoria.com

Italian standards meet creative dishes such as horseradish-crusted scallops at this dinner-only Sherman trattoria where the chef (of Ridgefield's defunct Insieme) also accepts menu requests; a friendly staff and cozy setting – recently brightened up after an ownership change – give it an intimate vibe, and the $41 'dinner for two' specials Tuesdays–Wednesdays provide economic incentive.

Arrosto Ⓜ *Italian*   ▽ 23 | 24 | 22 | $45

Port Chester | 25 S. Regent St. (William St.) | 914-939-2727 | www.arrostorestaurant.com

The wood-burning oven takes center stage at this "pretty" Port Chester Italian from Godfrey Polistina (founder of NYC's Carmine's), where you can choose among a "vast" array of "outstanding" family-style meat and fish roasts, sophisticated pizzas and "amazing" housemade pastas elevated by almost two dozen

| | FOOD | DECOR | SERVICE | COST |

wines by the glass; there's already a "lively bar scene" to go along with the "NY-esque" vibe, and it's all "priced fairly."

🔼 Artist's Palate Ⓧ *American* | 26 | 23 | 23 | $45 |

Poughkeepsie | 307 Main St. (bet. Catharine & Market Sts.) | 845-483-8074 | www.theartistspalate.biz

This "trendy" New American in Downtown Poughkeepsie is "a staple among the professional crowd" for "delectable", "original" eats set down amid "shabby-chic" decor that makes the renovated 1830s building "feel like SoHo North"; "service is tops", rates are "reasonable" and if you nab a table in back you can watch "down-to-earth" chef-owners Charlie and Megan Fells provide "theater" in the open kitchen; P.S. "make yourself happy: try the lobster mac 'n' cheese."

Asiana Cafe *Asian* | 21 | 18 | 20 | $34 |

Greenwich | 130 E. Putnam Ave. (Milbank Ave.), CT | 203-622-6833 | www.asianacafe.com

"Kid-friendly" and "quick", this Greenwich Pan-Asian is a "reliable" standby "when you don't want to cook", offering a "Chinese-American mash-up with a sushi bar" at "reasonable prices"; dissenters say the "trendy"-looking decor "could use some spiffing up", though, and some purists pan the fare as being "designed for the Waspy palate."

Asian Temptation *Asian* | 20 | 21 | 19 | $36 |

White Plains | City Ctr. | 23 Mamaroneck Ave. (bet. Main St. & Martine Ave.) | 914-328-5151 | www.asiantemptationrestaurant.com

There's a "hip" "techno feel" to this "sleek" White Plains canteen turning out "fresh" sushi, "unique" rolls and a "wide array" of "tasty" Asian fusion items with martinis and bubble tea in a "modern" setting with a koi pond; just be prepared for a "loud", "lively" "girls'-night-out crowd" and prices that are "not cheap" ("broccoli should not cost so much green").

NEW A Tavola *Italian* | - | - | - | M |

New Paltz | 46 Main St. (Chestnut St.) | 845-255-1426 | www.atavolany.com

Ensconced in the New Paltz space that once housed Beso, this stylish Italian launched by Bonnie and Nathan Snow (alumni of Manhattan's Sfoglia) is drawing raves with creative takes on regional dishes like octopus with chickpeas and pappardelle Bolognese, plus housemade gelato; a large wine rack forms a centerpiece downstairs in the bi-level setting, with a red accent wall and mismatched farm tables adding a warm, rustic note.

@ the Corner *American* ∇ | 20 | 20 | 20 | $38 |

Litchfield | 3 West St. (Rte. 61), CT | 860-567-8882 | www.athecorner.com

There's "something for everyone" on the menu at this Litchfield New American where aficionados are "delighted" by the "fun twists on old faves" and "friendly, attentive" service in the "cozy" setting with a "lively bar scene"; critics, though, find the fare "just ok" and evincing surprisingly "little imagination" for the "upper-moderate prices."

	FOOD	DECOR	SERVICE	COST

Aurelia *Mediterranean*

▽ 19 | 19 | 19 | $46

Millbrook | 3299 Franklin Ave. (bet. Church St. & Friendly Ln.) |
845-677-4720 | www.aureliarestaurant.com

"Good pastas" and "fabulous homemade gnocchi" are "highlights"
on the Mediterranean menu at this "nice" Millbrook spot that's still
a little "hit-or-miss" but "almost there"; even if it "won't set the town
on fire", locals advise "keep it simple", forgive "forgetful service"
and enjoy sitting "on the pretty terrace" "on a beautiful day"; P.S. a
recent change of chef is not reflected in the Food score.

Aurora *Italian*

21 | 21 | 21 | $44

Rye | 60 Purchase St. (bet. Elm Pl. & W. Purdy Ave.) | 914-921-2333 |
www.auroraofrye.com

For a "reasonably priced" bite in "upscale Rye", try this "reliable",
"modern" Italian turning out brick-oven pizzas and mains "with a
Northern spin"; it's especially "lovely for lunch" in warm weather
when the French doors are flung open, just beware of "loud acoustics" in the dining room during prime time.

Aux Délices Foods
by Debra Ponzek *American/French*

24 | 14 | 16 | $24

Darien | Goodwives Shopping Ctr. | 25 Old Kings Hwy. N. (Sedgewick Ave.),
CT | 203-662-1136
Greenwich | 3 W. Elm St. (Greenwich Ave.), CT | 203-622-6644
Riverside | 1075 E. Putnam Ave. (Riverside Ln.), CT |
203-698-1066
www.auxdelicesfoods.com

These "upscale" "delis for foodies" in Darien, Greenwich and
Riverside offer "healthy, tasty and imaginative" French–New
American dishes and "wonderful pastries" that'll earn "high-end
praise from your guests"; all locations received a freshening up in
late 2011 (which may outdate the Decor score), though "limited
seating" and the "attitudes" of the mostly "young, thin clients" have
many opting for takeout – and "unless you're a hedge-fund millionaire", it's "outrageously expensive"; P.S. a Westport location is
scheduled to open May 2012.

Aversano's *Italian*

21 | 21 | 21 | $28

Brewster | 1620 Rte. 22 (Rte. 312) | 845-279-2233 |
www.aversanosrestaurant.com

When brothers John and Paul Aversano expanded their Brewster
pizzeria into a "sit-down" eatery a couple of years ago, it "quickly
became a go-to" for "dependable", "classic Italian" fare, "and plenty
of it"; a staff that "aims to please" adds a "warm atmosphere" to the
simple space, while "pizzeria prices" "won't dent the wallet."

Avocado *Mexican*

▽ 22 | 18 | 22 | $26

Cornwall | 2576 Rte. 9W (bet. Academy & Willow Aves.) |
845-534-3350 | www.avocadorestaurant.com

An "extensive menu" of "real", "not run-of-the-mill", "fresh
Mexican" (including "great guacamole" and "authentic moles") has
is "happy addition" to Cornwall "creating a following" among lo-

FOOD DECOR SERVICE COST

cals; tabs are friendly, as is the staff serving the eats in colorful digs, or dispensing "fruity sangria" on the decks in summertime.

Azuma Sushi ⓜ *Japanese*   25 | 14 | 19 | $47
Hartsdale | 219 E. Hartsdale Ave. (bet. Bronx River Pkwy. & Central Park Ave.) | 914-725-0660 | www.azumasushihartsdale.com
There are "no gimmicks", just "amazing" "swimmingly fresh sushi" that's "on par with Manhattan's best" at this Hartsdale Japanese, an "über-tiny hole-in-the-wall" tucked in next to the train station; it's "popular with expats" and fans of "traditional" fare, but given the "arrogant" service and pricing worthy of a "second mortgage", "forget about bringing the kids."

Baang Cafe & Bar   *Asian*   23 | 21 | 19 | $48
Riverside | 1191 E. Putnam Ave. (Neil Ln.), CT | 203-637-2114 | www.decarorestaurantgroup.com
A "favorite for [over] 15 years", this "pricey" Riverside Pan-Asian still pulls "chic singles" into the colorful, "club"-like space with its "clever", "inventive" menu, "sexy" cocktails and "still-hoppin'" bar scene; it's "aptly named" say those who wince at the "deafening" decibel levels, while cynics who call it a "faded star" that's getting "long in the tooth" may be appeased by a 2012 renovation.

Baba Louie's Sourdough Pizza   *Pizza*   24 | 13 | 18 | $23
Hudson | 517 Warren St. (bet. 5th & 6th Sts.) | 518-751-2155 | www.babalouiespizza.com
See review in the Berkshires Directory.

Babette's Kitchen   *American*   ▽ 20 | 11 | 18 | $18
Millbrook | 3293 Franklin Ave. (bet. Church St. & Maple Ave.) | 845-677-8602 | www.babetteskitchen.com
"A fixture" in Millbrook, this little American bakery/cafe-cum-gourmet shop is a find for "freshly made" "breakfast treats", "upscale salads" and sandwiches at lunch, plus prepared dinners to go; after a move to larger digs, there are more tables in the country-kitchen setting, though takeout is still a boon for those "on the run."

Babycakes Cafe ⓜ *American*   - | - | - | M
Poughkeepsie | 1-3 Collegeview Ave. (Raymond Ave.) | 845-485-8411 | www.babycakescafe.com
Once a little cafe, this Poughkeepsie favorite of the Vassar crowd has grown up (and moved) to be a three-meals-a-day eatery dispensing New American fare from pastries and pancakes to porterhouse; the Tudor-esque exterior gives way to a bi-level space made warm with wood floors, red tabletops, Chinese lanterns and a bar with a copper backsplash; fair prices, live music Thursday–Saturday and sidewalk seating in summer are other lures.

Bacco Restaurant ⓜ *Italian*   21 | 16 | 22 | $34
Poughkeepsie | 718 Dutchess Tpke. (bet. Cherry Hill Dr. & Dorland Ave.) | 845-454-1882
It may be "nothing groundbreaking", but the "solid", "old-styl" Italian" served in "ample portions" at this "friendly" Poughkeeps

spot adds up to "good food at a good price"; a "quiet atmosphere" pervades the sage-green setting (most recently home to March Hare), but there's "limited room" and "no reservations, so be prepared to wait" on busy nights.

Bacio Trattoria M *Italian/Mediterranean*   23 | 15 | 23 | $38

Cross River | 12 N. Salem Rd./Rte. 121 (Rte. 35) | 914-763-2233 | www.baciotrattoria.com

"Warmth and charm" overcome the limitations of a "tiny, drab" interior at this "popular" Cross River trattoria, a "jam-packed neighborhood haunt" thanks to its "inexpensive" "homestyle" Italian-Med cooking; service is "family-friendly", and those who say the "noise detracts" from the experience think it's "a better bet in summer" when the patio is in full swing.

Z Back Yard Bistro Z M *American*   26 | 20 | 24 | $50

Montgomery | 1118 Rte. 17K (bet. Bailey Rd. & Rte. 208) | 845-457-9901 | www.holbertscatering.com

It's like "eating at a friend's house, if your friend happens to be a top chef", declare devotees of this "low-key" New American "diamond" "hidden" behind the Montgomery home of catering couple Jerry and Susan Crocker; the "imaginative" menu of "superb" fare comes "beautifully plated" via a "thoughtful" staff in a "tiny" space that seats just 18 ("reservations a must") or in the courtyard when it's warm.

Z Bagels & More *Deli*   21 | 8 | 17 | $12

Hartsdale | 224 E. Hartsdale Ave. (Rockledge Rd.) | 914-722-4444

Commuters fuel up at this "solid" deli across from the Hartsdale train station offering "excellent coffee", "delicious" bagels and an "extensive list of cream cheeses and spreads"; sure, it "could use a good cleanup", but most pass through "in a hurry" and "take out."

Bailey's Backyard M *American*   21 | 17 | 21 | $38

Ridgefield | 23 Bailey Ave. (Main St.), CT | 203-431-0796 | www.baileysbackyard.com

"Savory" New American fare is "served professionally" by an "amiable staff" at this "cozy" bistro on a quaint street in Downtown Ridgefield, where the owners "seem like they care"; the "casual" interior, which resembles a backyard "under a fun starry sky", is appealing, but it's so "small" that insiders caution "your wait will be outside" if you come at peak hours; reservations recommended.

Bambou Asian Tapas & Bar *Asian*   21 | 22 | 21 | $36

Greenwich | The Mill | 328 Pemberwick Rd. (Glenville Rd.), CT | 203-531-3322 | www.bambourestaurant.com

"Creative" Pan-Asian dishes (primarily some of the "best sushi in town") and "friendly", "unobtrusive" service draw families and others to this restored mill by the river in Greenwich's Glenville neighborhood, a "lovely modern hideaway" with a "large" outdoor patio; critics grouse that the "desserts leave something to be desired" and the "con-fusion" cooking can be "hit-or-miss", but "great lunch specials" make it a "good value" for many.

FOOD | DECOR | SERVICE | COST

NEW Bangall Whaling Company *American* — | — | — | M

Stanfordville | 97 Hunns Lake Rd. (Millis St.) | 845-868-3349 |
www.bangallwhalingcompany.com

Bringing upscale pub grub to the sleepy Stanfordville hamlet of
Bangall, this new American tavern turns out steaks, seafood and
burgers along with fancier fare in a quaint, 19th-century building;
patrons can pause by the fireplace in the lounge, head to the dining
room with its rustic beams and earth tones or hoist a cold one in the
bar; affordable tabs help ensure a whale of a time.

Bangkok Spice *Thai* ▽ 23 | 13 | 21 | $29

Shrub Oak | 1161 E. Main St. (New Rd.) | 914-245-3690 |
www.bangkokspicekitchen.com

Some of "the best Thai this side of the river" turns up at this Shrub
Oak option set in an old Victorian, where "flavorful" noodles and
curries are ferried by a "prompt, friendly" crew; though the spicing
may defer to "the American palate", it's "satisfying" nonetheless,
and "affordable" tabs make it a "locals'" favorite.

Bank Street Tavern *Eclectic* 18 | 18 | 19 | $35

New Milford | 31 Bank St. (bet. Main & Railroad Sts.), CT | 860-799-7991
Early boosters "bank on" this New Milford tavern serving "innovative" Eclectic fare and "great microbrews" at "reasonable" prices in
arguably the "best atmosphere in town"; but critics say it still "suf-
fers from growing pains" and "needs to decide what it wants to be."

Bao's Chinese Cuisine *Chinese* 20 | 15 | 19 | $26

White Plains | White Plains Mall | 200 Hamilton Ave.
(Dr. Martin Luther King Ave.) | 914-682-8858 | www.baosasiancuisine.com
"Not your ordinary Chinese restaurant", this "affordable" grotto in the
basement of the White Plains Mall slings "tasty", "authentic" cuisine
that celebrates "seasonal, fresh veggies" with "no heavy sauces"; a
staff that's "helpful" with ordering makes up for decor that's "a throwback to the '70s" and its somewhat "dismal" subterranean locale.

Barcelona Restaurant & 24 | 21 | 21 | $42
Wine Bar *Spanish*

Greenwich | 18 W. Putnam Ave. (Greenwich Ave.), CT | 203-983-6400
Stamford | 222 Summer St. (Broad St.), CT | 203-348-4800 ●
www.barcelonawinebar.com

"*Viva Espana!*" exclaim amigos over the "intense flavors" of the
Spanish tapas that "take hold of your taste buds" at this "jumping"
chainlet where the "young at heart in heat" share small plates, sangria and Iberian *vini* served by an "attentive" staff amid "eclectic, urbane" surroundings; frugal types grouse about "pricey" bites and
"high markups", but give an "*olé*" to half-price wines on Sundays.

Barnstormer Barbeque *BBQ* ▽ 21 | 14 | 21 | $21

Fort Montgomery | 1076 Rte. 9W (Garrison Rd.) | 845-446-0912 |
www.barnstormerbbq.com

"Come hungry", "ask what's been freshly smoked and order that", in-
struct regulars of this regional BBQ "temple of cholesterol" that'•

"alive and well in Fort Montgomery" after a move from Newbu
"tender, juicy pork ribs", "amazing wings" and other Carolina-mee
Kansas "finger-licking" fare is on offer, with "outgoing" servers, plent,
of paper towels and a roadhouse setting adding to the casual appeal.

Bar Rosso *Italian*   `- | - | - | E`

Stamford | 30 Spring St. (bet. Bedford & Summer Sts.), CT |
203-388-8640 | www.barrossoct.com

The former Bennett's in Stamford has been transformed into this upscale Italian serving rustic small plates, pastas and wood-fired
pizza, plus a carefully chosen list of Italian vinos (including 25 by the
glass); a staff schooled in food and wine pairings operates in a contemporary space featuring a 50-ft. bar and an outdoor patio.

Bartaco ● *Mexican*   `- | - | - | M`

Port Chester | 1 Willett Ave. (Abendroth Ave.) | 914-937-8226
NEW Stamford | 222 Summer St. (Broad St.), CT |
203-323-8226
www.bartaco.com

From the folks behind the ultrapopular Barcelona group comes this
beach-chic taqueria in Port Chester vending gussied-up Mexican
street fare in an airy space with an exhibition kitchen; it's full service
and features a lengthy bar with fresh-fruit cocktails and tequilas
poured until late plus a DJ spinning on weekends; P.S. Stamford is
new, and more branches are coming soon.

Bayou *Cajun/Creole*   `19 | 16 | 18 | $31`

Mt. Vernon | 580 Gramatan Ave. (W. Broad St.) | 914-668-2634 |
www.bayourestaurantny.com

"The place to go for your alligator fix", this "gritty" Mt. Vernon
Cajun-Creole serves up "down-and-dirty" grub that's "as close to
New Orleans as you're going to get" washed down with "lots of
beer"; the setting is equal parts "frat house" and "blues joint" with a
"friendly" vibe and live music adding up to "lots of fun."

Beach House Café *American*   `18 | 20 | 18 | $34`

Old Greenwich | 220 Sound Beach Ave. (Arcadia Rd.), CT | 203-637-0367 |
www.beachhousecafe.com

"You feel like you're at the beach" at this Old Greenwich American
that attracts a mostly local clientele (including a "stroller-crowd"
contingent) with a "comfortable" "shore-town" setting, "solid",
seafood-centric "pub fare" and a "laid-back staff that makes you feel
welcome", while evening bar action, "special nights" and live music
on weekends add to the "fun"; a few critics say the "menu gets old
fast", however, and complain about the "cacophonous" scene.

Bear Cafe *American*   `24 | 22 | 22 | $50`

Woodstock | 295 Tinker St./Rte. 212 (Striebel Rd.) | 845-679-5555 |
www.bearcafe.com

"Rock 'n' roll legends", "artists, actors" – maybe even "Uma
Thurman" – "might walk in" to this "laid-back" New American "hot
spot" on the "edge of Woodstock" that's been serving "consistently
licious" dishes since 1988; although it's "not cheap", "stream-

FOOD DECOR SERVICE COST

digs that are "rustic without being cutesy", a "lively bar", ...reful", "competent" service and a pavilion for summertime help ...ake it "a winner" whose "popularity is justified."

⛿ Bedford Post, The Barn *American*   23 | 24 | 21 | $48

Bedford | Bedford Post | 954 Old Post Rd./Rte. 121 (bet. Indian Hill Rd. & Rte. 137) | 914-234-7800 | www.bedfordpostinn.com

The "swankiest barn you've ever set foot in", this "trendy" Bedford New American cafe and bakery from Richard Gere attracts a "sophisticated crowd" of "local celebrities" for "delicious homemade pastries" and an "amazing" "farm-to-table" breakfast and lunch; many "wish the portions were bigger" and the service less "disorganized", but "pricey" though it be, the majority insists it's "worth the indulgence"; P.S. dinner is served on Mondays and Tuesdays.

⛿ Bedford Post, The Farmhouse Ⓜ *American*   25 | 26 | 23 | $78

Bedford | Bedford Post | 954 Old Post Rd./Rte. 121 (bet. Indian Hill Rd. & Rte. 137) | 914-234-7800 | www.bedfordpostinn.com

"Elegance and class" define the more formal of Richard Gere's Bedford Post eateries, a "charming" "getaway" that "romances its guests" with a "relaxed pace", "lovely ambiance" and "unfailingly excellent" New American cuisine focused on "local meat and produce"; a relatively new chef is in the kitchen, and there's still some murmuring about "small portions", occasionally "mediocre" service and tabs "not for the faint of wallet", but overall it's a "treat."

Beech Tree Grill *American*   22 | 18 | 20 | $31

Poughkeepsie | 1 Collegeview Ave. (Raymond Ave.) | 845-471-7279 | www.beechtreegrill.com

"Big flavors come out of a kitchen" "the size of a closet" at this usually "packed" Poughkeepsie New American and "Vassar hangout" dispensing "burgers you can count on" along with more "interesting offerings" and an array of "alluring ales" on tap; it's "an inviting", "enjoyable establishment" with a "bustling bar" that belies its narrow, "dive-y" looks.

Beehive *American/Eclectic*   21 | 16 | 21 | $33

Armonk | 30 Old Rte. 22 (Kaysal Ct.) | 914-765-0688 | www.beehive-restaurant.com

"New and improved" after a "major renovation", this Armonk "mainstay" is back with "large portions" of Eclectic–New American "upscale diner" fare that shows its "Greek roots" as well as covering the "comfort-food" "standards"; the "friendly" proprietors now preside over a "more spacious, airy" establishment that promises to be a "great place to meet."

Bellizzi *Italian*   15 | 12 | 15 | $23

Larchmont | 1272 Boston Post Rd. (Weaver St.) | 914-833-5800
Mt. Kisco | 153 Main St. (Dakin Ave.) | 914-241-1200
www.bellizzi.us

There's a "super-fun" playroom and "video-game mayhem" along wi... "standard" pizza and pastas at this child-centric Larchmont and ...

	FOOD	DECOR	SERVICE	COST

Kisco Italian twosome hosting birthday parties galore; adults who can't "tolerate noise, confusion and a hectic atmosphere" are in for an "instant headache", "liquor license" notwithstanding.

Bellota at 42 🗷 Ⓜ *Spanish* ‚ - | - | - | M

White Plains | Ritz-Carlton Westchester | 1 Renaissance Sq., 42nd fl. (Main St.) | 914-761-4242 | www.42therestaurant.com

This casual enclave in the bar of Restaurant 42 atop White Plains' glitzy Ritz-Carlton features chef Anthony Goncalves' idiosyncratic take on Spanish tapas; expect moderately priced Iberian snacks prepared with playful twists in an evocative setting framed by ashen birch trunks springing from pools of acorns ('bellota' simultaneously refers to acorns and the elite porkers that eat them).

Belvedere Restaurant Ⓜ *American* ▽ 20 | 26 | 22 | $57

Staatsburg | Belvedere Mansion | 10 Old Rte. 9 (Albany Post Rd.) | 845-889-8000 | www.belvederemansion.com

"You feel you've entered another time" at this "romantic" Gilded Age "mansion on the hill" in Staatsburg, thanks to an "inviting" dining room full of antiques and luxurious fabrics; although the New American fare can sometimes "miss the mark", overall the place is "a class act", with service as "sleek" as the setting and "gorgeous views of the Hudson and the Catskills" making it "a must for that special occasion."

Benjamin Steak House Ⓜ *Steak* 24 | 23 | 24 | $76

White Plains | 610 Hartsdale Ave. (Dobbs Ferry Rd./Rte. 100B) | 914-428-6868 | www.benjaminsteakhouse.com

"Running smoothly" from the get-go, this "outstanding" eatery gives Hartsdale a "true NYC steakhouse" (almost a "clone" of its Manhattan sibling), complete with "wonderful" beef, "delicious sides" and "excellent" service; the "clubby environment" can get "loud" and the tab is "not cheap", but most find it an "enjoyable" experience nonetheless.

🗷 Bernard's Ⓜ *French* 27 | 26 | 27 | $68

Ridgefield | 20 West Ln. (Main St.), CT | 203-438-8282 | www.bernardsridgefield.com

Chef-owner Bernard Bouissou turns out "superbly crafted" "classic" French fare "with a twist" at this Ridgefield "favorite" situated in an "upscale", "comfortable country-inn" setting; a "warm", "knowledgeable" staff, "outstanding wine list" and live piano on weekends help make it "the place to go for a special occasion" and "worth every penny"; P.S. the "more casual" Sarah's Wine Bar serves a separate, less-expensive bistro menu.

Bertucci's *Italian* 16 | 14 | 16 | $25

Danbury | 98 Newtown Rd. (I-84, exit 8), CT | 203-739-0500
Darien | 54 Boston Post Rd. (I-95, exit 13), CT | 203-655-4299
www.bertuccis.com

This "decent" Italian chain is a "surefire thing" for families with kids who get to "play with dough" at the table; insiders advise just "stick with" the brick-oven pizzas, "hot rolls" and "nice salads" (some dishes can seem "processed"), and you'll get a "solid", "predictable" meal for a "fair price."

it is", but even if you "wouldn't go out of your way for it", supporters say it's "pleasant" enough.

Cafe Maya *Mexican*   22 | 18 | 22 | $30
Wappingers Falls | 2776 W. Main St. (bet. McCafferty Pl. & North St.) | 845-632-3444
Maya Cafe *Mexican*
Fishkill | 448 Rte. 9 (Van Wyck Lake Rd.) | 845-896-4042
www.mayacafecantina.com
"Not your normal burrito joint", this "popular" Dutchess County duo dispenses "flavorful" Mexican "dishes with Mayan flair" alongside "exotic specials" and "fresh guacamole made at your table" – so "don't drown your taste buds" with the "fabulous margaritas"; a "super-friendly" staff and brightly colored digs add to the "fun", as does being "serenaded" by a mariachi band, while "bargain prices" keep 'em "packed."

Café Mezzaluna Bistro Latino 🅼 *Eclectic*   ▽ 23 | 18 | 23 | $29
Saugerties | 626 Rte. 212 (Division St.) | 845-246-5306 | www.cafemezzaluna.com
"Eclectic is a delightful understatement" to describe the "good home cooking" that comes with Latin flourishes at this "casual" Saugerties cafe; poetry readings and live music on weekends (it's "a haven for Joni Mitchell wannabes") add an arty aspect, while tabs are "affordable" and the "friendliest" "owners make sure everything is up to snuff."

Cafe Mio *American*   - | - | - | I
Gardiner | 2356 Rte. 44/55 (bet. Brodhead St. & Sand Hill Rd.) | 845-255-4949 | www.miogardiner.com
"A find" in "off-the-beaten-path" Gardiner, this informal American is "a great spot" for breakfast, brunch and lunch, turning out an array of "well-prepared" eats from egg dishes to wraps, sandwiches and burgers, most made with local, organic ingredients; presentation is "lovely" and the simple tile and wood setting suits aficionados who just "wish they were open for dinner."

Cafe Mirage *Eclectic*   22 | 12 | 20 | $36
Port Chester | 531 N. Main St. (Terrace Ave.) | 914-937-3497 | www.cafemirageny.com
A "funky setting in a converted gas station" forms the backdrop for this "happening" Port Chester Eclectic showcasing an "inventive" menu that foodies find "invariably delicious"; yes, it's "a little cramped", but a "staff that aims to please" makes up for it, and it's "open late" for the area too.

Cafe Mozart *Coffeehouse*   17 | 13 | 16 | $26
Mamaroneck | 308 Mamaroneck Ave. (Palmer Ave.) | 914-698-4166
A "lovely place to meet" "for coffee or brunch", this "cozy", "European"-style cafe in Mamaroneck is a "neighborhood" standby for "simple" salads, sandwiches and "caloric desserts"; perhaps the fare's "nothing to write home about", but the atmosphere's

"relaxed", live music on weekends is a "nice touch" and many find it especially "enjoyable" in summer when the sidewalk scene is in full swing.

Café of Love Ⓜ *American/French* | 22 | 21 | 21 | $46 |

Mt. Kisco | 38 E. Main St. (bet. Moger Ave. & Quaker Hill Ln.) | 914-242-1002 | www.cafeofloveny.com

Loyalists "love the cute, French feel" of this frilly Mt. Kisco bistro, "a real treat" thanks to its "beautifully presented" American-Gallic comestibles – including a farmhouse table loaded with "delectable" antipasti – served up in a "delightful" candlelit setting by "dishy waiters" who "pamper you"; though the "buzz" and the "bar scene" incur "brutal noise" on weekends, it's a "definite keeper", especially for a "ladies' night out."

Café on the Green *Italian* | 22 | 21 | 24 | $48 |

Danbury | Richter Park Golf Course | 100 Aunt Hack Rd. (Mill Plain Rd.), CT | 203-791-0369 | www.cafeonthegreenrestaurant.com

You may "need a GPS" to locate this "hidden culinary gem overlooking the rolling landscape" of the Richter Park Golf Course, but aficionados insist "it's worth the trek" for summer "drinks on the balcony" or "sophisticated" Northern Italian cuisine served by an "attentive", "professional" staff in a "relaxed" but "classy" setting; "beautiful views" of the 10th fairway and 18th green round out what most describe as a "superior dining experience."

Cafe Portofino *Italian* | 23 | 17 | 22 | $40 |

Piermont | 587 Piermont Ave. (Kinney St.) | 845-359-7300 | www.portofinoinpiermont.com

"Regulars attest to the quality" at this "low-key" Piermont "standby" offering "a little taste of Italy" via "traditional", "home-style cooking" served in a "comfortable" room; "waiting for a table can be frustrating", but there's a "nice bar" and "service is fast", so really all that's missing is "views" – if only "they took advantage of the riverside location."

🅩 Cafe Silvium 🅩 *Italian* | 26 | 17 | 22 | $39 |

Stamford | 371 Shippan Ave. (Park St.), CT | 203-324-1651 | www.cafesilvium.com

The "lines are legendary" at this *molto bene* Italian in Stamford's Shippan neighborhood, so "get there early" or "have a drink while you wait"; the "well-prepared, enormously comforting" fare is "as authentic as you can get" and comes in "generous" portions at "reasonable" prices, and the service is "friendly and seriously efficient", so even if some think the "casual" space is "not much to look at", seriously, "who cares?"

Cafe Tamayo Ⓜ *American* | 25 | 21 | 23 | $52 |

Saugerties | 91 Partition St. (Main St.) | 845-246-9371 | www.cafetamayo.com

For "a fine meal", "served with style", Saugerties citizens head to this "reliable" New American veteran, where they can watch chef James Tamayo in the kitchen creating a "delicious" daily menu based on local ingredients, while his "other half", Rickie, "makes sure diners are content"; the setup includes a sunroom and a "lovely garden", so the only "complaint" is "they're not open enough" – just May to December.

Caffé Azzurri *American*   22 | 20 | 22 | $49

Hartsdale | 20 N. Central Ave. (Hartsdale Ave.) | 914-358-5248 | www.caffeazzurri.com

Despite an "unassuming" facade on Central Avenue, patrons are "pleasantly surprised" by this Hartsdale New American restaurant where a "courteous" staff ferries "creative" signature dishes like whole roasted branzino in an "elegant" setting; prices can be "expensive", although there's a "generous prix fixe" special offered at dinner.

Caffé Macchiato Ⓜ *Italian*   - | - | - | I

Newburgh | 99 Liberty St. (Washington St.) | 845-565-4616 | www.caffemacchiatonewburgh.com

A "wonderful discovery in an unlikely neighborhood", this tiny Italian breakfast and lunch nook "nestled" in Newburgh's slowly reviving historic district "earns its excellent reputation" with "tasty" panini, frittatas or "to-die-for" waffles and pancakes at the weekend brunch; patrons perch at cafe tables in the simple storefront setting, where the mouthwatering display in the pastry case forms a focal point.

Caffe Regatta Ⓜ *Seafood*   22 | 19 | 21 | $42

Pelham | 133 Wolfs Ln. (Sparks Ave.) | 914-738-8686 | www.cafferegatta.com

As the name suggests, this "neighborhood gem" in Pelham is a find for "fine, fresh" seafood served in "lovely" nautically themed digs "quiet enough that you can talk"; despite some murmurs about "inconsistent" food and service, prices are modest, and it's a "nice, little spot" that's "versatile" enough "for a date" or a night with the family.

Calico Restaurant &   25 | 18 | 23 | $43
Patisserie Ⓜ *American/Eclectic*

Rhinebeck | 6384 Montgomery St./Rte.9 (Market St.) | 845-876-2749 | www.calicorhinebeck.com

"As excellent as it is small" – and it's "tiny" – this Rhinebeck bakery/cafe is an all-round "pleaser", serving chef Anthony Balassone's "well-crafted" Eclectic–New American dishes, and wife Leslie's "decadently rich desserts"; the "most tempting pastry case in the northeast" dresses up the "no-pretense" space, service is "outstanding" and tabs are a "deal", so overall, it's a "treat."

California Pizza Kitchen *Pizza*   17 | 13 | 16 | $24

Scarsdale | 365 Central Park Ave. (S. Healy Ave.) | 914-722-0600
Stamford | Stamford Town Ctr. | 230 Tresser Blvd. (bet. Atlantic St. & Greyrock Pl.), CT | 203-406-0530
www.cpk.com

"Clever", "unusual" pizzas (such as "BBQ chicken and Thai") and "creative" salads are the "stars" at this "gourmet" pie chain

	FOOD	DECOR	SERVICE	COST

that's a haven for the stroller set; it's "inexpensive", "prompt" and "consistent", though some complain the "wannabe eclectic offerings" have grown "tired" and the "overlit" surroundings just "don't have any charm."

Ca'Mea ☒ *Italian* 22 | 21 | 21 | $44

Hudson | The Inn at Ca'Mea | 333-335 Warren St. (City Hall Pl.) | 518-822-0005 | www.camearestaurant.com

Some "discriminating diners" say the fare at this "pleasant" Hudson Northern Italian is "excellent", with "delicious fresh pasta" and "truly special" specials, while others declare the eats "good, but not a knockout" and a little "pricey" "for the locale"; all agree the owners are "nice people", the dining rooms are "comfortable" and it's "a treasure in warm weather" when you can dine in the "memorable garden"; P.S. nine guestrooms allow for overnight stays.

Camillo's at the Crossroads ☒ *American* ▽ 18 | 12 | 19 | $37

Montgomery | 2215 Rte. 208 (Rte. 17K) | 845-457-5482 | www.camillosatthecrossroads.com

It may "look like a dump" from outside, but chef-owner Christopher Camillo's seasonal eats "hit the spot" at this old-style Montgomery American, although the menu might "benefit from a change" from time to time; decor in the three dining rooms is deemed "ordinary", but it's still "great for meeting with friends" or to take the kids.

Candlelight Inn ●⇕ *Pub Food* 22 | 8 | 15 | $21

Scarsdale | 519 Central Park Ave. (Old Army Rd.) | 914-472-9706

For "red-hot" wings "any way you want them" Scarsdale locals "love" this "been-there-forever", cash-only pub pulling a "mixed bag of patrons" ("bikers", "boomers", "families") for "all things fried", "good burgers" and "cheap beer" into the "wee hours of the night"; "ungodly waits" are a usual occurrence, but a "no-nonsense" staff "handles the crowds well", and even the "divey" digs don't keep the masses away.

Canterbury Brook Inn ☒☒ *Continental/Swiss* 23 | 20 | 23 | $40

Cornwall-on-Hudson | 331 Main St. (Quaker Ave.) | 845-534-9658 | www.thecanterburybrookinn.com

"Once you've found Cornwall, it's easy to find" this "long-established", "cozy" Continental where "year after year", chef-owner Hans Baumann serves "terrific" "comfort foods" with "a Swiss bent"; fireplaces boost the "warm, inviting" mood of "hospitality", while "modest prices" and "value" prix fixe meals midweek help make the spot "deserving of its reputation."

Capital Grille *Steak* 25 | 24 | 25 | $63

Stamford | Stamford Town Ctr. | 230 Tresser Blvd. (bet. Atlantic St. & Greyrock Pl.), CT | 203-967-0000 | www.thecapitalgrille.com

"Superb" cuts of beef are served to "lots of suits" at this "top-notch" chain that seems to be "hiding undercover as a locals' steakhouse and doing a good job of it"; boasting a "fantastic" wine list, "superior" service and a "manly club atmosphere", it's "wonderful" "for a date" or "impressing a client", so "if you're on an expense account, go for it."

Caravela *Brazilian/Portuguese* | 22 | 17 | 19 | $49 |

Tarrytown | 53 N. Broadway (bet. Central Ave. & Dixon St.) | 914-631-1863 | www.caravelatarrytown.com

"Pleasant" is the word for this Tarrytown "standby" supplying "authentic" Portuguese-Brazilian fare and "fine wines" from a "huge" list for over 25 years; though the "formal" "tuxedoed" service and "dark", "old-fashioned" setting are appealing to many, it can get "pricey."

Casa Rina of Thornwood *Italian* | 18 | 13 | 19 | $34 |

Thornwood | 886 Commerce St. (bet. Franklin Ave. & Kensico Rd.) | 914-769-4515 | www.casarinarestaurant.com

It's "like being back in the 1970s" at this Thornwood Italian where the "typical" traditional fare is "reasonably well done" and the "value"-priced early-bird special "can't be beat"; it's "nothing remarkable", but "bring the kids" and "you won't break the bank" when the check arrives.

Catamount *American* | ▽ 17 | 17 | 20 | $44 |

Mt. Tremper | Emerson Resort & Spa | 5340 Rte. 28 (Mt. Pleasant Rd.) | 845-688-2828 | www.emersonresort.com

Set on the grounds of Mt. Tremper's deluxe Emerson Resort & Spa, this easygoing Traditional American dishes up "a reliable burger" among other "moderately priced" standards from sandwiches to steaks; "pleasant" servers "who try hard" work the "comfortable", "woodsy" room, and although the eats can be "pedestrian", "a table on the terrace overlooking the Esopus Creek" makes up for much.

❷ Caterina de Medici Ⓢ *Italian* | 27 | 27 | 25 | $53 |

Hyde Park | Culinary Institute of America | 1946 Campus Dr. (Rte. 9) | 845-471-6608 | www.ciarestaurants.com

"You'll think you've died and gone to Tuscan heaven" at this "high-end", student-staffed eatery at the Hyde Park CIA, where "eager-to-please" budding chefs "strut their stuff" cooking and serving "top-of-the-line Italian" cuisine in a "beautiful" setting with "crystal chandeliers"; "earnestness" compensates for any "lack of polish", so overall, it's "five-star dining at two-star prices" – and the menu in the less-formal Al Forno room "is a steal"; P.S. closed weekends.

Catherine's Ⓢ Ⓜ *American* | 23 | 19 | 21 | $37 |

Goshen | 153 W. Main St. (New St.) | 845-294-8707 | www.catherinesrestaurant.net

"Goshen residents take pride" in this midpriced "staple" where chef Stephen Serkes "outdoes himself", creating "craveable", "quality" Traditional American "comfort" "provender" dispensed in such "mammoth portions" you can "plan on taking half your dinner home"; the "funky", "casual" pub downstairs is "anti-romantic" but upstairs is "attractive", and both are tended by a "well-trained" staff that "knows its business"; no wonder it's a "neighborhood standby."

	FOOD	DECOR	SERVICE	COST

Cathryn's Tuscan Grill *Italian*   23 | 20 | 22 | $45

Cold Spring | 91 Main St. (bet. Fair & Garden Sts.) | 845-265-5582 | www.tuscangrill.com

"A wise choice if you're antiquing" in "colorful" Cold Spring, this "local haunt" is famed for its "innovative" Tuscan cooking, "humongous Italian wine list" and "interesting small plates" served in the "spacious" new lounge; a "cheerful" staff is backed by "on-the-ball restaurateur" Cathryn, who "chats up patrons" in a "relaxing" setting that is "not over-the-top fancy" or in the "charming garden" in summer.

Catskill Rose Ⓜ *American*   - | - | - | M

Mt. Tremper | 5355 Rte. 212 (Wittenberg Rd.) | 845-688-7100 | www.catskillrose.com

You may spot "a music luminary" at this Mt. Tremper New American owned by culinary couple Peter DiSclafani and Rose-Marie Dorn, given that it's an "old established hangout" for nearby Woodstock types; the signature house-smoked duckling is "a must" on a menu of "sometimes wonderful", "moderate-to-cheap" fare, and although the room is "ordinary", in summer, you can sit in the courtyard overlooking the organic vegetable garden.

Cava Wine Bar & Restaurant *Italian*   22 | 21 | 21 | $46

New Canaan | 2 Forest St. (East Ave.), CT | 203-966-6946 | www.cavawinebar.com

A "mainstay" on New Canaan's Restaurant Row, this Northern Italian draws "couples, small groups and ladies'-night-out gatherings" with "a wonderful wine selection" and a "good mix of casual and more formal fare", served by an "amiable staff" in a "cavernous setting" that gets "loud"; a few critics decry it as "inconsistent" and "overpriced", but others regard it as a "real gem", and the summer sidewalk seating "makes it that much better."

CB Kitchen Bar *Southern*   - | - | - | M

New City | 190 South Main St. (bet. Laurel Rd. & 3rd St.) | 845-499-2294 | www.cbkitchenandbar.com

A more casual offshoot of Café Barcel in Nyack, this affordable New City spot cooks up Southern favorites from fried chicken and mac 'n' cheese to house-smoked BBQ; families settle into maroon booths on one side of the storefront space, while sports fans can watch a game in the bar on the other, and on Fridays and Saturdays, night owls file in at 10 PM for live classic rock.

NEW Cedar Street Grill *American*   - | - | - | M

Dobbs Ferry | 23 Cedar St. (B'way) | 914-674-0706 | www.cedarstreetgrillny.com

It's a family affair at this well-priced Dobbs Ferry New American where chef Matt Kay along with brother Joseph and mom Catherine serve back-to-basics comfort fare and barbecue like roast chicken and pulled pork sliders; the space has an unpretentious tavern feel with wood walls and trim, while sidewalk seating is an agreeable option in warmer weather.

FOOD | DECOR | SERVICE | COST

Cena 2000 *Italian*   23 | 23 | 23 | $49

Newburgh | 50 Front St. (3rd St.) | 845-561-7676 |
www.cena2000.com

"Elegant" Northern Italian cuisine, "wonderful service" and "magnificent views" of the Hudson add up to a "special" combo at this sister to Il Cenàcolo situated in a "pretty" spot on the Newburgh waterfront; it can get "crowded on weekends", the dining room is "small" and, "yes, it's pricey", but worth "a splurge", especially for a "romantic" evening on the patio – and *mamma mia, the desserts!*"

Centro Ristorante &   20 | 18 | 19 | $37
Bar *Italian/Mediterranean*

Greenwich | The Mill | 328 Pemberwick Rd. (Glenville Rd.), CT |
203-531-5514 | www.centroristorante.com

This "modern" Med–Northern Italian "pleases everybody" with "basic", "reliable" fare at "reasonable prices", "accommodating" service and a "colorful, lively" setting, with crayons and paper tablecloths that are "as much fun for adults as for kids" and "alfresco" dining in the warmer months looking onto a waterfall; though some "can't figure out why" it's so "popular", most consider it a "real find for informal dining."

Chaiwalla Ⓜ⊄ *Tearoom*   ▽ 25 | 23 | 24 | $25

Salisbury | 1 Main St. (Under Mountain Rd.), CT | 860-435-9758
Aficionados advise "don't miss" this "small, sweet" cozy teahouse in Salisbury offering "original, simple" lunch and brunch fare ("tomato pie to die for"), "made with love (and butter)" "on the premises" and served in the "owner's actual kitchen"; just "leave room for the exquisite desserts" and one of the "excellent" teas; open weekends-only in the winter.

Charlotte's Ⓜ *European*   21 | 25 | 20 | $48

Millbrook | 4258 Rte. 44 (bet. Deep Hollow & Kennels Rds.) |
845-677-5888 | www.charlottesny.com

"Crazy chef" Mikael Möller mans the stove while wife Alicia plays "charming, attentive hostess" at this "very pretty" Millbrook European offering an ever-changing menu of "tasty" "country cooking" along with "wine and beer from all over the world"; it's "cozy in winter", thanks to "roaring fires", while sitting outdoors in summer "overlooking the hills" and horse farm is "a delight."

Chat American Grill *American*   18 | 19 | 18 | $38

Scarsdale | 1 Christie Pl. (Eastern Pkwy.) | 914-722-4000 |
www.chatamericangrill.com

Chat 19 *American*

Larchmont | 19 Chatsworth Ave. (Boston Post Rd.) | 914-833-8871 |
www.chat19.net

A pub "with flair" describes this clubby Larchmont standby and its "prettier" Scarsdale offshoot offering a "broad", "something-for-everyone" American menu from burgers to "inventive" entrees, all "reasonably priced" and backed by "fun" drinks; it's "handy for parents" and their brood, but later on is "packed to the brim with nipped-and-tucked" "singles", when the "buzz" can be "deafening."

Chateau Hathorn Ⓜ Continental ▽ 23 | 27 | 24 | $53

Warwick | 33 Hathorn Rd. (bet. County Rte. 1A & Rte. 94) |
845-986-6099 | www.chateauhathorn.com

There's an atmosphere of "old-world charm" at this "luxurious"
"manor house" in Warwick where the "delicious" Swiss-accented
Continental fare is almost upstaged by the "exquisite decor",
whether in the "large", "castlelike" ballroom or a "romantic" "nook" in
the "cozy library", Victorian piano room or bar; "impeccable service"
and a "legendary wine cellar" help make it "worth the high price."

☒ Cheesecake Factory American 17 | 17 | 17 | $30

White Plains | The Source | 1 Maple Ave. (Bloomingdale Rd.) |
914-683-5253
West Nyack | Palisades Ctr. | 1612 Palisades Center Dr. (Hwy. 59) |
845-727-1000
www.thecheesecakefactory.com

"Humongous portions and humongous lines" characterize these
American chain links where the "textbook"-size menu offers
"lots of choices" and a "broad price spectrum" to keep families
"stuffed and happy"; the "herd 'em in, herd 'em out" feel isn't for everyone and critics knock "mass-produced" fare and "overdone" decor, but overall it's a "crowd-pleaser", especially when it comes to
the "amazing" namesake dessert, even if you need to "take it home
for much later."

Chef Antonio Italian 20 | 14 | 22 | $34

Mamaroneck | 551 Halstead Ave. (Beach Ave.) | 914-698-8610

"Still solid" is the word on this 50-year-old Mamaroneck "work-
horse" known for its "traditional" Southern Italian cooking in
"generous" helpings and coddling staff that "treats everyone like
a regular"; "reasonable prices" are a plus, but many find the
"dated" decor (and "some of the clientele") "in desperate need of
a face-lift."

Chef Luis American 25 | 18 | 23 | $46

New Canaan | 129 Elm St. (bet. Main & Park Sts.), CT | 203-972-5847 |
www.chefluis.net

Fans swear "you never want to leave" "charming" chef-owner Luis
Lopez's New American on New Canaan's main drag showcasing his
"eclectic", "flavorful" Latin- and Med-inflected fare in an expanded
space with a bar and full liquor license; if a few find Luis' habit of
naming dishes after regulars "insular", they appreciate the "friendly,
efficient" staff; P.S. outdoor seating is warmed by heat lamps.

Chez Jean-Pierre French 24 | 21 | 23 | $51

Stamford | 188 Bedford St. (Spring St.), CT | 203-357-9526 |
www.chezjeanpierre.com

Aficionados advise "go for the classics" at this "charming" French
bistro in Downtown Stamford, aka "Paris without the Seine" to fans
who laud the "savory" cuisine, "charming" owner and "courteous,
professional" servers, who are "helpful" in selecting from the "reasonable" wine list; a few feel the "smallish" room "could use an up-

| | FOOD | DECOR | SERVICE | COST |

date", while others caution "bring a full wallet", though "awesome" half-price wines on Sundays help lower the tab.

Ⅴ Chiboust *French/Mediterranean*　　24 | 18 | 21 | $49

Tarrytown | 14 Main St. (B'way) | 914-703-6550 | www.chiboust.com
Surveyors are smitten with this "sweet, little" "sliver" of a space in Tarrytown known for its "delicious", "sophisticated" takes on French-Med "bistro standards" backed by "tempting" "patisserie-quality" desserts "beckoning" from a big glass case up front; add in a "warm welcome", a "stylish" yet "unpretentious" setting plus "reasonable" tabs and it's no wonder it's so "popular"; P.S. try it "before a show at the Music Hall."

China Rose *Chinese*　　21 | 18 | 20 | $32

Rhinecliff | 1 Shatzell Ave. (Kelly St.) | 845-876-7442 |
www.chinaroserestaurant.com
"Addictive goat-cheese wontons" star among the "flavorful", "original" eats at this affordable Rhinecliff Chinese where "polite", "prompt service" and a "lively bar" alleviate "waits", as do the "generous sake margaritas" ("watch out", "they sneak up on you"); the "decor isn't anything to write home about", but even those who find the fare "so-so" say the Hudson River view from the porch is "so magical, you don't mind."

NEW China White Noodle Bar *Chinese*　　- | - | - | E

Purchase | 578 Anderson Hill Rd. (bet. New & Purchase Sts.) |
914-437-9700
Greenwich | 249 Railroad Ave. (bet. Arch St. & Field Point Rd.), CT |
203-674-8577
www.chinawhiteusa.com
Chinese fare crafted with a modern sensibility – as well as organic vegetables and grass-fed beef – is the draw at this upscale Greenwich, CT and Purchase, NY duo; it has a sophisticated, all-white setting, and though it's from restaurateur/scene-maker Jody Pennette (Gabriele's, Lolita Cocina), the vibe is relaxed, the service friendly and there's takeout too.

Ching's Table *Asian*　　24 | 17 | 19 | $37

New Canaan | 64 Main St. (Locust Ave.), CT | 203-972-8550
Wild Ginger Dumpling House *Asian*
Darien | 971 Post Rd. (Center St.), CT | 203-656-2225
"Classic items are given twists and added depth" at this Pan-Asian pair that's "always jammed on weekends" thanks to "fresh", "inventive" dishes at "reasonable prices" served in a "friendly environment", and though the decor may be "nothing to write home about", at least it's "not embarrassing"; the presence of "lots of families with kids", however, results in noise levels some liken "to the Apollo moon launch", which is why "takeout, takeout, takeout" is the mantra of many.

Chuck's Steak House *Steak*　　18 | 14 | 18 | $36

Danbury | 20 Segar St. (bet. Lake & Park Aves.), CT | 203-792-5555 |
www.chuckssteakhouse.com

(continued)

Chuck's Steak House

Darien | 1340 Boston Post Rd. (I-95), CT | 203-655-2254 |
www.chucksdarien.com

Loyalists of this "tried-and-true" steakhouse chain tout it as a
"much less expensive alternative to the overpriced" competition, offering "tender" beef "nicely cooked" and a "wonderful salad bar" in
a "casual", "family-type" setting; foes find the fare "forgettable",
describe the digs as a "dark and dreary" "flashback to the early '70s"
and warn that servers appear "overwhelmed" when "the place gets
full – which it usually is."

Chutney Masala *Indian*

23 | 22 | 22 | $39

Irvington | 4 W. Main St. (off Rte. 9) | 914-591-5500 |
www.chutneymasala.com

Indian cuisine gets some "delicious, modern twists" at this Irvington
entry featuring a "heady mix" of "beautifully prepared" dishes that
"warm the heart and stomach"; it's set in a "cool" turn-of-the-
century warehouse building "right on the Hudson" decorated with
"fabulous, old" black-and-white photos and brimming with "welcoming" hospitality, so even if it's a touch "pricey" for the genre,
there's still "nothing like it" elsewhere.

Ciao! *Italian/Pizza*

19 | 15 | 19 | $35

Eastchester | 5 John Albanese Pl. (Main St.) | 914-779-4646 |
www.ciaoeastchester.com

It's all about the "dough-twirling" chefs in the glass-enclosed
kitchen at this "casual", well-priced Eastchester pizzeria that's
especially "good for kids" who "watch the action" while their
parents tuck into "thin-crust" pies and other "simple" Italian
items with "nice bottles of wine"; the "family-friendly" mood can
be "too noisy" for some, although those in the know say upstairs
is more "civil."

Cienega Latin Cuisine *Nuevo Latino*

- | - | - | E

New Rochelle | 179 Main St. (Lispenard Ave.) | 914-632-4000 |
www.cienegarestaurant.com

Architects and Brooklyn restaurateurs Vivian Torres and Pedro
Muñoz (Luz in Ft. Greene) have transformed an awkward triangular-
shaped space in New Rochelle into this sleek Nuevo Latino eatery
painted in modern, muted browns with votives illuminating the bar;
expect upper-end dishes like Peruvian corn chowder and rum- and
sugar-cane-glazed lamb chops matched with an ambitious cocktail
list; early surveyors give it a "thumbs-up."

NEW Cinnamon Indian Cuisine *Indian*

- | - | - | M

Rhinebeck | 5856 Rte. 9 (Fox Hollow Rd.) | 845-876-7510

Regional specialties and Sri Lankan dishes dress up the traditional
Indian menu at this fairly priced newcomer near Rhinebeck,
where lunch buffets on most weekdays and at dinner on Sunday
allow novices to sample the dishes; the digs (once home to
Tanjore) are done up in soothing cinnamon and spice tones, with

FOOD DECOR SERVICE COST

Asian paintings adorning the walls and friendly owners adding to the welcoming atmosphere.

☑ City Limits Diner *Diner* | 19 | 15 | 18 | $27 |

White Plains | 200 Central Ave. (bet. Harding Ave. & Tarrytown Rd.) | 914-686-9000
Stamford | 135 Harvard Ave. (I-95, exit 6), CT | 203-348-7000
www.citylimitsdiner.com

"You're sure to run into someone you know" at these "ever-popular" "diners on steroids" in Stamford and White Plains dispensing "sophisticated takes" on "wholesome" "comfort-fare" classics like "breakfast 'round the clock" and "tempting", "made-from-scratch desserts"; if prices are relatively "high", so is the "quality", and a "cheerful" chrome-bedecked setting and "kid-friendly" service keep them "tried-and-true."

Clamp's Hamburger Stand *Burgers* | – | – | – | I |

New Milford | Rte. 202 (Sawyer Hill Rd.), CT | no phone

There's no phone, signage or even an address at this iconic, circa-1939 New Milford stand, whose "roadside ambiance seals the deal" for some, though most are hooked by the burgers with a "nice char on them", which are "not fancy" and "probably not healthy", just "really good", especially when topped with "excellent sautéed onions"; be sure to "get there in the summer", for it's closed from September to April.

☒☒☒ Club Car | – | – | – | E |
Restaurant Lounge *American*

Mamaroneck | 1 Station Plaza (Mamaroneck Ave.) | 914-777-9300 | www.clubcarny.com

Mamaroneck's restored landmark train station from 1888 is the setting for this New American newcomer offering both a casual tavern and menu, plus a more-formal dining room with entrees like pork chops and ahi tuna in the $24–$40 range; the space retains some original architectural features including a multicolored glass window above the main entrance and a ticket counter–turned-bar where partyers can revel after dinner to DJ-spun tunes and live music.

☒☒☒ Coals ☒ ☒ *Pizza* | – | – | – | I |

Port Chester | 35½ N. Main St. (Adee St.) | 914-305-3220 | www.coalspizza.com

This Port Chester offshoot of a Bronx pie shop showcases thin-crust pizzas cooked on an open grill with a few wacky spins like a Fluffernutter dessert version made with Nutella and mascarpone cheese; modest pricing, comfy couches and mismatched bookshelves lend it a certain quirky appeal.

Cobble Stone ☻ *American* | 15 | 13 | 16 | $26 |

Purchase | 620 Anderson Hill Rd. (bet. Lincoln Ave. & Purchase St.) | 914-253-9678 | www.thecobblestonerestaurant.com

"Convenient to SUNY Purchase" and the PepsiCo Sculpture Gardens, this "old-fashioned" tavern attracts students and theatergoers for a "nothing-fancy" American lineup of "good burgers", "cold beer" and

	FOOD	DECOR	SERVICE	COST

the like; judging from the scores, the "food needs work", but tabs are "low" and service "quick", so it's "fine for what it is."

Colony Grill ⬤ *Pizza* — 24 | 7 | 13 | $18

Stamford | 172 Myrtle Ave. (bet. Elm & Frederick Sts.), CT | 203-359-2184 | www.colonygrill.com

People "drive for hours" and endure "long waits, crowds" and "surly service" at this "hole-in-the-wall" in an "industrial" area of Stamford for its "amazing", "addictive" thin-crust pizzas, which have earned it a "cult following", even if a few skeptics pan the pies as "over-rated"; some say the "bar" setting is "not a great place to take the kids", but cognoscenti report the new Fairfield location has "much better atmosphere" and is family-friendly.

Columbus Park Trattoria Ⓢ *Italian* — 25 | 20 | 23 | $47

Stamford | 205 Main St. (Washington Blvd.), CT | 203-967-9191 | www.columbusparktrattoria.com

At this "always friendly Downtown Stamford gem", "authentic dishes not usually found outside Italy" and "divine homemade pastas" have been "consistently palate-pleasing for decades", and the "all-in-the-family operation" "bends over backward trying to please its guests"; some complain of "New York" prices and "cramped" quarters that get "noisy" when "crowded", but most insist its "tasty perfection" is "not to be missed."

🆕 Comfort Ⓜ *American* — - | - | - | M

Hastings-on-Hudson | 583 Warburton Ave. (Maple Ave.) | 914-231-7711 | www.comfortrestaurant.net

New owners have resurrected this Hastings New American, keeping much of the original menu, which focuses on easygoing market-fresh fare like hanger steak and herbed chicken matched with a bounty of veggie sides; prices remain moderate, and though the simple wood-and-brick space got a spruce-up, it remains as cozy as before.

Commissary ⓈⓂ *American* — - | - | - | M

Tappan | 65 Old Tappan Rd. (bet. Brandt Ave. & Stephens Ln.) | 845-398-3232 | www.commissary65.com

Chef Daniel Foti has settled into the Tappan space where Village Grille used to be with this New American serving seasonal fare such as Atlantic cod and grilled rib-eye along with homemade desserts; a burgundy-and-pumpkin paint job snazzes up the simple setting, as does the low-key jazz and blues soundtrack.

Community Table *American* — ▽ 27 | 20 | 21 | $51

Washington | 223 Litchfield Tpke. (Wilbur Rd.), CT | 860-868-9354 | www.communitytablect.com

At this Washington New American, "inventive" chef Joel Viehland's "ever-changing menus" of "uniformly excellent" dishes emphasizing "fresh food from local farms" are "meant to entice knowing locavores"; opinions are split on the spare room made with green building materials ("original and attractive" vs. "charmless" and "noisy"), but for most it's a "splendid addition to the Litchfield County dining scene", now taking reservations; P.S. closed Tuesdays and Wednesdays.

Northeast"; there's almost "no atmosphere" (and no hard liquor), although service is "friendly" and tabs are "as cheap as they come."

Emilio Ristorante ☑ *Italian*   25 | 20 | 25 | $53

Harrison | 1 Colonial Pl. (bet. Harrison Ave. & Purdy St.) | 914-835-3100 | www.emilioristorante.com

"A throwback to the Italian restaurants of yesteryear", this "charming" Harrison "treasure" turns out "excellent" "classic" dishes (including "antipasti you can make a meal of") in a "cozy" warren of rooms in a restored Colonial home; yes, it's "expensive", but with such an "accommodating" staff, it's "worth it" for "special occasions."

Emma's Ale House   *Pub Food*   18 | 16 | 18 | $32

White Plains | 68 Gedney Way (Mamaroneck Ave.) | 914-683-3662 | www.emmasalehouse.com

"It's basically a sports bar", but nonetheless this "solid neighborhood joint" in White Plains "doesn't disappoint" with "polished" American "pub grub", an "excellent beer selection" and gratis baskets of "warm pretzels" that are "worth the price of the meal"; factor in a "congenial" atmosphere with pictures of the owner's canine lining the walls, and it works for a "casual" night out.

Empire Hunan   *Chinese/Japanese*   20 | 17 | 19 | $26

Yorktown Heights | 1975 Commerce St. (Hanover St.) | 914-962-5500

Boosters "bring a group" to this "popular" Yorktown Heights "arena" of a restaurant, a "longtime source" for "large portions" of "reliable" Chinese-Japanese eats adjusted "for suburban tastes", plus sushi; cynics suggest that "inexpensive" prices are "the chief attraction."

Encore Bistro Français   *French*   23 | 19 | 22 | $43

Larchmont | 22 Chatsworth Ave. (Boston Post Rd.) | 914-833-1661 | www.encore-bistro.com

A "delightful taste of Paris", this "tiny" Larchmont "charmer" transports guests with "wonderful" French cuisine and "just enough snooty service to add the final touch of authenticity"; "ever-present crowds" mean its "teensy storefront" space done up with vintage posters has a tendency to be "much too noisy", but "value pricing" compensates; P.S. lunch is "quieter" and a downright "bargain."

Enzo's   *Italian*   20 | 15 | 21 | $45

Mamaroneck | 451 Mamaroneck Ave. (Halstead Ave.) | 914-698-2911

An "affable" staff "makes you feel at home" at this "old-world" Mamaroneck Italian that "hasn't changed in eons", offering "robust", if "not exactly original", fare in "portions ample enough to feed Pavarotti"; however, in light of the "high-end prices", a number of surveyors note the "tired" Tuscan-inspired setting "could use a little freshening" up.

Eos Greek Cuisine   *Greek*   24 | 19 | 22 | $39

Stamford | 490 Summer St. (bet. Broad & Spring Sts.), CT | 203-569-6250 | www.eosgreekcuisine.com

Fans cheer "*opa*" for the "modern" Greek fare ("you'll wish you could hold eight forks" when devouring the octopus) at this "family-run" midpriced venue in Downtown Stamford's Restaurant Row; while the "Mykonos white" contemporary decor leaves a few cold, the staff "aims to please", plus there's "outdoor seating in warm weather."

Epstein's Kosher Deli *Deli* | 19 | 8 | 15 | $23 |

Hartsdale | Dalewood Shopping Ctr. | 387 N. Central Ave. (Rte. 119) | 914-428-5320 | www.epsteinsdeli.com
Yonkers | 2574 Central Park Ave. (Fort Hill Rd.) | 914-793-3131 | www.epsteinskosher.com

Some "of the last" of the "NYC-style" delis, these separately owned "shrines" to "Jewish comfort food" in Hartsdale and Yonkers are "cherished" for their "classic corned-beef" sandwiches "with all the trimmings" and other "homestyle" kosher eats that "warm the heart"; service is "gruff" and the "old-school" setting is strictly "utilitarian", but it works for a "nostalgia trip."

☒ Equus *American/French* | 25 | 28 | 25 | $80 |

Tarrytown | Castle on the Hudson | 400 Benedict Ave. (Martling Ave.) | 914-631-3646 | www.castleonthehudson.com

"Old-world elegance" is alive and well at this "hilltop oasis" in Tarrytown, a "real castle" whose "fairy-tale" setting includes "gorgeous views" of the Hudson and a "baronial" dining room with "flowers everywhere"; service is "spectacular" and the "exorbitantly" priced French–New American cuisine suitably "fit for a king", so even if it's a tad "stodgy" for some, you can't beat it for a "special occasion"; P.S. brunch is a "less-formal" affair.

☒ Escoffier Restaurant Ⓢ Ⓜ *French* | 27 | 25 | 26 | $63 |

Hyde Park | Culinary Institute of America | 1946 Campus Dr. (Rte. 9) | 845-471-6608 | www.ciarestaurants.com

The "crème de la crème" at the Hyde Park CIA, this "dressy" "foodie's delight" presents "first-rate", "fine French cuisine" prepared by "future Iron Chefs", with the "cavalry" (aka "chef-professors") "to back 'em up"; the decor recently underwent an "elegant" "buffing", so add "delightful", "retro service" from "earnest" students, and although it's "expensive", it's "perfect" for a "celebration."

España Ⓜ *Spanish* | 20 | 19 | 21 | $42 |

Larchmont | 147 Larchmont Ave. (Boston Post Rd.) | 914-833-1331 | www.espanatapas.com

For something "different" in Larchmont, try this "inviting" Spaniard for "authentic" tapas, "fantastic wines" and a multitude of paellas served in a "lovely" space; an "attentive" staff is a perk, although critics complain of "hit-or-miss" fare ("choose carefully") and bills that "can add up quickly."

Euro Asian *Asian* | 17 | 18 | 17 | $33 |

Port Chester | Waterfront at Port Chester | 30 Westchester Ave. (bet. Townsend St. & Traverse Ave.) | 914-937-3680 | www.asianbistrony.com

A "mix" of traditional and "fusion" Asian dishes with "gorgeously presented" sushi characterizes this "lively" Port Chester eatery situated in a slick, wood-lined space that feels "cool" for the neighbor-

FOOD | DECOR | SERVICE | COST

hood; in spite of the "great location" near the multiplex, detractors decry the service as "lackluster", and the fare as inconsistent.

Eveready Diner ● *Diner* | 20 | 19 | 20 | $21

Brewster | 90 Independence Way (Dykeman Rd.) | 845-279-9009
Hyde Park | 4189 Albany Post Rd./Rte. 9 (bet. Calmer Pl. & South Dr.) | 845-229-8100
www.theeverydiner.com

Even "self-proclaimed food snobs" get "nostalgic" at this "chrome-and-neon" slice of "Americana" in Hyde Park and its equally "retro" Brewster outpost, both celebrating the diner's "glory days in spades" with "crammed menus" offering "piles" of "stick-to-your-ribs grub", malteds, egg creams and such; "cheerful service" and "gentle prices" add to the "consummate experience", while 24-hour service on weekends lives up to the name.

F.A.B. *American/French* | 19 | 19 | 19 | $45

Mt. Kisco | 222 E. Main St. (bet. Hyatt Ave. & Lenox Pl.) | 914-864-1661 | www.fabbistro.com

With wood-paneled walls, a tin ceiling and a "New York City–feel" this "upscale-casual" Mt. Kisco yearling has established "a bit of a scene" at the "busy" bar while satisfying other appetites with a "fairly standard" French–New American bistro menu, which, like the "agreeable" service, can be "hit-or-miss"; a notable "noise level" and "expensive" prices seem more "so-so" than fab.

The Farmer's Wife *American* | ▽ 21 | 12 | 18 | $20

Ancramdale | 3 County Rd. 8 (Rte. 32) | 518-329-5431 | www.thefarmerswife.biz

Columbia County caterer Dorcas Sommerhoff, "an honest-to-goodness farmer's wife", is behind this "quirky" "country deli" "in the middle of nowhere" (aka "the tiny hamlet of Ancramdale"), offering the "epitome of farm-fresh, wholesome" American food at breakfast and lunch along with "terrific" prepared dinners and baked goodies to take home; the tiny storefront with its four tables was recently smartened up, although on warm days, some prefer to sit outside.

NEW Farm to Table Bistro *American* | - | - | - | M

Fishkill | 1083 Rte. 9 (Smithtown Rd.) | 845-297-1111 | www.ftbistro.com

No surprise, the focus is on regional ingredients at this Fishkill New American newcomer, with dishes like pan-seared duck and short ribs prepared with meats, veggies, eggs and breads sourced from local farms, bakeries and dairies; reclaimed wood, barrels, beams and backlit stained glass give the bar rural appeal, while vintage farm tools dress up the main dining room; P.S. there's also a private wine room and sidewalk seating in summer.

Ferrante *Italian* | 20 | 21 | 18 | $44

Stamford | 191 Summer St. (Broad St.), CT | 203-323-2000 | www.ferranterestaurant.com

For "*delizioso* dining" in a "great location", fans tout this Northern Italian in Downtown Stamford, which earns bravos for its "attrac-

FOOD | DECOR | SERVICE | COST

"tive" oak-pillared interior, highlighted by abundant fresh flowers and windows that open to the street in summer, "above-average" cuisine and "friendly" service; detractors demur, however, calling it "inconsistent" and "overpriced."

The Fez *Mediterranean/Moroccan* ▽ 20 | 19 | 22 | $37

Stamford | 227 Summer St. (Broad St.), CT | 203-975-0479 | www.thefez1.com

"Inventive" Moroccan and Mediterranean tapas and an "eclectic" wine list are served in a "sexy" space that "looks like it was lifted from a Middle Eastern souk" at this "interesting, affordable" option in Downtown Stamford; the "omnipresent" owner and "attentive" staff make sure "all diners have a good time", while rotating belly dancers, live music and bring-your-own-vinyl-record nights add to the "unusual, terrific" experience.

Fife 'n Drum *American* 18 | 18 | 21 | $44

Kent | 53 N. Main St./Rte. 7 (Rte. 341), CT | 860-927-3509 | www.fifendrum.com

At their "reliable favorite" in Kent, the Traymon family "really does treat you like one of them", offering a "comfortable" Traditional American menu, including duck and Caesar salad served tableside by "tuxedo-clad" waiters, and an "extensive wine list"; patriarch Dolph plays jazz piano in the "classic" "men's-club" setting, and while a few critics find it "overrated and overpriced", most consider this "step back in time" a real "treat"; closed Tuesdays.

Fifty Coins *American* 16 | 13 | 18 | $25

Ridgefield | 426 Main St. (Big Shop Ln.), CT | 203-438-1456 | www.fiftycoinsrestaurant.com

"Local families" and "laid-back ladies who do casual lunch" flock to this "afforable", casual American in Ridgefield for a "quick bite" of "basic but tasty" "pub-style" eats and craft beers (including gluten-free), served by a "friendly" staff in a "horsey-theme" setting (it's named after a racehorse); neighsayers, though, knock the fare as merely "so-so" and bemoan the "noise" and "kids"; P.S. the New Canaan location closed in 2011.

59 Bank *American* 19 | 18 | 19 | $34

New Milford | 59 Bank St. (Railroad St.), CT | 860-350-5995 | www.59bank.com

A "comfortable" "locals' place", this New Milford American is a popular stop for "drinks" and "reliable", "down-home" eats such as panini, flatbread pizzas and salads at "moderate" prices; the staff is "friendly", though some say the service can be "spotty" and suggest the menu could "use an update"; P.S. live music on weekends.

Fig & Olive *Mediterranean* - | - | - | E

Scarsdale | Vernon Hills Shopping Ctr. | 696 White Plains Rd. (Burnham Rd.) | 914-725-2900 | www.figandolive.com

This Scarsdale outpost of the Manhattan-based chainlet is set in sophisticated, sunwashed digs with seating at private tables or at a marble tasting bar; the upscale Med menu features a multitude of small plates, plus mains like grilled lamb on rosemary skewers and branzino with aged balsamic matched with regional wines.

Fin *Japanese* | 23 | 12 | 19 | $33 |

Stamford | 219 Main St. (Washington Blvd.), CT | 203-359-6688 | www.fin-sushi.com

"Fin fans" "cannot get enough" of the "beautifully presented", "super-fresh" sushi at this Stamford Japanese and declare it "one of the best buys" for a "simple meal without fuss"; "friendly", "helpful" service and "reasonable" prices are additional pluses, but critics carp over "cramped seating" and "no real decor", lamenting that the "pristine" fare "deserves grander surroundings."

Finalmente Trattoria ⓜ *Italian* | 24 | 21 | 22 | $47 |

Sleepy Hollow | 31 Beekman Ave. (Lawrence Ave.) | 914-909-4787

A "tiny place with a big heart", this "sophisticated" Sleepy Hollow trattoria charms customers with "excellent", "contemporary" Italian fare prepared with "the freshest ingredients" and delivered by an "attentive" staff; factor in relatively moderate bills, and fans only "wish they took reservations"; P.S. patio seating eases the "tight" quarters in summer.

Flames Steakhouse *Steak* | 22 | 18 | 20 | $64 |

Briarcliff Manor | 533 N. State Rd. (bet. Chappaqua Rd. & Ryder Ave.) | 914-923-3100 | www.flamessteakhouse.com

"Year after year", the "prime meats" "sizzle" at this "solid" Briarcliff steakhouse, and though the sides are only "so-so", a "fantastic wine selection" paired with "personable" service keep the "crowds" coming; some find it "way too costly", citing "casual" decor and "uneven" offerings, but satisfied fans insist the beef "is worth it."

Flatiron ⓜ *American/Steak* | 23 | 20 | 25 | $42 |

Red Hook | 7488 S. Broadway/Rte. 9 (Rte. 199) | 845-758-8260 | www.flatironsteakhouse.com

"A rare steakhouse that doesn't break the bank", this "welcoming" Red Hook American serves "superb" cuts of beef with "a petite-portion option", "an array of juicy burgers" (including a duck and a veggie version) plus other "delicious", "well-prepared" fare – even "fresh oysters"; the "city-chic" decor strikes some as "blah", but "cheerful", "smooth service" more than makes up for it.

⨅ 42 ⓩ *American* | 22 | 27 | 22 | $72 |

White Plains | Ritz-Carlton Westchester | 1 Renaissance Sq., 42nd fl. (Main St.) | 914-761-4242 | www.42therestaurant.com

"So very ritzy" with its "stunning views" and "sophisticated vibe", this "elegant" 42nd-floor dining room at the Ritz-Carlton in White Plains makes you want to "dress up" to celebrate "special occasions" and savor "talented" chef Anthony Goncalves' "inventive riffs" on New American cuisine; however, service "varies from visit to visit" (sometimes "personable", other times "snooty"), which can be irksome given the "sky-high prices."

	FOOD	DECOR	SERVICE	COST

Francesca's Ⓜ *Italian/Pizza*   21 | 12 | 20 | $31

Rhinebeck | 88 Aster Way (Rte. 9) | 845-876-2129

"Think *Cheers* with food instead of beer" and you get a sense of this "old-fashioned" Rhinebeck "Italian comfort-food joint" that's a favorite for its "down-home, simple" dishes dispensed in "truly large portions"; a "warm", "welcoming" staff and affordable rates help keep the "no-frills", "glorified-pizzeria" setup "crowded."

Frank Guido's Little Italy *Italian*   21 | 15 | 21 | $32

Kingston | 14 Thomas St. (B'way) | 845-340-1682 | www.frankguidoslittleitaly.com

A "vast menu" of "family-style" Italiana lures locals to this Midtown Kingston "hangout" dishing up same in "portions that will have you rolling out in a wheelbarrow"; brick walls in the renovated factory setting "echo with camaraderie" (aka "noise") and "close" tables mean you're "squished", but the "helpful" staff and "good value" compensate.

Frankie & Fanucci's   21 | 17 | 19 | $24
Wood Oven Pizzeria *Pizza*

Hartsdale | 202 E. Hartsdale Ave. (bet. Fenimore & Rockledge Rds.) | 914-725-8400

Mamaroneck | 301 Mamaroneck Ave. (Palmer Ave.) | 914-630-4360 www.fandfpizza.com

A "welcome addition" to the Westchester "pizza scene", this Hartsdale parlor puts out "terrific" Neapolitan-style thin-crust pies that are "a cut above" the competition (and prices are a step up too); it's "kid city" in the "casual" dining room most nights, so "noisy", "crowded" conditions should come as no surprise; P.S. the Mamaroneck branch is newer, and also serves pasta.

Frankie & Johnnie's Steakhouse *Steak*   24 | 22 | 22 | $66

Rye | 77 Purchase St. (Purdy Ave.) | 914-925-3900 | www.frankieandjohnnies.com

Boosters "bank on" this "top-notch" Rye steakhouse in a former savings and loan for "perfectly cooked" "prime" beef and "delicious" sides bolstered by a 650-label wine list; its "inviting" white-tablecloth setting and "attentive" service make it well suited to a "client" lunch, but you'll need to "bring the boss' credit card."

Ⓩ Frank Pepe Pizzeria *Pizza*   24 | 11 | 17 | $21

Yonkers | 1955 Central Park Ave. (bet. Heights Dr. & Northrop Ave.) | 914-961-8284

Ⓩ Frank Pepe Pizzeria Napoletana *Pizza*

NEW **Danbury** | 59 Federal Rd. (White Turkey Rd.), CT | 203-790-7373 www.pepespizzeria.com

"There's magic in that coal-fired brick oven" swear fans of these New Haven pizzeria offshoots, putting out what many claim is "the most memorable pie you'll ever inhale" – featuring thin, chewy crusts "with the right hint of smokiness" and toppings like "fresh shucked" clams – that's worth enduring "long waits" and "grumpy"

some of "the crispiest pizza" around; indeed, it's not fancy", but it's "a local hangout."

NEW Hudson 🖼 Ⓜ *American*   - | - | - | E

Briarcliff Manor | 25 Studio Hill Rd. (Haymount Terr.) | 914-502-0080
This spare-no-expense revamp of a grand 1912 estate is set on four acres of Hudsonside property in lush Briarcliff Manor; an all-star team heads up the kitchen under chef Scott Riesenberger – lately of NYC's Corton – and delivers seasonal, local cuisine at multiple price points, meaning that while the main dining room's haute cuisine might cost you, frugal diners can also sit in the bar and order a burger.

Hudson Grille *American*   20 | 22 | 20 | $37

White Plains | 165 Mamaroneck Ave. (bet. E. Post Rd. & Maple Ave.) | 914-997-2000 | www.hudsongrilleny.com
"More upscale" than your "average Mamaroneck Avenue pub", this "handsome" White Plains New American proffers an "expansive" lineup of "surprisingly good" fare, from crab cakes to rib-eyes; a "knowledgeable" staff is a plus, and there's also an "active" bar crowded with "singles"

NEW Hudson Hil's Café *American*   - | - | - | M

Cold Spring | 129-131 Main St. (Kemble Ave.) | 845-265-9471 | www.hudsonhils.com
Using the local produce and grass-fed meats that they sell in their adjacent market, chef Bob Hayes and his wife (and cafe namesake), Hilary, launched this Cold Spring American, where sunny-yellow and white digs set a cheerful mood for fairly priced egg-centric breakfasts, with salads and sandwiches at lunch; fancier fare such as trout stuffed with spinach and Camembert plus steak frites and other bistro favorites are served at dinner on weekends, and some weekdays in season.

Hudson House Inn *American*   22 | 23 | 22 | $46

Cold Spring | 2 Main St. (West St.) | 845-265-9355 | www.hudsonhouseinn.com
"Overlooking the Hudson" in "darling" Cold Spring, this "classy but relaxed" New American set in a "quaint" 1832 inn keeps customers "happily stuffed" with "tasty", "well-thought-out" fare that's "as good as" the "romantic views"; "prompt" service, plus a "spiffy dining room" with a "cozy" fireplace and a porch for summer, help make it a "mainstay for locals."

Hudson House of Nyack Ⓜ *American*   23 | 22 | 23 | $48

Nyack | 134 Main St. (Franklin St.) | 845-353-1355 | www.hudsonhousenyack.com
"Personable" co-owner/pastry chef Matt Hudson "treats everyone like a regular" at this Nyack New American dispensing "delicious", "modern" fare followed by "off-the-hook" desserts; the "marvelously decorated" former village hall with its "cool" jail wine cellar and small bar has an "urban" vibe that's so "lively" that even being "cramped feels like fun"; maybe it's "not cheap, but it never disappoints."

	FOOD	DECOR	SERVICE	COST

Hudson's Ribs & Fish *Seafood/Steak*   19 | 18 | 21 | $36

Fishkill | 1099 Rte. 9 (bet. Old Rte. 9 & Smithtown Rd.) | 845-297-5002 |
www.hudsonsribsandfish.com

It's "nothing fancy" but the "parade" of "well-prepared" surf 'n' turf
specialties is "done with aplomb" at this "tried-and-true" Fishkill
eatery where meals kick off via "out-of-this-world" popovers with
strawberry butter; portions are "hearty" and rates "reasonable", so
as long as "you're not looking for chichi decor", it's a "dependable
choice" that's "fun" for families; P.S. the Decor score does not reflect a post-Survey update.

Hudson Street Cafe *American*   - | - | - | I

Cornwall-on-Hudson | 237 Hudson St. (bet. Duncan & Maple Aves.) |
845-534-2450 | www.hudsonstreetcafe.com

After working with Slow Food guru Alice Waters in Berkeley, CA, chef
Donna Hammond is displaying her "excellent culinary talents" at this
affordable American cafe in Cornwall-on-Hudson, where she caters
to carnivores, kiddies, vegans and the allergic alike; a broad menu of
"very good" breakfast and lunch choices, plus heartier fare at BYO
dinners Thursday–Saturdays, come served in a homespun setting.

Hudson Water Club *American*   18 | 22 | 18 | $44

West Haverstraw | Haverstraw Marina | 606 Beach Rd. (Rte. 9W) |
845-271-4046 | www.hudsonwaterclub.com

Boaters can "dock and dine" at this "informal" New American seafooder at the Haverstraw Marina, whose "huge", "trendy" digs with
walls of windows attract a "young crowd" of landlubbers as well; the
eats are "solid if not exciting", so the "spectacular view" of the Hudson
is "the most compelling reason" to go; P.S. closed January–March.

Hunan Larchmont *Chinese/Japanese*   17 | 12 | 17 | $25

Larchmont | 1961 Palmer Ave. (West Ave.) | 914-833-0400 |
www.hunanlarchmont.com

A longtimer on the "suburban Chinese" circuit, this Larchmont entry
offers "predictable", "fairly average" cooking and sushi that fits the
bill when you want a "quick dinner after catching a movie down the
street"; "rushed" service "without a smile" and digs that could bear
some "remodeling" prompt many to opt for takeout.

Ichi Riki *Japanese*   19 | 13 | 18 | $34

Elmsford | Elmsford Plaza | 1 E. Main St./Rte. 119 (Rte. 9A) |
914-592-2220 | www.ichirikisushi.com

"Better-than-average" sushi and "traditional" Japanese fare are
served up by "attentive" waitresses in "kitschy" "geisha" dress at
this Elmsford Japanese offering solid "bang for your buck"; it's "convenient", even if the "tired" strip-mall setting could "use a face-lift."

Il Bacio Trattoria *Italian*   20 | 15 | 19 | $30

Bronxville | 1 Park Pl. (Pondfield Rd.) | 914-337-4100 |
www.ilbaciotrattoria.com

"Always mobbed", this Bronxville Italian is "kid-friendly to the ex-
treme" with "lots of families" cramming in "elbow to elbow" for

FOOD DECOR SERVICE COST

"imaginative" pizzas, salads and pasta; service can be "variable", and "don't expect peace and quiet", but for a "casual", "value"-priced meal, the majority maintains "you can't go wrong"; P.S. don't miss the "great, homemade gelato."

Z Il Barilotto ☒ Italian
27 | 23 | 25 | $48

Fishkill | 1113 Main St. (North St.) | 845-897-4300 | www.ilbarilottorestaurant.com

They're "at the top of their game" at this "fantastic" Fishkill cousin to Aroma Osteria, where a "polished staff" serves "sublime" Italian dishes and "scrumptious specials" matched by a "terrific wine list"; "lovely, exposed brick" lends the restored 1800s carriage house a "casual but smart" feel, and although "you can rack up a bill" and it's often "noisy", those who "go again and again" say it's a "stellar experience."

Il Castello ☒ Italian
24 | 19 | 25 | $54

Mamaroneck | 576 Mamaroneck Ave. (Waverly Ave.) | 914-777-2200 | www.ilcastellomenu.com

This "tiny" "jewel of a place" in Mamaroneck "packs a big punch" with "delicious" "Northern Italian delicacies" and an "excellent wine list" delivered via an "impeccable" staff; rich woods, modern decor and "civil sound levels" provide an "impress-a-date" setting at a cost that's "not that expensive" for the neighborhood.

Z Il Cenàcolo Italian
28 | 24 | 26 | $62

Newburgh | 228 S. Plank Rd./Rte. 52 (bet. I-87 & Rte. 300) | 845-564-4494 | www.ilcenacolorestaurant.com

"Consistently *molto buono*", this "first-class" Newburgh Northern Italian may look "unimposing outside" but "sets the bar very high", greeting diners in "nicely decorated" digs with a "groaning board" of "second-to-none" antipasti and an "impressive staff" that recites a "long list" of "mouthwatering" specials; it's "expensive, yes, but cheaper than a trip to Tuscany, and no pat-down."

Il Forno ☒ Italian
21 | 16 | 21 | $32

Somers | 343 Rte. 202 (Rte. 100) | 914-277-7575 | www.ilfornosomers.com

This "moderately priced" Somers trattoria "has the right formula" for a "casual, family-style" spot, including "first-rate" brick-oven pies and "huge portions" of "wholesome" Italian eats, "enthusiastically served"; the digs may be "pizzerialike", but the atmosphere is "warm", so folks "keep going back."

Il Portico Italian
23 | 21 | 23 | $49

Tappan | 89 Main St. (Oak Tree Rd.) | 845-365-2100 | www.ilportico.com

A "wonderfully quaint" onetime stagecoach stop serves as the backdrop for "good", "authentic" Northern Italian cooking at this "lovely" if lesser-known Tappan spot located in a "historical neighborhood"; it's a tad "expensive", and portions are perhaps "tiny", but softly lit, flower-bedecked dining rooms add to the "perfect ambiance" that helps make it "worth a trip."

Il Sogno *Italian/Mediterranean*

24 | 19 | 23 | $49

Port Chester | 316 Boston Post Rd. (S. Regent St.) | 914-937-7200 | www.ilsognony.com

Still somewhat under the radar, this Port Chester "sleeper" is an "unexpected find" for "excellent" Italian-Med cuisine (including "wonderful specials") set down in a "sleek", "subdued" interior of stone and wood; given the "first-rate" service from a "passionate" staff, many don't mind if it's "a few dollars more" than the competition.

Il Sorriso Ⓜ *Italian*

21 | 19 | 21 | $46

Irvington | 5 N. Buckhout St. (Main St.) | 914-591-2525 | www.ilsorriso.com

An "old standby that won't let you down", this Irvington Italian is known for its "tasty", if "predictable", menu served up in "comfortable", "sedate" surroundings, or out on a Hudson River–facing terrace that's a real "treat" in summer; "reasonable costs" and service "with a smile" make for an "enjoyable" experience all around.

Il Tesoro *Italian*

25 | 20 | 23 | $41

Goshen | 6 N. Church St. (Main St.) | 845-294-8373 | www.iltesoro.us

"Although tiny", this Goshen "go-to" turns out "amazing Northern Italian" dishes that have such a "big effect" it makes "the lack of space tolerable"; an "excellent" staff "treats everyone like family" in "pleasant surroundings" with brick and mustard walls, the pace is "leisurely" and the desserts are "to die for"; in short, it really "lives up to its name."

Imperial Wok *Chinese/Japanese*

17 | 15 | 17 | $28

North White Plains | 736 N. Broadway (bet. McDougal Dr. & Palmer Ave.) | 914-686-2700

"No surprises", just a "giant menu" of "typical" Chinese and Japanese "favorites" served up in "large portions" keeps this North White Plains "neighborhood" "standby" "bustling"; sure, the "decor could use improvement" but "reasonable" prices make it "worth a visit" or a call for "speedy delivery."

NEW Impulse Hibachi *Japanese*

- | - | - | M

White Plains | 32 Mamaroneck Ave. (bet. Main St. & Martine Ave.) | 914-285-1888 | www.impulsehibachi.com

A red granite bar, leather couches and dim lighting set a sexy mood at this posh White Plains Japanese hibachi and lounge across from the City Center; dexterous chefs perform knife tricks and build fiery onion volcanoes while preparing seafood and myriad meats at lighted grill tables beneath a wall-length mural of feudal Japan.

India House Restaurant *Indian*

22 | 16 | 20 | $33

Montrose | 2089 Albany Post Rd. (Trinity Ave.) | 914-736-0005 | www.indiahouseny.com

Groupies "gobble up" the "marvelously complex" Indian "favorites" at this "trusted" Montrose standby also famed for its "better-than-usual" lunchtime buffet; the "faded", "kitschy" setting "hasn't changed in forever", but a "thoughtful" staff and "fair prices" compensate.

some partake at the long, copper-topped bar, others prefer a table or sofa in the brick-walled lounge in back, while the hideaway courtyard beckons in warm weather.

Karuta *Japanese*
▽ 18 | 12 | 18 | $33

New Rochelle | North Ridge Shopping Ctr. | 77 Quaker Ridge Rd. (North Ave.) | 914-636-6688

"The owner is a delight" at this New Rochelle Japanese that's "nice to have in the neighborhood" thanks to its "reasonably priced" sushi and cooked items; it's a mainstay for takeout, even if some shrug the food and setting are "nothing special."

Kelly's Corner *Pub Food*
▽ 17 | 12 | 19 | $22

Brewster | 1625 Rte. 22 (Rte. 312) | 845-278-4297 | www.kellyscorner.com

A "local watering hole" that "doesn't try to be something it's not", this "traditional", Irish-accented American pub in Brewster dishes up "better-than-average" grub in "abundant" amounts at good "value" "for the money"; "friendly" staffers and a "casual" setting with wooden booths make it "great for kids" too, but "go early, it fills up" fast "at prime time."

The King & I *Thai*
17 | 16 | 18 | $31

Nyack | 93 Main St. (bet. Broadway Ave. & Cedar St.) | 845-358-8588 | www.kingandinyack.com

"Thai is hard to come by" in Nyack, so those "in the mood" head to this storefront playing it "safe" with "satisfying" "standards" whose "level of spice can be adjusted to your taste" and "won't break the budget", either; if the "traditional decor" doesn't suit, "a seat at the window allows for people-watching."

Kirari *Japanese*
▽ 20 | 11 | 19 | $34

Scarsdale | 30 Garth Rd. (bet. Bronx River Pkwy. & Popham Rd.) | 914-725-3730 | www.kirarisushi.com

This "reliable, neighborhood" Scarsdale Japanese keeps customers coming with "decent" "classic" sushi at "affordable" rates, including a lunch box that's a "steal"; although many wish they'd "innovate" the decor and menu, it's still a mainstay for takeout.

Kira *Japanese*
23 | 14 | 20 | $35

Armonk | Armonk Town Ctr. | 575 Main St. (School St.) | 914-765-0800

The "wide range" of "original", "fantastically fresh" sushi and specialty rolls may just "spoil you for anywhere else" at this "casual" Armonk Japanese; service can be "brusque" and the strip-mall setting is "nothing to write home about", but the fare's "well priced" so it's about "as good as it gets in the 'burbs."

Kisco Kosher *Deli*
17 | 10 | 15 | $25

White Plains | 230 E. Post Rd. (bet. B'way & Mamaroneck Ave.) | 914-948-6600 | www.kiscokosher.com

"Overstuffed sandwiches", matzo-ball soup and other "traditional" kosher comestibles turn up at this "reliable" White Plains deli and catering outfit serving the area for over 30 years; decor is nonexistent and the food's "a few kreplach from perfection" (and not cheap either), but when you "need a fix", it's one of the "only games in town."

Kit's Thai Kitchen *Thai*
21 | 12 | 18 | $25

Stamford | Turn of the River Shopping Ctr. | 927 High Ridge Rd. (Cedar Heights Rd.), CT | 203-329-7800 | www.kitsthaikitchen.com

"When the Thai craving hits", aficionados head to this "fast and friendly" Stamford strip-maller, aka "Bangkok on a budget", turning out "plentiful" portions of "fresh", "addictive" fare that "packs a punch" ("if it says it's hot, it's hot!"); many find the space "cramped" and "not terribly inviting", likening dining on the outdoor patio to "eating in a roadway", which may help explain why it does such "lively take-out business."

Kona Grill *American/Asian*
17 | 19 | 18 | $33

Stamford | Stamford Town Ctr. | 230 Tresser Blvd. (bet. Atlantic St. & Greyrock Pl.), CT | 203-324-5700 | www.konagrill.com

"Kids and parents love the big fish tank" behind the sushi bar in the "large", aquatic-themed space of this Stamford American-Asian chain link, which also boasts a "hopping" outdoor patio and an "unusually friendly" staff; happy hour offers "some of the best deals around", drawing a "professional crowd" into the mix, and while a few pan the fare as "uninspired" and overpriced", others deem the sushi "excellent" and the rest of the menu "better than expected."

Koo *Japanese*
23 | 18 | 19 | $47

Rye | 17 Purdy Ave. (2nd St.) | 914-921-9888 | www.nouveausushi.com
Danbury | 29 E. Pembroke Rd. (Hayestown Rd.), CT | 203-739-0068 | www.koodanbury.com

Acolytes insists there's "lots to coo about" at these separately owned Japanese jewel boxes in Rye and Danbury, from the "undeniably fresh", "exotic" sushi like "works of art" to the servers who "anticipate your needs"; given the "tony" addresses and "stylish" clientele, the "exceptionally high" prices should come as no surprise.

Kotobuki Ⓜ *Japanese*
24 | 12 | 21 | $36

Stamford | 457 Summer St. (bet. Broad & Spring Sts.), CT | 203-359-4747 | www.kotobukijapaneserestaurant.com

Chef-owner Masanori Sato "must have his own boat" to get such "fabulous fresh fish" marvel mavens of this Downtown Stamford spot serving some of the "most authentic sushi and Japanese food in the region"; sure, "there are fancier places" around, but those who find the digs "dreary" will appreciate the recent refresh (which may not be reflected in the Decor score), and as the owner and his family "treat you like family" and the "price is right", "don't let the appearance put you off."

Kraft Bistro Ⓩ *American/Mediterranean*
21 | 20 | 18 | $49

Bronxville | 104 Kraft Ave. (bet. Park Pl. & Pondfield Rd.) | 914-337-4545 | www.kraftbistro.com

This "romantic" boho-chic bistro in Bronxville "entices" a "sophisticated" clientele with its copious candles and twinkly lights setting the scene for "inventive" Mediterranean-New American cuisine;

FOOD | DECOR | SERVICE | COST

however, service can be "less-than-pleasant" and some can't shake the feeling that it's "priced higher than it should be."

Kujaku *Japanese* ▽ 18 | 14 | 18 | $36

Stamford | 84 W. Park Pl. (Summer St.), CT | 203-357-0281 | www.kujakustamford.com

While the "hokey teppanyaki" show in the "back room" "can be fun for the kids" at this Stamford Japanese, many grown-ups opt for the front, where they can order "fresh" sushi and "decent" cooked fare; a few dismiss it as "mediocre", but to others the "more-than-reasonable" prices, "especially at lunch", make it "a place to recommend."

NEW KYO Sushi *Japanese* - | - | - | M

Hartsdale | 17 E. Hartsdale Ave. (Central Ave.) | 914-682-8952 | www.kyosushitown.com

Hartsdale has a new sushi stop in this midpriced newcomer from brothers Darryl and Derek Wu; look for all the raw stuff in signature rolls and slabs, plus homemade noodles, curry bowls and bento-box lunch specials; P.S. Metro-North riders should note that it also offers commuter curbside delivery.

Kyoto Sushi *Japanese* ▽ 21 | 15 | 19 | $32

Kingston | 337 Washington Ave. (Lucas Ave.) | 845-339-1128 | www.kyotokingston.com

"Who knew you could get good sushi" in Uptown Kingston, exclaim those discovering the "ample" "fresh" fish at this affordable Japanese; a "simple" setting is brightened up by a "smiling", "gracious" staff, so the only "nuisance" is "parking on the street."

NEW La Bella Havana *Cuban* - | - | - | M

Yonkers | 35 Main St. (Warburton Ave.) | 914-920-9777 | www.labellahavana.com

Shrimp empanadas, ropa vieja and other island favorites are washed down with mojitos at this cozy, well-priced Yonkers Cuban done up in a charmingly faded style with old-timey streetlights, exposed-brick walls and a tropical bar decked out with bamboo and straw; lunch specials and live Latin jazz on weekends are other draws.

La Bocca *Italian* 23 | 19 | 21 | $46

White Plains | Renaissance Corporate Ctr. | 8 Church St. (bet. Hamilton Ave. & Main St.) | 914-948-3281 | www.laboccaristorante.com

"Tucked away" inside the Renaissance Corporate Center in Downtown White Plains is this "cozy" Italian restaurant where an "attentive" staff ferries "authentic", "mouthwatering" fare, "much of it from the North"; it's not cheap, but pays off with a "warm, inviting" ambiance that's equally suited to "work lunches" and "date night."

La Bretagne Ⓜ *French* 24 | 16 | 25 | $54

Stamford | 2010 W. Main St. (bet. Harvard Ave. & Havemeyer Ln.), CT | 203-324-9539 | www.labretagnerestaurant.com

"Just like the French restaurant your parents took you to", this country French in Stamford presents "well-prepared" classics such as duck à l'orange carved tableside and Dover sole "to die for", a "top-notch" wine selection, "attentive service" and a quiet setting that enables you to "carry on a conversation"; a 2012 face-lift perks up the "tired" room, while fans declare "whiners should get past the age of the patrons" and appreciate what they call one of the "best deals in town."

La Camelia ⊠ Spanish   23 | 20 | 21 | $49

Mt. Kisco | 234 N. Bedford Rd./Rte. 117 (Knowlton Ave.) | 914-666-2466 | www.lacameliarestaurant.net

This "quaint" Mt. Kisco Spanish "treasure" is "worth seeking out" for "wonderful" "traditional Iberian fare" and "top tapas" buttressed by "interesting" Spanish wines and "super sangria"; "friendly" service is paced to let you "take your time" to fully enjoy the "warm" ambiance worthy of a "special occasion."

🏆 La Crémaillère ⊠ French   27 | 26 | 26 | $81

Bedford | 46 Bedford-Banksville Rd. (Round House Rd.) | 914-234-9647 | www.cremaillere.com

"Memorable evenings" transpire at this "gold standard" of "fine dining" in Bedford, where "superb" "traditional" French cuisine is elevated by an "extensive wine cellar" and "outstanding" service in a "beautiful" farmhouse that "oozes charm"; "such excellence comes at a price", but for a "special treat" "you can't ask for much more"; P.S. jackets suggested.

La Duchesse Anne Restaurant French   ▽ 19 | 16 | 18 | $62

Mt. Tremper | La Duchesse Anne | 1564 Wittenberg Rd. (Rte. 212) | 845-688-5260 | www.laduchesseanne.com

Offering "well-prepared", slightly pricey "country French fare" to match its location in a "beautiful spot, surrounded by woods", this 1850s Mt. Tremper inn is a favorite of weekenders who enjoy "a drink on the porch" or "fireside" in winter; Victorian decor adds to the "upstate atmosphere" and "utterly charming" chef Fabrice Vittoz makes up for variable service, so "what's not to like?"

La Fontanella Italian   24 | 21 | 25 | $57

Pelham | 115 Wolfs Ln. (bet. 1st & 2nd Sts.) | 914-738-3008 | www.lafontanellapelham.com

"Elegant" all the way, this longtime Pelham Italian "pays attention to detail" with "classic" Northern-style cuisine and "fantastic specials" "beautifully served" in a "formal", "white-tablecloth" setting; no surprise, it's "a little expensive", but it works when you want to feel "pampered."

La Herradura Mexican   18 | 18 | 18 | $26

Mamaroneck | 406 Mamaroneck Ave. (Spencer Pl.) | 914-630-2377
New Rochelle | 1323 North Ave. (Northfield Rd.) | 914-235-3769
New Rochelle | 563 Main St. (Center Ave.) | 914-235-2055

For "hearty plates" of "down-to-earth" Mexican cooking, devotees deem this "colorful", casual chainlet a downright "bargain", "spiffy", "Aztec-inspired" digs and "service with a smile" seal the deal and make it a standby for families.

atmosphere, with cozy fireside dining a lure in winter, the patio appealing in summer and dinner theater a bi-monthly bonus.

Lolita Cocina & Tequila Bar *Mexican*   22 | 23 | 19 | $46

Greenwich | 230 Mill St. (bet. Henry & Water Sts.), CT | 203-813-3555 | www.lolitamexican.com

"Young hipsters" flock to Greenwich's Byram neighborhood to "see and be seen" (but not heard, with music at "dance-club noise level", including live bands Thursdays and DJs on weekends) at this "hoppin' spot" offering Mexican fare with "kitschy", "unusual twists"; a "fabulous tequila list" and an "intriguing bordello atmosphere" fuel the "dark", "sexy" vibe, so despite service that "can be spotty" and a check that's "pricey for what you get", most agree it's "so worth the trip."

Long Ridge Tavern *American*   14 | 19 | 16 | $38

Stamford | 2635 Long Ridge Rd. (Rte. 104), CT | 203-329-7818 | www.longridgetavern.com

This old converted barn on a Stamford back road with a "cozy fireplace" and "lots of antiques" just "screams out for some good downhome cooking", but while the American "tavern grub" "straight out of the '50s" "does the trick" for some, to others it seems as if "the chef is lost in the woods without a GPS"; still, "in an area with no restaurants" it's a "comfortable" "oasis" for many, with a "welcoming staff", live music on weekends and "pretty outdoor seating" in the warmer months.

Los Abuelos *Mexican*   ▽ 18 | 10 | 22 | $28

Ossining | 38 N. Highland Ave. (bet. Eastern Ave. & Ellis Pl.) | 914-488-5874

"There's always a line out the door" on weekends at this "mom-and-pop" Ossining Mexican whipping up "good portions" of "fresh", "homemade" *comida*; prices are low, but note that a beer and wine-only license only means "no margaritas at this fiesta."

Louie & Johnnies' Ristorante *Italian*   ▽ 22 | 19 | 21 | $37

Yonkers | 887 Yonkers Ave. (Trenchard St.) | 914-423-3300 | www.louieandjohnnies.com

"Be prepared for a doggy bag" at this Yonkers *cucina* right "near the raceway" turning out "down-home" Italian standards in "swanky" digs with white tablecloths and a granite martini bar; though the mood is "pleasant" and it's vaunted for "value", some sniff it's "quantity, not quality" here.

Louie's on the Avenue *American/Steak*   21 | 21 | 21 | $45

Pearl River | 160 E. Central Ave. (bet. Henry & John Sts.) | 845-735-4344 | www.louiesontheavenue.com

"If you like steak" and you're in Rockland County, this "comfortable" Pearl River chop shop is a "charming" option, with "something for everyone" on the Traditional American menu; all comes "well served" by "professionals" in a "quiet" Victorian house whose five "cozy" dining rooms are "interestingly decorated" with musical instruments, or on the porch, weather permitting.

	FOOD	DECOR	SERVICE	COST

Lubins-N-Links ⓂⓊ *Hot Dogs* ▽ 24 | 13 | 24 | $11

Tarrytown | 38 Main St. (S. Washington St.) | 914-909-4198 |
www.lubinsandlinks.com

"Do yourself a favor and learn what a lubin is" pronounce fans of this
"tiny" Tarrytown nook specializing in a housemade creation of slow-
roasted beef on a bun, plus "delicious" weenies with a "bewildering"
array of toppings; prices are "cheap", and service is "with a smile",
while the lack of indoor tables makes the all-weather patio appealing.

ⓩ Luca Ristorante Italiano Ⓢ *Italian* 26 | 24 | 26 | $58

Wilton | 142 Old Ridgefield Rd. (Godfrey Pl.), CT | 203-563-9550 |
www.lucaristoranteitaliano.com

For "a little bit of Italy" in "sleepy" Downtown Wilton, *paesani* head
to Luca and Sandra Morrone's storefront "gem" where "sensational", "delectable delicacies" ("light, flavorful sauces", "superb
pastas"), "wonderful desserts" and a "strong wine list" are served
by a "friendly, professional" staff in an "attractive", "romantic" room
with "flattering lighting"; the tabs are "high-end", but most agree
the "quality justifies the cost."

Lucky Buddha *Asian* ▽ 24 | 23 | 21 | $38

Thornwood | Thornwood Town Ctr. | 1008 Broadway
(American Legion Way) | 914-495-3365 |
www.luckybuddha-us.com

Choose from "hibachi-style dining" or the sushi bar at this "un-
expectedly sophisticated" Asian tucked into a Thornwood strip
mall offering a "wide variety" of dishes that dip into Japanese,
Chinese and Thai traditions; it's set in a "dimly" lit", "dramatic"
Buddha-themed setting, but between the kids and the "clubby"
music (DJs on weekends), it can be "loud", and tabs are on the
"pricey" side too.

Lucky's *Diner* 18 | 19 | 18 | $18

Stamford | 209 Bedford St. (bet. Broad & Spring Sts.), CT |
203-978-0268 | www.luckysclassic.com

"You'll feel like you jumped on Doc's time machine" and landed in
the "'50s" at this "inexpensive" "burger joint of burger joints" in
Downtown Stamford, slinging "juicy" hamburgers, "piping hot fries"
and "thick, tasty" milkshakes in a "loud, bright" setting with juke-
boxes "playing old-time rock 'n' roll"; the staff is "friendly", and
though some dismiss the eats as "ordinary", others find it "fun for
kids and unpretentious adults."

Luc's Café Ⓢ *French* 24 | 21 | 21 | $44

Ridgefield | 3 Big Shop Ln. (bet. Bailey Ave. & Prospect Ave.), CT |
203-894-8522 | www.lucscafe.com

For a "little bit of France" in Ridgefield, Francophiles head to this
basement bistro for "authentic, rustic French cooking" served by
a staff with "appropriately thick accents" (and, some say, "snotty"
demeanors); once you get past the "long lines", you can rub elbows
with celebs ("frequent Keith Richards sightings" are reported),
but "don't stretch or you'll hit your neighbor" in the "noisy",

	FOOD	DECOR	SERVICE	COST

NEW Mythos *Greek*

| - | - | - | M |

Thornwood | 1006 Broadway (Garrigan Ave.) | 914-747-2122 | www.mythosgreekrestaurant.net

A lengthy list of well-priced, traditional Greek specialties is on offer at this family-friendly Thornwood newcomer set in a large dining hall–style room with blue-and-white checkered tablecloths, wall niche statuary and framed photos of Grecian tourist sites; a display case showing off trays of classic pastries as well as live Greek music every last Saturday of the month are other nice touches.

Nanuet Hotel *Italian*

| 21 | 10 | 15 | $23 |

Nanuet | 132 S. Main St. (bet. 1st & Prospect Sts.) | 845-623-9600

"People from near and far" "flock" to this Nanuet Italian, "famous" for its "amazing" thin-crust pizza at prices you "can't beat"; true, it takes "a looong time" to come, and the former hotel "hole-in-the-wall" setting "doesn't look too appealing", but there's "ice-cold draft beer" for grown-ups plus video games to amuse "noisy kids", so "who cares?"; "bring earplugs and enjoy."

Napa & Co. ☒ *American*

| 24 | 23 | 22 | $56 |

Stamford | 75 Broad St. (bet. Bedford & Summer Sts.), CT | 203-353-3319 | www.napaandcompany.com

Oenophiles "know they're going to have a great night" once they "see the wall of wine" at this "trendy" Stamford New American where "creative", "locally sourced" farm-to-table fare and "excellent pairings" are served by a "professional" staff; while some critics find it "too noisy" and "overpriced", claiming it's trying too hard "to be NYC", others promise a "memorable meal", whether it's a "casual dinner or more formal night out."

Nautilus Diner ● *Diner*

| 16 | 13 | 17 | $23 |

Mamaroneck | 1240 W. Boston Post Rd. (bet. Richbell Rd. & Weaver St.) | 914-833-1320

An "impossibly long menu" of "old-style" American favorites is the hook at this "quintessential" Mamaroneck diner, a 24/7 mainstay set in "glossy" digs and manned by a "sweet" crew; even if the fare's rather "run-of-the-mill", it's a "local staple" – come on a weekend and you'll certainly "see someone you know."

Neko Sushi *Japanese*

| 21 | 14 | 19 | $31 |

New Paltz | 49 Main St. (Chestnut St.) | 845-255-0162

Neko Sushi & Hibachi *Japanese*

Wappingers Falls | 1817 South Rd./Rte. 9 (Vassar Rd.) | 845-298-9869
www.thenekosushi.com

"Smiling sushi chefs and sparkling fresh fish" plus some "offbeat" choices please at this affordable Japanese duo also earning "kudos for offering brown-rice sushi"; "entertaining" hibachi tables add a "kid-friendly" note to the Wappingers branch, so although the ambiance in each "lacks warmth" and service can be "slow", "the food makes it ok."

	FOOD	DECOR	SERVICE	COST

NEW Nemea Greek Taverna Greek ▕ - ▏ - ▏ - ▏ E ▕

Mamaroneck | 599 E. Boston Post Rd. (Beach Ave.) | 914-698-6600 |
www.nemeataverna.com

At this stylish arrival in Mamaroneck, Sterling Smith (ex New
Rochelle's Sterling Inn) offers both contemporary and classic dishes
like moussaka, lamb burgers and mussels with ouzo plus a Helleno-
centric wine list; the look is urbane with exposed brick and sculp-
tural light fixtures, plus sidewalk seating in summer.

Neo World Bistro & Sushi Bar Asian ▕ 23 ▏ 18 ▏ 20 ▏ $35 ▕

Mt. Kisco | 69 S. Moger Ave. (Britton Ln.) | 914-244-9711 |
www.neobistro.com

Truly "unique" for Mt. Kisco, this spot is "worth a visit" for its "surprisingly elegant and delicious" Asian cuisine including a "delightful
Korean bibimbop" and "outrageous, creative sushi" (banana and
crab rolls, anyone?); the basement digs are minimalist and the service is straight-ahead, but converts claim "the food makes up for it."

Nessa Italian ▕ 21 ▏ 18 ▏ 19 ▏ $50 ▕

Port Chester | 325 N. Main St. (Horton Ave.) | 914-939-0119 |
www.nessarestaurant.com

Very "romantic", this "wonderful, little" midpriced Port Chester Italian
puts out "simple", "modern" dishes and "standout wines" in a sultry
space awash in candlelight; service can be hit-or-miss, and the "noise
is incredible", so "bring earplugs", or try the patio in the summer.

New World Home ▕ 22 ▏ 18 ▏ 21 ▏ $38 ▕
Cooking Co. American/Eclectic

Saugerties | 1411 Rte. 212 (Chestnut Hill Rd.) | 845-246-0900 |
www.ricorlando.com

"Local celeb chef" Ric Orlando "rocks" it at his "upbeat" Saugerties
New American–Eclectic, offering "adventurous" "tastes from
around the world" that are "a treat for vegans", with "plentiful
options for meat lovers" and "folks who like a little spice in their
lives"; "terrific service", "cooler-than-cool", "crunchy-granola decor" and regular "divertissements" (live music and dancing) make
for a "happy crowd."

Niko's Greek Taverna Greek ▕ 20 ▏ 14 ▏ 20 ▏ $35 ▕

White Plains | 287 Central Ave. (Aqueduct Rd.) | 914-686-6456 |
www.nikostaverna.com

"Like the Greek family you never knew you had", this modestly ap-
pointed White Plains kitchen coddles guests with "hearty" Hellenic
fare and service that "bends over backwards to take care of you"; it's
"always packed", although the "charming" outdoor tables ease the
crush in summer.

Nina Eclectic ▕ 25 ▏ 23 ▏ 24 ▏ $45 ▕

Middletown | 27 W. Main St. (bet. Canal & North Sts.) | 845-344-6800 |
www.nina-restaurant.com

"Haute cuisine in Middletown – who knew?" ask those discovering
chef Franz Brendle's Eclectic "standout", which adds a "fashionable"

note to the neighborhood with "phenomenal" fare ferried by a staff that "genuinely tries to please"; the "pretty", brick-walled space has a "sophisticated" air, especially when it's full of weekenders, so although a tad costly, it "thrives"; "these people are doing something right."

Nino's *Italian* ▽ | 20 | 14 | 20 | $37

South Salem | 355 Rte. 123 (Glen Dr.) | 914-533-2671 | www.ninos123.com

"Locals like" this "laid-back" South Salem Italian laying out a "wonderful variety" of "filling" "homestyle" fare, and several praise the brick-oven pizzas; the staff is "competent" but it's "not much on atmosphere" so some might prefer "takeout"; P.S. scores do not reflect a recent ownership and chef change.

Nino's ⓈItalian 21 | 18 | 20 | $46

Bedford Hills | 13 Adams St. (Rte. 117) | 914-864-0400

"Wood-fired pizzas" with "a little zest" plus "dependable" "old-school" Italian cuisine appeal to "families" and "couples" alike at this "popular" Bedford Hills storefront that manages to maintain a "cozy, warm atmosphere"; a lively "bar business" encourages those in the know to "opt for the back room" when they want "a quieter dinner."

Noda's Japanese Steakhouse *Japanese* 19 | 14 | 20 | $35

White Plains | White Plains Mall | 200 Hamilton Ave. (Dr. Martin Luther King Ave.) | 914-949-0990 | www.nodarestaurant.com

All the usual "theatrics" turn up at this well-priced White Plains teppanyaki where the "entertaining", "knife-twirling" show makes it a magnet for birthday parties; the "filling" Japanese fare and sushi is "good" enough, although judging from the scores, the decor has "seen better days."

NEW NoMa Social *Mediterranean* - | - | - | M

New Rochelle | Radisson Plaza Hotel | 1 Radisson Plaza (Cedar St.) | 914-576-3700

New Rochelle's Radisson Hotel just splurged on a $2 million makeover, the focus of which is its restaurant, formerly known as City Chow House; at press time in April, chef Bill Rosenberg (of Port Chester's dearly departed F.I.S.H.) is set to debut a mid-priced Mediterranean menu focusing on seafood specialties in a modern, new space.

ⓏNo. 9 Ⓜ *American* 27 | 23 | 25 | $49

Millerton | Simmons' Way Village Inn | 53 Main St. (bet. Dutchess & N. Maple Aves.) | 518-592-1299 | www.number9millerton.com

Ensconced in the dining room of Millerton's "luxury" Simmons' Way Inn, chef Tim Cocheo's "fantastic" entry offers a "daring" French- and Austrian-accented New American menu and "pulls it off superbly", with "sublime", "mouthwatering" cooking that draws "fans from a 10-town radius"; the "congenial", "sophisticated country setting", "personal service" and "midweek prix fixe offering even greater value" have devotees declaring "its name is off by one – it should be a 10!"

	FOOD	DECOR	SERVICE	COST

Norimaki 🗲 *Japanese* | - | - | - | M |
Washington | 4 Green Hill Rd. (Titus Rd.), CT | 860-868-0555
Chef Makoto Sekikawa and his "charming" wife, Jinyi, have resurrected their former NYC Japanese in Washington Township, and sushi savants laud it as "an extraordinary addition to the Litchfield dining scene", serving "wonderfully fresh", "artfully presented" sushi, as well as a "consistently interesting" menu of cooked fare that "shifts with the seasons"; cognoscenti whisper "do not tell anyone, but this is the real deal."

Northern Spy Cafe Ⓜ *American* | ∇ 18 | 17 | 18 | $38 |
High Falls | 155 Main St./Rte. 213 (Orchard St.) | 845-687-7298 | www.northernspycafe.com
Part "watering hole", part "sweet" eatery, this "relaxed" High Falls New American turns out a "limited menu" of "well-prepared if not especially memorable" "standards" along with "good" "vegetarian choices", like the "favorite free-range tofu wings"; a "courteous" staff mans the old farmhouse where a "cozy" fireplace, an "inviting screened porch" and "nice exhibits on the walls" keep the surroundings "pleasant" year-round.

North Star *American* | 20 | 18 | 21 | $47 |
Pound Ridge | 85 Westchester Ave. (Pine Dr.) | 914-764-0200 | www.northstarny.com
"Delivering on both taste and atmosphere", this "casual bistro" in Pound Ridge is a "hub of activity" where selections from a "creative" New American menu come via "friendly" servers; for some "it's all about the live music" on Thursdays and Sundays and the half-price "wine deal" on Tuesdays, but it's also "jammed on weekends."

Oakhurst Diner *Diner* | ∇ 16 | 16 | 15 | $24 |
Millerton | 19 Main St. (Center St.) | 518-592-1313
"Not your everyday diner", this "retro" Millerton coffee shop takes an "interesting approach" with its three squares a day, mixing "comfort" "classics" (eggs Benedict, grass-fed burgers and such) with "imaginative", "upmarket" eats like "venison chili" and "deftly spiced vegetable" dishes for "cheap"; new owners gave the 1950s "vintage" interior a cosmetic overhaul, so all that's "lacking" is service at times.

🄕 Ocean House Ⓜ *Seafood* | 27 | 16 | 24 | $46 |
Croton-on-Hudson | 49 N. Riverside Ave. (Farrington Rd.) | 914-271-0702
It may "not look like much from the outside", but this "New England"–style seafooder in Croton specializes in "incredibly fresh fish" so "delectable" "you'd think you were in Nantucket"; service is "pleasant" and its BYO policy makes for "affordable" bills, but it's so "tiny" you'll need to dine with "your elbows tucked in", and the no-reservations policy means "come early or plan to wait."

Okinawa Japanese Restaurant *Japanese* | 20 | 19 | 17 | $37 |
Mt. Kisco | 39 S. Moger Ave. (Main St.) | 914-666-8188

(continued)

FOOD | DECOR | SERVICE | COST

(continued)

Okinawa Hibachi Steakhouse *Japanese*

Ossining | 218 S. Highland Ave. (Rockledge Ave.) | 914-762-9888 |
www.okinawaossining.com

Japanese fare comes with a side of "fireworks" at this hibachi pair
where "entertaining" chefs put on "quite the show" for the kids, and
there's "fresh" sushi for the grown-ups; the "hip, attractive" setting
of the new Ossining offspring is a cut above the Mt. Kisco original,
but the "well-intentioned" service can be "lax" at both, especially
when "packed" with "birthday parties."

The Olde Stone Mill *American*   17 | 22 | 17 | $47

Tuckahoe | 2 Scarsdale Rd. (Lake Ave.) | 914-771-7661 |
www.theoldestonemill.com

The "quaint" historic setting in an 1803 cotton mill is the standout
at this Tuckahoe American steakhouse whose "cozy, romantic"
"date-night" vibe is enhanced by a fireplace and a "delightful" patio;
it's all "so charming that you really want the food to be great", although the majority maintains the fare is "only so-so", and a tad
"pricey" unless you opt for the sunset menu.

Old '76 House *American*   18 | 22 | 18 | $47

Tappan | 110 Main St. (Old Tappan Rd.) | 845-359-5476 |
www.76house.com

What with "the ghost of Major André", the "memorabilia", "timbers
and fireplaces", Tappan's "beautifully restored" Revolutionary War-
era "publick house" is a "find for history buffs"; "service is average"
and the "typical" Traditional Americana has its "ups and downs, but
the atmosphere is always there" (and jazzed up by music on weekends), so nab "a wingback chair", quaff a "generous" drink and "savor."

Olé Molé *Mexican*   19 | 10 | 17 | $22

Stamford | 1030 High Ridge Rd. (Olga Dr.), CT | 203-461-9962 |
www.olemole.net

"Reliable" and "relatively authentic" Mexican fare, "friendly" service
and "affordable" prices make this Stamfordite a "great value in an
expensive town", especially for families with "kids", but purists pan
the offerings as "white-bread" eats for "people who don't like
spices"; cognoscenti also caution "eat in at your own peril", for you
may need a "shoehorn" to "squeeze in" to the "tiny storefront",
which is why many opt for "takeout."

Oliva Cafe Ⓜ *Mediterranean*   24 | 18 | 21 | $47

New Preston | 18 E. Shore Rd. (New Preston Hill Rd.), CT | 860-868-1787 |
www.olivacafe.com

The Mediterranean fare is "spectacularly tasty, yet simple" at this
"hidden gem in New Preston", where the atmosphere is "friendly"
and "welcoming" in the "lovely setting" of an old Colonial with a balcony and terrace for outdoor dining; the prices are "so reasonable
you want to eat there daily", and while some grouse that the "menu
hasn't changed in ages", others reason that this is "as adventurous
as it gets in the NW hills."

	FOOD	DECOR	SERVICE	COST

Olive Market ⓂSpanish
24 | 20 | 22 | $30

Georgetown | 19 Main St. (Redding Rd.), CT | 203-544-8134 |
www.theolivemarketct.com

You can "shop while your garlic pizza cooks" at this "informal", mid-priced Spanish cafe housed in a cheese shop/gift store in the village of Georgetown serving "unique" South American–influenced breakfast fare, "zesty" sandwiches and more, plus "fabulous" tapas dinners Thursdays–Saturdays; chef-owner Fernando Pereyra "adds charm and warmth" to the "quaint", "casual" setting, and the rest of the staff is "friendly and attentive."

☑ Ondine Ⓜ French
26 | 23 | 26 | $70

Danbury | 69 Pembroke Rd. (Wheeler Dr.), CT | 203-746-4900 |
www.ondinerestaurant.com

At this Danbury "classic", the "unpretentious" staff "gets good service right" while the kitchen creates "fabulous", "traditional" French cuisine "the way it used to be", and the "creative, elegant" $62 dinner prix fixe and $39 Sunday dinner help keep the tab from getting *trop chèr*; those who find the decor "stodgy" will be encouraged by a face-lift in 2011 (which may not be reflected in the Decor score), though others are "comfortable" in the "sophisticated" setting and deem it a "superior restaurant for special occasions."

☑ 121 Restaurant & Bar American
22 | 19 | 20 | $43

North Salem | 2 Dingle Ridge Rd. (Rte. 121) | 914-669-0121 |
www.121restaurant.com

A "perennial favorite" for North Salem "families and the horsey crowd", this "upscale pub" trots out "consistently good" New American fare, from "creative" wood-fired pizzas to braised short ribs; a "well-trained" staff, a "cozy fireplace" and "porch dining" make for a "congenial atmosphere", though an "energetic bar scene" gets "loud on weekends" and the "wait for a table" can be "frustrating."

On the Way Café Ⓜ⌖ American/European
– | – | – | I

Rye | 34 Ridgeland Terr. (bet. Forest Ave. & Playland Pkwy.) |
914-921-2233 | www.onthewaycaferye.com

With polished lamps and a smooth white marble counter as focal points, this former luncheonette across from the entrance to Rye Playland has morphed into a sleek American-European cafe; the daytime menu is well priced and runs the gamut from frittatas to wraps to beef carpaccio with plenty of espresso to wash it all down; P.S. cash only.

Opus 465 American
18 | 17 | 17 | $42

Armonk | 465 Main St. (Orchard Dr.) | 914-273-4676 |
www.opus465.com

There are "different rooms for different moods" at this "reliable" Armonk American providing a "loud" "after-work watering hole" downstairs and a "cozier" upstairs in which to enjoy "substantial" "comfort-food" classics; critics claim the decor's "a little tired", but weekend bands are a plus and patrons "love eating outside" in good weather.

	FOOD	DECOR	SERVICE	COST

Orem's Diner ● *Diner* | 15 | 12 | 17 | $19 |

Wilton | 167 Danbury Rd. (Wolfpit Rd.), CT | 203-762-7370 |
www.oremsdiner.com

The "definitive diner", this "Wilton institution" offers a "huge menu"
and servings (forget "portion control") ferried by a "warm, friendly
staff", all making it a "home away from home" for local families; it's
also a "quick", "reliable" choice for business breakfasts (open from
6 AM), so just add in "reasonable prices" to answer the question:
"why is this place so crowded?"

Oriental House Ⓜ *Japanese/Korean* | - | - | - | I |

Pine Bush | 78 Main St./ Rte. 52 (bet. Center St. & Maple Ave.) |
845-744-8663

For "excellent sushi" and "nicely seasoned" Japanese and Korean hibachi, Pine Bush denizens head to this no-frills, "mom-and-pop establishment" where the owners "work tirelessly"; everything comes
"cooked to order" (read: slowly), so just "relax and have another
sake or Kirin" while you wait.

Oriole 9 *European* | ▽ 20 | 16 | 19 | $29 |

Woodstock | 17 Tinker St. (Mill Hill Rd.) | 845-679-5763 |
www.oriole9.com

This "casual" Woodstock European breakfast and lunch spot proffers
"interesting" "farm-fresh" salads, sandwiches and "corned beef hash
to die for"; service is "solid" and the "funky" setting "comfy", especially if you get a banquette full of pillows, so although "it's a bit
pricey", it's "the best place in town to relax" with "a cup of coffee."

Orissa Ⓜ *Indian* | 24 | 23 | 20 | $41 |

Dobbs Ferry | 14 Cedar St. (B'way) | 914-231-7800 | www.orissany.com
"Elegant and modern", this Dobbs Ferry Indian specializes in "interesting" riffs on the traditional, yielding "delicious", "quirky" dishes
like chutney bison burgers and spice-rubbed strip steak; "spotty"
service can be a drawback, but an unusual red-and-yellow space
"beautifully" designed by its architect owner redeems, as do prices
regarded as reasonable for the neighborhood.

Osaka *Japanese* | 22 | 16 | 23 | $33 |

Rhinebeck | 22 Garden St. (Rte. 308/W. Market St.) | 845-876-7338
Tivoli | 74 Broadway (Pine St.) | 845-757-5055
www.osakasushi.net

"Lots of regulars" attest that "the sushi is pretty darn good" at this
"reliable" Dutchess County duo also offering "excellent tempura" and
other "tasty" fare; the "simple, quiet" settings are "intimate", which
at the Rhinebeck branch can mean "small", but even so, the "consci-
entious owners" and "friendly" staff "make you feel comfortable."

Osteria Applausi Ⓢ *Italian* | ▽ 24 | 19 | 22 | $48 |

Old Greenwich | 199 Sound Beach Ave. (Arcadia Rd.), CT |
203-637-4447 | www.osteriaapplausi.com

"Everything is freshly made", including mama's "lovely" pasta, at
this "authentic" Italian "mainstay" (sibling of Columbus Park) situ-

ated on the "small-town main street" of Old Greenwich; there's sleek new "darker" decor, and the staff's "personal attention is welcoming", just be sure to "get reservations", and don't be surprised if the tab's "a bit pricey."

Outback Steakhouse *Steak* | 17 | 14 | 18 | $31 |

White Plains | 60 S. Broadway (Westchester Ave.) | 914-684-1397
Yonkers | 1703 Central Park Ave. (bet. Balint Dr. & Sadore Ln.) | 914-337-3244
Danbury | 116 Newtown Rd. (I-84), CT | 203-790-1124
Wilton | 14 Danbury Rd. (bet. Fawn Ridge Ln. & Heathcoate Rd.), CT | 203-762-0920
www.outback.com

"Reliable" (if "not prime") seasoned steaks provide "real value for the dollar" at this "Aussie-themed" "middle-of-the-road" chain where folks love to "overindulge in the bloomin' onion"; it's too "kitschy" and "packaged" for pickier patrons and the "cute" service is "hit-or-miss", but "you can take all of your kids and your neighbors too" since you'll blend right into the "noisy" surroundings.

Pagoda *Chinese* | 17 | 11 | 16 | $25 |

Scarsdale | 694 Central Park Ave. (Old Army Rd.) | 914-725-8866 | www.pagoda-ny.com

A "run-of-the-mill" Chinese menu gains a lift from a handful of "healthy" preparations plus some "interesting" Shanghainese and dim sum offerings at this Scarsdale "strip-mall" Sino that's long been a local "standby"; however, given an "overwhelmed" staff and overall slippage in scores, some suggest it's gone "downhill" in recent years.

Painted Bistro Ⓜ *Eclectic* | ▽ 18 | 18 | 19 | $36 |
(fka O'Leary's)

Red Hook | 7100 Albany Post Rd./ Rte. 9 (Old Post Rd. S.) | 845-758-4155 | www.paintedbistro.com

"Pretty good" is the word on this "friendly" Red Hook Eclectic launched by "CIA-pedigreed" caterers Mark and Carol O'Leary; Asian and Mediterranean accents light up the "limited menu", while fireplaces, wide-plank floors and mocha walls make for "pleasing", country-chic decor in the refurbished roadhouse; factor in a "first-rate bar" and it's "a welcome addition."

Painter's *Eclectic* | 19 | 20 | 20 | $31 |

Cornwall-on-Hudson | 266 Hudson St. (Ave. A) | 845-534-2109 | www.painters-restaurant.com

With its "interesting" Eclectic menu and "a drink list that doesn't stop", there's "something for everyone, including the kids", at this "laid-back" Cornwall Inn "hangout" offering "reliably tasty" grub delivered by "terrific" staffers; completing the picture are aptly "arty" digs with "ever-changing" exhibits, "discreet corners" for "romantics", a "lively bar" for imbibers and a "charming" porch for summer.

	FOOD	DECOR	SERVICE	COST

Palmer's Crossing *American* `21` `20` `21` `$38`

Larchmont | 1957 Palmer Ave. (Larchmont Ave.) | 914-833-3505 | www.palmerscrossing.com

"Reliable" is the word on this white-tablecloth Larchmont American featuring a "solid", "something-for-everyone" menu in an "upscale" bi-level space with a "crowded" bar; perhaps it's "not a destination" restaurant, but tabs are moderate and service "accommodating", while live music on weekends "makes it all that much better."

The Pantry ⑤Ⓜ *American* `24` `14` `19` `$24`

Washington Depot | 5 Titus Rd. (Rte. 47), CT | 860-868-0258

A "long-standing favorite for breakfast" and the "see-and-be-seen lunch place" in "charming" Washington Depot, this "kind of pricey" American deli "run by lovely people" offers prepared dishes and baked goods that are "marvelous" enough to "blind one to the glam and glitz of the clientele"; "interesting" "gifts, chocolates and housewares" are "displayed on shelves right next to your table", and though the "small" space is "always crowded", most agree "it's hard not to love" this place.

NEW Panzur ⑤Ⓜ *Spanish* `-` `-` `-` `M`

Tivoli | 69 Broadway (Pine St.) | 845-757-1071 | www.panzur.com

Adding to Tivoli's culinary diversity, this new Spaniard turns out tapas and small plates along with housemade charcuterie and nose-to-tail porcine fare ranging from pig's ears to whole roasted suckling piglets, all complemented by Iberian wines, craft beers and specialty cocktails; the pale-gray digs mix sleek and rustic, with a copper-trimmed bar and a farm table for slicing the hams and cheeses.

NEW Park 143 Bistro *American* `-` `-` `-` `M`

Bronxville | 143 Parkway Rd. (Palmer Rd.) | 914-337-5100

This glam Bronxville New American flaunts leopard-skin banquettes, lipstick-red barstools and arty handmade light fixtures; chef Derek Townsend (ex 10 Downing Street in NYC) offers a mid-priced menu of seasonal small plates plus homemade pastas, steaks and bacon-and-egg-topped short-rib burgers all backed by creative cocktails infused with herbs, chiles and the like; P.S. there's also a notable Sunday brunch.

Pascal's Ⓜ *French* `23` `21` `24` `$48`

Larchmont | 141 Chatsworth Ave. (Palmer Ave.) | 914-834-6688

The "charming" owners "make you feel welcome" at this "lovely" Larchmont bistro offering "wonderful", "traditional" French cuisine including a weekday prix fixe that's a "value"; it caters to an "older" crowd that appreciates service that's "never rushed" and a "quiet" atmosphere that's "good for conversation."

Passage to India *Indian* `22` `14` `21` `$32`

Mt. Kisco | 17 E. Main St. (bet. Kisco & Moger Aves.) | 914-244-9595 | www.passagetoindia.us

"Spicy" subcontinental fare is prepared "with finesse" at this "solid" Mt. Kisco Indian ensuring "enjoyable" meals thanks to a "helpful" staff and a "quiet" atmosphere "conducive to conversation"; insiders insist the best "reason to go" is the "reasonable" lunch buffet.

Pasta Cucina *Italian*   18 | 16 | 18 | $34

Stony Point | Patriot Sq. | 32 S. Liberty Dr. (Central Dr.) | 845-786-6060
Suffern | 8 N. Airmont Rd. (bet. NY Thrwy. & Rte. 59) | 845-369-1313
www.pastacucina.com

Best "come hungry" to these separately owned Rockland County Italians, because the "good, basic" fare comes in such "plentiful" platefuls, "even big eaters" can "plan to take home half"; they're "kid-friendly and parent-satisfying", so although gourmands grumble the grub's a "predictable" "snore", service only "fair" and the digs "loud" and "crowded", the "value makes them a hit."

Pasta Vera *Italian*   20 | 13 | 18 | $34

Greenwich | 48 Greenwich Ave. (W. Putnam Ave.), CT | 203-661-9705 | www.pastavera.com

While this "convenient midpricer" Italian on Greenwich Avenue does a "booming counter business", it also offers a "nice sit-down menu" featuring "standard", "no-fuss, no-pretension" dishes, which come in "ample portions", and "reasonably priced" wines; there's "always a table available" in the "airy", "sparse" digs, but some report that "service can be uneven."

Pas-Tina's Ristorante *Italian*   19 | 13 | 18 | $30

Hartsdale | Hartsdale Plaza | 155 S. Central Ave. (Washington Ave.) | 914-997-7900 | www.pas-tinas.com

"Still going strong" after almost 20 years, this "family-friendly" Hartsdale Italian is a "reliable" pick for pastas prepared in "a million different ways" in portions "big enough for doggy bags"; a "crowded", "noisy" strip-mall setting is part of the package, but the "attractive prices" – including an early-bird special that's "hard to beat" – make it "well worth it."

Pastorale Bistro & Bar Ⓜ *French*   23 | 22 | 23 | $51

Lakeville | 223 Main St. (Lincoln City Rd.), CT | 860-435-1011 | www.pastoralebistro.com

Weekenders call this Lakeville French bistro the "essential Friday-night stop on the way to the country house", while locals laud it as a "perfect spot for a relaxing dinner"; "inventive" Gallic fare is served in the "rustically romantic" antique house with a "beautiful" outdoor deck, where management and staff offer a "warm welcome, whether or not they know your name", and while a few feel it's "slipping", many others consider it a "pleasant surprise in the middle of nowhere."

Peekamoose *American*   24 | 23 | 20 | $51

Big Indian | 8373 Rte. 28 (Lasher Rd.) | 845-254-6500 | www.peekamooserestaurant.com

"One of the coolest places" "in the middle of nowhere" (aka Big Indian), this "quality" Traditional American "find" is mostly patronized by "second-homer" types who file in for "fabulous fare with flair" and don't mind that it's "not cheap"; the "multiroom barn of a

FOOD | DECOR | SERVICE | COST

place" with its beams and views is "charming", so the one "down-side" is that the "staff can't always keep up."

Peekskill Brewery *American* 19 | 17 | 20 | $33

Peekskill | 55 Hudson Ave. (bet. Railroad Ave. & S. Water St.) | 914-734-2337 | www.thepeekskillbrewery.com

Lots of "top-notch" local and house-brewed beers plus "tummy-warming" Traditional American eats prove a "winning combination" at this "boisterous" brewpub in Downtown Peekskill, where a staff that's "knowledgeable" and "friendly" keeps the mood "warm"; prices are "fair", and the weekday hoppy hours offer even deeper discounts.

Pellicci's *Italian* 19 | 12 | 18 | $30

Stamford | 96-98 Stillwater Ave. (bet. Alden & Spruce Sts.), CT | 203-323-2542 | www.pelliccis.com

Since 1947, this family-run "old-fashioned red-sauce house" on Stamford's West Side has been a veritable "Rock of Gibraltar", serv-ing up "generous portions" ("always have leftovers") of "standard Italian fare", including "family-style" menus that "cannot be beat for taste or value" according to fans; the owners are "nice to everyone", and those who jibe that it's "past its prime" will be happy to see the redo in late 2011.

Penang Grill *Asian* 22 | 15 | 20 | $28

Greenwich | 55 Lewis St. (Greenwich Ave.), CT | 203-861-1988

The "cute", "low-frills" digs are "too small for such gigantic flavor" say fans of this BYO Pan-Asian on a side street off Greenwich Avenue offering an "enjoyable" "Indo-Malay-Thai-Chinese-American mashup" with an "emphasis on vegetables"; while a few carp that the "food is not what it has been", "bargain prices" and a staff "so nice it's almost unreal" help make it a "great value" in the minds of many; P.S. cognoscenti counsel it "gets fairly crowded, so opt for takeout."

Peppino's Ristorante *Italian* 20 | 15 | 21 | $37

Katonah | 116 Katonah Ave. (Jay St.) | 914-232-3212 | www.peppinosristorante.com

"Popular with locals", this "comfy, casual" Katonan depends on a staff of "real pros" to deal out its "nice-sized portions" of "classic" Northern Italian specialties; after 20 years the converted train-station quarters "feel a little old", even with the Tuscan touches, but the "value for the money" compensates.

Peter Pratt's Inn Ⓜ *American* 25 | 22 | 24 | $58

Yorktown | 673 Croton Heights Rd. (Rte. 118) | 914-962-4090 | www.prattsinn.com

Brimming with "character", from its "nestled-in-the-woods" loca-tion to its "lovely" fireplace-blessed interior, this Yorktown New American is a "perennial favorite" for "fabulous" "locally sourced" fare elevated by an "impressive wine list" and "gracious" service; it's expensive, and you'll need to "test the GPS" to find it, but smitten customers "can't wait to go back."

	FOOD	DECOR	SERVICE	COST

Pete's Saloon & Restaurant *American*   `18` `16` `20` `$29`

Elmsford | 8 W. Main St. (Rte 9A) | 914-592-9849 |
www.petessaloon.com

"After a lousy day at work", surveyors seek out this "easygoing" Elmsford old-timer where "cold beer" comes alongside "satisfying" American grub in a "comfy" tavern setting; although prices "won't strain your pocketbook", live music later on makes it "way too noisy" for some.

P.F. Chang's China Bistro *Chinese*   `18` `19` `17` `$33`

White Plains | Westchester Mall | 125 Westchester Ave. (Bloomingdale Rd.) | 914-997-6100
Stamford | Stamford Town Ctr. | 230 Tresser Blvd. (bet. Atlantic St. & Greyrock Pl.), CT | 203-363-0434
www.pfchangs.com

"Light, delicious", "Americanized" Chinese food keeps fans "coming back", especially for the "standout" lettuce wraps, to this "trendy", "stylish" chain; though not everyone is convinced ("overpriced", "ordinary", "loud"), the "consistent" service is a plus, as is the "smart" menu "catering to people with allergies" and other needs.

The Phoenix *American*   `-` `-` `-` `M`

Mt. Tremper | Emerson Resort & Spa | 5340 Rte. 28 (Mt. Pleasant Rd.) | 877-688-2828 | www.emersonresort.com

Risen again after being closed to the public for a couple of years, this American at Mt. Tremper's posh Emerson Resort & Spa serves a changing menu of reasonably priced regional fare with signatures like crab cakes and braised bison short ribs, along with simpler fare in the tavern; unchanged is the opulent, jewel-toned Silk Road–inspired interior and the deck overlooking Esopus Creek; P.S. breakfast is available every day, but dinner is Thursdays–Saturdays only.

Piatto Grill *Italian*   `20` `20` `22` `$40`

Yorktown Heights | 90 Triangle Ctr. (Rte. 202) | 914-248-6200 |
www.piattogrill.com

"Come with a group" to share in the "family-style" dishes at this "casual", "contemporary" Yorktown Heights Northern Italian (with bows to Argentinean and Iberian cuisine), or make it a "romantic night for two", tucking into "individual" portions set out on white-linen tablecloths; moderate prices and a "comfortable" lounge have patrons proclaiming "*viva Italia.*"

Piero's Ⓜ *Italian*   `24` `9` `22` `$41`

Port Chester | 44 S. Regent St. (bet. Ellendale Ave. & Franklin St.) | 914-937-2904

"Don't be deceived" by the "dive"-y digs, this "no-frills" Port Chester Italian is "an insider's favorite", garnering praise for its "outstanding" "red-sauce" repasts and a "wonderful" staff that sets it out in "huge portions"; a "personable" owner and "gently priced" menu make up for "eating on your neighbor's lap", and the many "regulars" attest it's "not to be missed."

	FOOD	DECOR	SERVICE	COST

The Pine Social *American* ▽ 23 | 23 | 22 | $41

New Canaan | 36 Pine St. (bet. Grove & Park Sts.), CT | 203-966-5200 | www.pinesocial.com

New Canaanites are "pleasantly surprised" by the "turnaround" of the former Rocco's into this "casual", "medium-priced" New American where "good, solid" fare is served by the "same welcoming staff"; there's live guitar Thursdays–Fridays in the "clubby" setting with a "nice big bar", and some predict this "makeover" will "attract a younger, more social crowd" than its predecessor.

Pinocchio ⓜ *Italian* 21 | 18 | 22 | $47

Eastchester | 309 White Plains Rd. (Highland Ave.) | 914-337-0044

"Lovely and warm", this Eastchester Italian "pleasantly surprises" patrons with "fine", "top-quality" "traditional" cuisine and coddling service overseen by "warm host" and owner Tarcisio Fava; it's "a bit more upscale than other neighborhood places", so higher prices should come as no surprise.

Piper's Kilt ⓓ *Pub Food* 22 | 11 | 16 | $23

Eastchester | 433 White Plains Rd. (Mill Rd.) | 914-779-5772

"The burgers are legendary" at this longtime Eastchester pub, a "total dive" where "everything else is secondary", although the "basic bar food" and "well-made drinks" certainly have their fans; be prepared for "interminable waits" for a table, but at least "the price is right."

Piri-Q ⓜ *Portuguese* ▽ 20 | 16 | 19 | $29

Mamaroneck | 360 Mamaroneck Ave. (bet. Maple & Mt. Pleasant Aves.) | 914-341-1443 | www.piriqrestaurantgrill.com

Good ol'-fashioned barbecue gets a "tasty" Portuguese twist at this Mamaroneck eatery from Rui Correia (of the shuttered Oporto) specializing in fire-roasted chicken and ribs doused in "delicious" signature piri-piri sauce; it's a "cute" spot done up in traditional terra-cotta tile, and "value"-priced takeout inspires "return visits."

ⓩ Plates ⓜ *American* 25 | 21 | 22 | $56

Larchmont | 121 Myrtle Blvd. (Murray Ave.) | 914-834-1244 | www.platesonthepark.com

"A true gem", this "pleasantly grown-up" Larchmont American "just keeps getting better" with "inventive, beautifully presented" seasonal cuisine (and "outstanding" desserts) courtesy of chef-owner Matthew Karp; it's set in a "lovely" "historic" home overlooking a "charming" park, so in spite of some service hiccups and "pricey" bills, most find it "well worth the cost", and the once-a-week BYO special is a steal.

Plumbush Inn Restaurant ⓜ *American* 21 | 25 | 23 | $50

Cold Spring | Plumbush Inn | 1656 Rte. 9D (Peekskill Rd.) | 845-265-3904 | www.plumbushinn.com

Take a "woodsy setting" in Cold Spring, add a "beautiful", "Victorian mansion" with "pretty" rooms "warmed by fireplaces", an oak-paneled bar and a veranda overlooking the gardens, and you've got "pure magic" as a backdrop for "enjoyable" Traditional America▾

fare; throw in "efficient, cordial" service that makes you "feel elegant and pampered", and it's "well worth the money", especially for a "romantic occasion."

Plum Tree *Japanese* | 20 | 18 | 20 | $36 |

New Canaan | 70 Main St. (Locust Ave.), CT | 203-966-8050 | www.plumtreejapanese.com

Though it's "far from the sea", this "family-friendly" Japanese is "close to the hearts of New Canaan's sushi-starved folks" for its "fine, fresh" fin fare served by an "attentive" staff in a "relaxing" setting that includes an "oasislike" outdoor rock garden, a private room decorated with hand-painted paper and an indoor fish pond that "keeps the kids occupied"; a few consider it merely "adequate", while others find it downright "delightful."

(P.M.) Wine Bar Ⓜ *Spanish* | - | - | - | M |

Hudson | 119 Warren St. (bet. 1st & 2nd Sts.) | 518-301-4398 | www.pmwinebar.com

Although it's more about tasting "fine wines" than feasting, you'll find a "talkative crowd" munching on "succulent" small plates between sips at this "cool" Spaniard in Hudson; it's a "wonderful oasis for adults to meet and greet", grab something "appetizing" and perhaps "play Scrabble" in the back room.

NEW Polpettina *Italian* | - | - | - | M |

Eastchester | 102 Fisher Ave. (Maple Ave.) | 914-961-0061 | www.polpettina.com

This Brooklyn-esque arrival in Eastchester is chock-full of easygoing charm with reclaimed wood paneling, exposed brick and quirky doodads like a vintage lard can on display; look for three taps pouring Captain Lawrence beer and deep pours of wine paired with well-priced Italian comfort foods like meatballs and pizza crafted from locally sourced ingredients, including the Hudson Valley curds the kitchen stretches into its housemade mozzarella.

Polpo *Italian* | 24 | 21 | 21 | $63 |

Greenwich | 554 Old Post Rd. (W. Putnam Ave.), CT | 203-629-1999 | www.polporestaurant.com

"Well-executed" Italian fare, "fresh" seafood and an "excellent" wine list "served with panache" are found at this "Greenwich power scene" where "hedge-fund managers" ("and the women who pretend to love them") and other "Ferrari-driving" sorts gather around a "wonderful old boys' piano bar" and revel in the "warm" setting full of "old-world style and charm" (and "noise", some complain); opinions are split on the service – "informative and friendly" vs. "arrogant" and "pretentious" – and "unless you are on expense account or a millionaire", the "prices can be excessive."

The Pond Restaurant Ⓜ *Continental* | ▽ 14 | 17 | 17 | $30 |

Ancramdale | 711 Rte. 3 (Blodget Rd.) | 518-329-1500

Even first-timers are "greeted as long-standing friends" at this Columbia County Continental in "rural" Ancramdale, where the

FOOD | DECOR | SERVICE | COST

"large menu" of "home cooking" is "usually good" and "you get lots for the money"; the log-sided house is rustic, with repurposed windows for dividers and (yes) a pond to dine by come summer.

Pony Express *American*
22 | 6 | 15 | $15

Pleasantville | 30 Wheeler Ave. (bet. Bedford & Manville Rds.) | 914-769-7669 | www.ponyexpresstogo.com

A "fresh" take on fast food, this "tiny" Pleasantville American uses organic and all-natural ingredients in its "delicious" sliders, "snappy" hot dogs and other "quick-bite" fare whipped up by chef Philip McGrath (Iron Horse Grill); decor's barely a step above a "hole-in-the-wall", but "bargain" prices make it handy, especially "before or after a movie" at the nearby Jacob Burns; P.S. online ordering and curbside delivery are added conveniences

Poppy's *Burgers*
∇ 24 | 12 | 14 | $13

Beacon | 184 Main St. (Cliff St.) | 845-765-2121 | www.poppyburger.com

Chef Poppy Yeaple "keeps it simple, local and fun" at his organic burger joint on "Beacon's Restaurant Row" slinging "delicious" patties from grass-fed beef, "hand-cut french fries" and a smattering of daily specials; expect counter service and foil-wrapped food in the tiny plain-Jane cafe, where cheap tabs and a pinball machine offset occasional "long waits."

Porter House *American/Pub Food*
19 | 17 | 20 | $30

White Plains | 169 Mamaroneck Ave. (E. Post Rd.) | 914-831-5663 | www.porterhousebar.com

"When you're in the mood for a burger and a beer", this White Plains pub on the Mamaroneck Avenue strip comes through with "typical", well-priced Americana in "big" portions; it's "more of a bar than a restaurant", so expect a "lively" vibe with lots of "singles", especially "after work" and on weekends, while summertime sees a "hopping" crowd on the patio.

Portofino Pizza & Pasta *Italian/Pizza*
22 | 10 | 19 | $18

Goldens Bridge | North County Shopping Ctr. | Rtes. 22 & 138 (Anderson Ln.) | 914-232-4363 | www.portofinopizzera.net

"A bigger slice you will not find" swear fans of this "reasonably priced" Goldens Bridge pizza joint that's "been there forever" and is run by "some of the nicest guys around"; it's "not the most stylish" restaurant and counter service "can be slow", so some stick with "takeout."

Portofino Ristorante Ⓜ *Italian*
23 | 15 | 23 | $32

Staatsburg | 57 Old Post Rd. (River Rd.) | 845-889-4711 | www.portofinorest.com

"A wide array" of "well-prepared" red-sauce "standards" in "nice-sized portions" make this "old-fashioned" Italian restaurant "hidden" in "rural Staatsburg" a "local favorite"; prices are affordable, and the "gracious, helpful" staff adds a "polite" note in digs that are "unpretentious", but "comfortable" enough that "everyone enjoys themselves.

FOOD | DECOR | SERVICE | COST

Post Corner Pizza *Pizza* | 20 | 10 | 18 | $22 |

Darien | 847 Boston Post Rd. (Mansfield Ave.), CT | 203-655-7721 | www.postcornerpizza.com

"Families love" this casual Darien "tradition" that's been around "forever" offering "heavenly" Greek-style deep-dish pizza, along with other "good-value" salads, gyros and such; service is "quick", and "you can't hurt the furniture since it hasn't changed in years", ergo, it's "noisy and crowded" "when the kids' sports teams let out."

Posto 22 *Italian* | 21 | 18 | 21 | $39 |

New Rochelle | 22 Division St. (bet. Huguenot & Main Sts.) | 914-235-2464 | www.posto22.com

This "cute" trattoria in Downtown New Rochelle recalls "Little Italy" with "solid" "home cooking" set down in a "tight" space that's "boisterous" on weekends; even if detractors declare it "nothing special", prices are "reasonable", the staff "pleasant" and it's just the kind of place that makes you "happy."

Post Road Ale House *American* | - | - | - | M |

New Rochelle | 11 Huguenot St. (bet. Pratt & Rhodes Sts.) | 914-633-4610 | www.postroadalehouse.com

This New Rochelle pub offers a democratic American menu spanning wings, steaks and seafood (including raw-bar items) backed by microbrews and cocktails; the space evokes an updated tavern with exposed brick and other industrial touches, while moderate bills complete the package.

⬛NEW Pranzi *Italian* | - | - | - | E |

White Plains | Trump Tower | 8 City Ctr. (Court St.) | 914-328-4000 | www.pranzirestaurant.com

Bold and buzzy, this cosmopolitan newcomer in the base of White Plains' Trump Tower serves a vast Italian menu from Carmine Paglia (ex Polpo in Greenwich, CT); expect to find expense-accounters snuggled in black banquettes, dipping into a generous, Italo-centric wine list along with pizza, pasta and traditional dishes like branzino with shrimp, scallops and clams in saffron broth.

Primavera *Italian* | 24 | 23 | 21 | $50 |

Croton Falls | 592 Rte. 22 (bet. Birch Hill & Deans Corner Rds.) | 914-277-4580 | www.primaverarestaurantandbar.com

An "upscale" Croton Falls crowd convenes at this "inviting" Northern Italian–Med where choosing from a "vast" array of "delicious" specials is helped along by "willing", "on-target" servers; the major quibble is over the "Manhattan prices", which don't faze those who are "always impressed."

Priya Ⓜ *Indian* | ∇ 19 | 10 | 16 | $28 |

Suffern | 36 Lafayette Ave. (bet. Chestnut St. & Rte. 202) | 845-357-5700 | www.priyaindiancuisineny.com

Ok, the "decor isn't that pleasing", but the "fantastic variety" of "delicious, authentic" Indian fare at this Suffern spot "definitely is", particularly as it comes spiced to order; "great buffets for lunch and

FOOD DECOR SERVICE COST

weekends" are a bonus, as is "attentive service", while those who don't go for "dated" digs say it's "good for takeout."

Puccini *Italian*

| - | - | - | E |

Rhinebeck | 22 Garden St. (Market St.) | 845-876-3055 | www.puccinirhinebeck.com

No surprise, the strains of music by you-know-who drift through the dining room of this Rhinebeck restaurant dispensing upscale regional Italian classics like veal milanese and fettuccini carbonara along with seasonal specials; the L-shaped space is chic in pastel tones with posters from La Scala continuing the opera motif, while in summer, umbrella tables in the courtyard garden add another harmonious note.

Pumpernickel *Pub Food*

| 15 | 14 | 14 | $24 |

Ardsley | Ardsley Mall | 925 Saw Mill River Rd. (Sylvia Ln.) | 914-479-5370 | www.pumpernickelrestaurantardsley.com

"Stick to the burgers" and the homemade root beer at this Ardsley "mom-and-pop" "sports bar" slinging "decent" pub grub that's priced well for "families"; it's "comfortable" enough, although critics claim "mediocre" grub and "spotty" service mean it's "nothing to write home about."

Q Restaurant & Bar *BBQ*

| 22 | 12 | 17 | $26 |

Port Chester | 112 N. Main St. (bet. Adee St. & Willette Ave.) | 914-933-7427 | www.qrestaurantandbar.com

"Feasting" on "dream-worthy" barbecue is the order of the day at this Port Chester portal for "fall-of-the-bone" ribs and other "down-and-dirty" 'cue plus an "excellent selection of microbrews"; "bare-bones" decor and "cafeteria-style ordering" are part of the "sloppy" "fun", and "kids love it", while adults chortle over the "low prices."

Quattro Pazzi *Italian*

| 23 | 18 | 20 | $37 |

Stamford | 269 Bedford St. (Prospect St.), CT | 203-324-7000 | www.quattropazzi.com

There's "lots of choices" on the menu of this "moderately priced" Italian serving "reliable, quality dishes" in a "warm, friendly setting"; it inhabits a roomy, bi-level Stamford space that nonetheless gets "crowded" at peak hours.

Que Chula es Puebla *Mexican*

| 23 | 16 | 20 | $30 |

Sleepy Hollow | 180 Valley St. (bet. Chestnut & Depeyster Sts.) | 914-332-0072 | www.quechulaespueblarestaurant.com

"Not your same-old Mexican", this "friendly" Sleepy Hollow *cucina* kicks out "authentic, well-spiced" eats that go well with an "intoxicating variety of tequilas" and (on weekends) the tunes of "excellent mariachi musicians"; service in the colorful space is usually "adept", if sometimes "overwhelmed", and "reasonable prices" seal the deal.

Quinta Steakhouse *Portuguese/Steak*

| 21 | 17 | 20 | $46 |

Pearl River | 24 E. Central Ave. (bet. Main & William Sts.) | 845-735-5565 | www.quintasteakhouse.com

Rockland County residents who "want a good steak" at "reasonable cost" find "quality meats" at this "neighborhood" Pearl River chophouse, although it's the "interesting mix" of Portuguese offerings that set it apart; red banquettes brighten the simple setting, the "owners are nice" and the "$10 lunch special" is a "bargain."

Raccoon Saloon   *Pub Food*   21 | 15 | 19 | $34

Marlboro | 1330 Rte. 9W (Western Ave.) | 845-236-7872

An "old-time staple" in Marlboro, this "rustic" New American saloon serving "good" pub food is renowned for its "tasty, big burgers", "New Orleans–caliber sweet-potato fries" and "homemade ketchup" delivered by a "polite" crew; it "looks a bit downtrodden", but "go during the day" for views of the waterfall out back, or at night to make the most of the "hopping bar."

Rainwater Grill   *American*   16 | 19 | 19 | $39

Hastings-on-Hudson | 19 Main St. (Whitman St.) | 914-478-1147 | www.rainwatergrill.com

This "casual, comfortable" Hastings New American inhabits "contemporary" digs with a "vibrant bar scene" and a menu brimming with "interesting choices"; service is "efficient", so surveyors give it "an 'A' for effort", but wish the food was less "hit-or-miss" and hope it lives up to its "potential."

NEW Rambler's Rest   *Irish*   - | - | - | M

Monroe | 590 Rte. 208 (Mountain Rd.) | 845-782-1345
Poughquag | 2578 Rte. 55 (Palmer Circle) | 845-478-2223
www.ramblersrestny.com

Though somewhat new, these mid-Hudson Irish pubs conjure the old country with mahogany paneled walls, coffered ceilings, stone fireplaces and stained glass forming a backdrop for hearty vittles like shepherd's pie, fish 'n' chips and lamb stew; an array of draft ales and whiskeys completes the illusion, along with music, entertainment and a menu for the wee ones.

NEW Ramiro's 954   - | - | - | M
Latin Bistro   Ⓜ *Nuevo Latino*

Mahopac | 954 Rte. 6 (Country Rd. 6) | 845-621-3333 | www.ramirorestaurant.com

Chef Ramiro Jiminez (formerly at La Puerto Azul in Salt Point) has launched his own midpriced Nuevo Latino newcomer on Mahopac's main drag, offering updated classics from Central America, the Caribbean and Spain along with recipes from his Mexican grandmother; the main room is tricked out in fruity colors with a lively bar and a view of the kitchen, while a mini art gallery brightens the more sedate upstairs dining room.

Rani Mahal   *Indian*   23 | 14 | 21 | $32

Mamaroneck | 327 Mamaroneck Ave. (Palmer Ave.) | 914-835-9066 | www.ranimahalny.com

Curry-lovers praise the "wonderful" "variety" at this Mamaroneck Indian doling out "dependably delicious" subcontinental fare with "nice twists on traditional dishes"; most overlook the "odd" subterranean locale since servers are "helpful" and the "weekday buffet is a foodie's delight and a bargain to boot."

	FOOD	DECOR	SERVICE	COST

Ray's Cafe *Chinese*
19 | 8 | 17 | $26

Larchmont | 1995 Palmer Ave. (Parkway St.) | 914-833-2551 | www.rayscafeny.com

Customers count on this Larchmont Chinese for relatively "healthy" Shanghainese dishes with a focus on "fresh" veggies and gluten-free offerings that are "better than most"; considering the "so-so service" and "dreary" settings that are "begging for a makeover", most opt for takeout.

Reality Bites *Eclectic*
▽ 20 | 15 | 18 | $28

Nyack | 100 Main St. (Cedar St.) | 845-358-8800 | www.realitybites.com

There's a real "community" feel to this "cute, little" Nyack "concept" spot mixing "moderately priced" Eclectic eats, from "tasty" small plates to mains, with a side of entertainment via screenings of rock DVDs plus "fabulous live music" on Fridays; Christmas lights add sparkle to the "casual" setting, and "if all the TVs are distracting", there are "sidewalk tables", weather permitting.

ⓩ Rebeccas ⓢ Ⓜ *American*
26 | 21 | 23 | $80

Greenwich | 265 Glenville Rd. (bet. Pemberwick & Riversville Rds.), CT | 203-532-9270 | www.rebeccasgreenwich.com

The "superb", "tantalizing flavors" and "beautiful presentations" on chef/co-owner Reza Khorshidi's "imaginative menu" make this Greenwich New American a "culinary paradise", one that's "run like a well-oiled machine" by his "gracious" wife and partner, Rebecca, and their "professional" staff; "exquisite flowers" grace the "lovely environment", but some grouse that "regular customers" are favored, while wallet-watchers wince at the "*très* haute prices."

Red Brick Tavern *American*
▽ 20 | 13 | 19 | $32

Rosendale | 388 Main St. (bet. Central & Keator Aves.) | 845-658-8500 | www.redbrickrosendale.com

"Noisy bar, dark restaurant, good food" sums up this Rosendale New American where the "hearty" cooking comes in almost "comically large portions"; yes, it's a "dive"-y setting, but the "staff is welcoming" and the atmosphere "pleasant", so the "diverse crowd" that convenes doesn't care.

Red Devon Ⓜ *American*
23 | 24 | 20 | $52

Bangall | 108 Hunns Lake Rd./Rte. 65 (bet. James Cagney Way & Mills Ln.) | 845-868-3175 | www.reddevonrestaurant.com

Set amid farmland in "out-of-the-way" Bangall, this "entirely green" New American offers "organic", "nose-to-tail" fare in the "sleek" dining room, Thursday–Sunday, plus "fantastic" breakfasts and lunches in the adjoining market/cafe, all served at a "relaxed pace"; it's "a bit fancy for the country" and "Manhattan central" on weekends, but "if you're a locavore with a credit card", it's "a worthy option."

Red Dot Restaurant & Bar *Eclectic*
17 | 15 | 15 | $31

Hudson | 321 Warren St. (bet. City Hall Pl. & 3rd St.) | 518-828-3657

"Artists, antiques dealers" and "rowdy revelers" are among the "regulars" reporting to this Hudson "hangout" for "casual" New American–

Eclectic "comfort food", or the "delish" Sunday brunch; the mood is "low-key and fun" in the two "small" rooms and the "lovely garden" in back, so when it's "impossible to get your waiter's attention", just watch the "entertaining clientele."

❷ Red Hat on the River American   23 | 26 | 22 | $54

Irvington | 1 Bridge St. (River St., off Main St.) | 914-591-5888 | www.redhatbistro.com

Drinks on the rooftop are a "summer must" at this Irvington "stunner" situated in "magical" surroundings on the Hudson and turning out "delightful" "Frenchified" New American cuisine; its "lofty" exposed-brick space in a former factory exudes a "Manhattanesque" vibe, although some could do without occasionally "snotty" "SoHo" service and prices as "breathtaking" as the vistas.

Red Hook Curry House Indian   21 | 11 | 16 | $22

Red Hook | 28 E. Market St./Rte. 199 (bet. Church St. & S. B'way) | 845-758-2666 | www.redhookcurryhouse.com

Indian eateries are scarce around Red Hook, so it's "good to have" this "reliable" BYO "standby" serving "simple", "spicy" cuisine with plenty of vegetarian choices; "huge portions" and a "wonderful", "bargain" buffet on Tuesdays and Sundays keep it "popular with Bard college students and locals", who overlook the "old" digs but wish the staffers would "smile once in a while."

Red Lotus Thai   21 | 19 | 20 | $32

New Rochelle | 227 Main St. (Stephenson Blvd.) | 914-576-0444 | www.redlotusthai.com

Neighborhood fans "frequent" this New Rochelle Thai for "flavorful" basic dishes "pleasantly served" "in a pretty red room"; "tight parking is a downside", but modest prices make up for it, and many "love it for takeout."

Red Onion American   23 | 21 | 20 | $44

Saugerties | 1654 Rte. 212 (Glasco Tpke.) | 845-679-1223 | www.redonionrestaurant.com

An "imaginative" New American menu of "anything from a nicely cooked burger to a stunning duck confit" attracts a "happening" crowd to this Saugerties "treasure" manned by an "efficient" team; "vintage diner tables" help set a "warm", "bistro" mood in the "charming" "old country house" with its "quiet" porch, "prices are reasonable" and drinks "out-of-this-world" – in short, it "ain't bad at all."

Red Plum Asian   21 | 22 | 22 | $33

Mamaroneck | 251 Mamaroneck Ave. (bet. Palmer & Prospect Aves.) | 914-777-6888 | www.redplumrestaurant.com

An "interesting" array of Pan-Asian specialties – from "unusually fresh" sushi to pad Thai – awaits at this "modern" Mamaroneck sib of Toyo Sushi also pouring specialty cocktails at a marble bar; even if prices are "higher" than its next-door neighbor, the vibe is "pleasant in a Zen kind of way", and it's something of a "go-to" the area.

☒ Red Rooster Drive-In ⬒ *Burgers* `18` `11` `15` `$13`

Brewster | 1566 Rte. 22 (Rte. 312) | 845-279-8046

"Road food just as it should be" is the lure at this "nifty", 1960s Brewster drive-in dishing up "good burgers", "perfect dogs", "fresh, fried onion rings" and "frosty shakes" "like you remember from your childhood"; "kids love it" and grown-ups who enjoy the "retro vibe" "feel nostalgic" picnicking outside (seating's minimal) then taking "a whirl through the miniature golf course" next door.

Reka's *Thai* `19` `15` `20` `$34`

White Plains | 2 Westchester Ave. (Main St.) | 914-949-1440 | www.rekasthai.com

A White Plains "fixture" since 1987, this modest but "welcoming" Thai features "classic", "authentic" cooking – and "plenty of it" – "spiced as you request"; most don't mind the distinctly "unfancy" basement digs, because prices are low, and the lunch specials "can't be beat."

NEW RéNapoli *Pizza* `-` `-` `-` `I`

Old Greenwich | 216 Sound Beach Ave. (W. End Ave.), CT | 203-698-9300 | www.renapoli.com

A World Pizza Champion crafts artisan pies in Old Greenwich – thick, puffy Roman, thin, charred Neopolitan and New York–style all topped with fine cheeses and meats and baked in an imported wood-fired oven or a gas-fired brick oven; BYO keeps costs down, and since the spartan storefront has just 20 seats, takeout and catering are popular.

☒ Restaurant North ⬛Ⓜ *American* `26` `22` `25` `$60`

Armonk | 386 Main St. (bet. Bedford Rd. & Elm St.) | 914-273-8686 | www.restaurantnorth.com

A "terrific addition" to the Northern Westchester scene, this "chic" "hot spot" from Union Square Cafe alums brings "destination dining" to Armonk with "sublime" "farm-to-table" New American fare, a "fantastic" wine list and a "sharp, solicitous" staff; it's "pricey" and the din can be "deafening" (upstairs is more "serene"), but the biggest hurdle may be scoring a reservation.

☒ Restaurant X & `27` `24` `26` `$63`
Bully Boy Bar Ⓜ *American*

Congers | 117 Rte. 303 N. (Hilltop Rd.) | 845-268-6555 | www.xaviars.com

"X is for extraordinary" exclaim those "floored" by Peter Kelly's "magical" Congers New American that's like "Xaviars on a budget" but turning out equally "transcendent" food; "inviting" rooms in the "lovely" "country" house are tended by a "savvy" staff willing to "bend over backwards", and although it's "high priced", the $25 prix fixe lunch and Sunday's "food orgy" of a brunch are truly a "great deal."

Rhinecliff Hotel Bar *European* `19` `22` `17` `$38`

Rhinecliff | The Rhinecliff | 4 Grinnell St. (Shatzell Ave.) | 845-876-0590 | www.therhinecliff.com

A "far cry from the Rhinecliff of yore", this once-derelict "vintage hotel" has been transformed into "a jovial gathering place" by Brit▪

| | FOOD | DECOR | SERVICE | COST |

David and James Chapman, who dispense European "comfort food" like fish 'n' chips along with "local libations"; while the food is "variable" and the service "so-so", the "historic feel" and "terrific view" of the Hudson from the terrace make "everyone happy."

Rigatoni *Italian*
∇ 21 | 15 | 22 | $37

Pelham | 124 Fifth Ave. (bet. 2nd & 3rd Sts.) | 914-738-7373

The "caring staff" makes you "feel at home" at this Pelham Italian proffering "not trendy" but "reliable family fare" including pizzas from a "wood-burning oven"; prices are gentle, so its "unassuming" looks don't deter those looking for something "dependable."

Risotto *Italian*
∇ 21 | 17 | 24 | $38

Thornwood | 788 Commerce St. (Columbia & Franklin Aves.) | 914-769-6000 | www.risotto-restaurant.com

"Small and cozy", this otherwise "standard" Thornwood Italian is distinguished by six "consistently good" risottos offered daily, sparkling "homemade" desserts and service that "shines"; the "pedestrian" decor doesn't interfere with a "pleasant" "laid-back" atmosphere, and "affordable" tabs don't hurt at all.

Ristorante Buona Sera 🅼 *Italian*
22 | 16 | 22 | $39

Mt. Vernon | 546 Gramatan Ave. (Broad St.) | 914-665-9800 | www.ristorantebuonasera.com

They "make you feel like family" at this Mt. Vernon "red-sauce joint" that would be equally at home "on Arthur Avenue", what with its "good", "old-fashioned" fare and vibe that "takes you back 40 years"; "affordable" bills lure "a loyal, local following" even if a smidge suggest it's a tad "overrated."

Ristorante Lucia *Italian*
∇ 18 | 19 | 18 | $37

Bedford | 454 Old Post Rd. (bet. Pea Pond & Stone Hill Rds.) | 914-234-7600 | www.ristorantelucia.com

"Dependable family dining" with pizza, pastas and "homemade gelato" is the thing in the "casual" portion of this Bedford Italian, while more ambitious "quiet, adult" repasts are served in a room reserved for "fine dining"; "lackluster" service is a damper, but the fireplaces are a draw, as is a take-out or delivery option.

River City Grille *American/Eclectic*
19 | 17 | 20 | $42

Irvington | 6 S. Broadway (bet. Main St. & Sycamore Ln.) | 914-591-2033 | www.rivercitygrille.com

"There's something for everyone" at this Irvington Eclectic offering a "broad", "ambitious" menu with "interesting twists" on New American "comfort" plates; with a "comfortable", colorful setting and moderate prices, it "strikes a perfect balance" for a night out.

The River Club 🅼 *American*
14 | 15 | 16 | $36

Nyack | 11 Burd St. (bet. Hudson River & River St.) | 845-358-0220 | www.nyackriverclub.net

A "priceless view" of the Hudson "with the graceful Tappan Zee bridge in the distance" makes this "waterside" Nyack American "somehow addictive", despite "pedestrian" eats and "unpredictable service"; a

FOOD DECOR SERVICE COST

makeover of the dining room may outdate Decor scores, while the deck remains a "great place to kick back with friends."

The River Grill *American* `20` `22` `19` `$41`
Newburgh | 40 Front St. (2nd St.) | 845-561-9444 | www.therivergrill.com
The Hudson River views are so "inspirational" at this "enjoyable" spot on Newburgh's waterfront that they almost upstage chef Mark Mallia's "eclectic" New American cooking; service can be "spotty", but prices are "fair" and it's a particular "pleasure" in summer to sit on the patio and "watch the boats" go by.

Riverview Ⓜ⇗ *American* `24` `20` `23` `$50`
Cold Spring | 45 Fair St. (Northern Ave.) | 845-265-4778 | www.riverdining.com
"One of the best" eateries in Cold Spring, this "welcoming" New American is a "home away from home" for those who file in for "fantastic" fare or "excellent wood-fired pizza"; a "personable" crew, a "simple, elegant" setting and "gorgeous" views of Storm King and the Hudson are other reasons patrons "always leave happy."

NEW Rizzuto's *Italian/Pizza* `20` `19` `18` `$36`
Stamford | 1980 W. Main St. (Myano Ln.), CT | 203-324-5900 | www.rizzutos.com
The "aroma from the brick oven makes you hungry as soon as you enter" this Stamford Italian offering "something for everyone", including "yummy pizzas", and in a setting that's "upscale without being stuffy", drawing lots of "families" as well as a "nice bar crowd"; calling the cooking "hit-or-miss" and the service "anything but professional", however, critics lament that it "looks like it wants to be a chain."

Roasted Peppers *American* `21` `16` `20` `$34`
Mamaroneck | 320 Mamaroneck Ave. (Spencer Pl.) | 914-341-1140 | www.roastedpeppersny.com
This "welcome" addition along Mamaroneck Avenue's ever-expanding restaurant strip specializes in "creative" New American cooking with Latin American "twists" (like their signature roast pepper); the "casual" space with exposed brick and sun-inspired tones is "comfortable" enough, and "inexpensive" prices complete the package.

NEW Rock and Rye Tavern Ⓜ *American* `–` `–` `–` `M`
New Paltz | 215 Huguenot St. (Old Kingston Rd.) | 845-255-7888 | www.rockandrye.com
An old-fashioned vibe prevails at this New Paltz New American offering charcuterie and small plates along with seasonal bistro fare in an atmospheric stone house; patrons can sip a classic cocktail or cask beer in the tavern room with its wood-burning stove, opt for one of the two pretty dining rooms or sit on the patio when it's warm.

Roger Sherman Inn Restaurant *Continental* `24` `25` `23` `$59`
New Canaan | Roger Sherman Inn | 195 Oenoke Ridge (Holmewood Ln.), CT | 203-966-4541 | www.rogershermaninn.com
A "big old historical country house" is the "luxurious, comfortable" setting for a "top-notch" dinner or "magnificent" brunch at this "dig-

nified" New Canaan Continental offering "wonderful" fare and "unobtrusive, watchful" service in a "beautiful", "white-tablecloth" space with a "lovely outdoor porch"; while a few sound the "snooze alert" for the "old-school" scene, a younger, "preppy" crowd ("Muffy? Is it really you?") gathers in the "casual" bar for a "well-done" bistro menu and "live music."

Roma ☒ *Pizza*

| 18 | 10 | 17 | $26 |

Tuckahoe | 29 Columbus Ave. (Underhill St.) | 914-961-3175 | www.romarestaurantinc.com

The "delectable, thin-crust" pizza is the "best bet" at this Tuckahoe Italian "joint" where otherwise the red-sauce fare is rather "ordinary"; service can be cold "if they don't know you", and decor "needs an update" ("hello 1970s"), but at least the portions provide value.

Ron Blacks ◑ *Pub Food*

| ▽ 16 | 19 | 18 | $32 |

White Plains | 181 Mamaroneck Ave. (bet. Maple Ave. & Rutherford St.) | 914-358-5811 | www.ronblacks.com

The many craft beers on tap "are a wonder to behold" at this "roomy" White Plains pub also proffering "bar food" in "comfortable" digs with lots of wood and walls full of antique clocks; so even if the grub's "underwhelming", it's still a "cool place to hang out."

Rosa's La Scarbitta ☒ *Italian*

| - | - | - | M |

Mamaroneck | 215 Halstead Ave. (Ward Ave.) | 914-777-1667

Rosa Merenda left Spadaro in New Rochelle to open this midpriced Mamaroneck Italian with a similarly homey vibe; the menu focuses on regional peasant cuisine like ricotta gnocchi and wild boar accompanied by wine and cocktails and capped with homemade desserts.

Rosendale Cafe *Vegetarian*

| ▽ 15 | 12 | 14 | $26 |

Rosendale | 434 Main St./Rte. 213 (Hardenburgh Ln.) | 845-658-9048 | www.rosendalecafe.com

Sure, it's a bit of a "throwback to the '60s", and the "homestyle" vegetarian fare is "nothing too exciting", but this "casual" Rosendale "joint" is "reliable" for "affordable" eats in fittingly "funky" digs; sometimes "too-cool-for-school" service can be a bummer, but the "top-notch live music on weekends" makes it "fun", "even for carnivores."

☑ Rosie's Bistro Italiano *Italian*

| 23 | 20 | 22 | $46 |

Bronxville | 10 Palmer Ave. (Paxton Ave.) | 914-793-2000 | www.rosiesbronxville.com

Locals "love everything about" this "warm, bustling" Bronxville Italian, from the "consistently delicious" cuisine offering "excellent quality for the price", to the "inviting" atmosphere; factor in an "attentive" staff that's "welcoming toward families", and it's no wonder it's a neighborhood "favorite."

Route 100 *American*

| ▽ 22 | 18 | 23 | $35 |

Yonkers | 2211 Central Park Ave. (Roxbury Dr.) | 914-779-2222 | www.route100newyork.com

They "make you feel welcome" at this Yonkers "sleeper" that comes "highly recommended" by locals thanks to its "excellent" American standards priced to offer "tremendous value" (especially during happy hour); "accommodating" service and an overall congenial vibe overcome its modest strip-mall digs.

Route 22 *Pub Food*   14 | 17 | 16 | $27

Armonk | 55 Old Rte. 22 (Kaysal Ct.) | 914-765-0022 | www.rt22restaurant.com

A "cross between a truck stop, a diner and Chuck E. Cheese", this Armonk pub is where parents "take the kids for a burger" "served in cute car boxes" amid "lots of distractions"; "erratic" service and "noisy" environs drive adults sans children to "go elsewhere."

Royal Palace *Indian*   20 | 13 | 19 | $35

White Plains | 77 Knollwood Rd. (Dobbs Ferry Rd./Rte. 100B) | 914-289-1988 | www.royalpalacecuisines.com

"Lots" of "flavorful" choices – especially at the "limitless" buffets at both lunch and dinner – keep loyalists coming to this "friendly" White Plains Indian; its spare setting could likely use an "update", but at least it's "convenient to the movies", and priced well too.

☑ Rraci ⓜ *Italian*   26 | 22 | 25 | $50

Brewster | 3670 Rte. 6 (bet. Branch & Thomas Rds.) | 845-278-6695 | www.rracisrestaurant.com

"You can tell they care" at this "high-end" Brewster Italian offering a "bit of heaven" via "delicious, homemade pasta" and such "wow"-worthy seafood "they must own the boat"; those who find the "attractive" low-lit setting too "cave"-like and "deafening" at times can head to the "lovely garden", while practically "perfect" service and prices that are a "bargain for the quality" help make it "a winner."

Ruby's Oyster Bar & Bistro *Seafood*   23 | 20 | 21 | $48

Rye | 45 Purchase St. (Smith St.) | 914-921-4166 | www.rubysoysterbar.com

Locals "love" this "pearl" of an oyster bar in Rye, a "fashionable" stop for bivalves "galore", "wonderful" bistro-style seafood and "generous pours" on drinks; it owes its "sophisticated", "city" vibe to a "hopping bar" scene and a "yuppie" clientele, just know that "noisy" acoustics can make "earplugs" a necessity.

Rue des Crêpes *French*   19 | 20 | 18 | $25

Harrison | 261 Halstead Ave. (Harrison Ave.) | 914-315-1631 | www.ruedescrepes.com

A "delightful hideaway", this "quaint, little" cafe in Harrison puts out "borderline-addictive" crêpes "prepared in every way imaginable" and other French fare in a "casual" muralled interior decked out with Parisian touches; modest prices are a perk, although service can be a sore spot and the "Epcot"-y decor is a little "overly cute" to some.

Ruth's Chris Steak House *Steak*   25 | 22 | 24 | $65

Tarrytown | Westchester Marriott | 670 White Plains Rd. (bet. I-287 & Old White Plains Rd.) | 914-631-3311 | www.ruthschris.com

Carnivores "love the sizzling platters" of "oh-so-good buttery steaks" at this "top-quality" chophouse chain that comes through with "winning" sides too; delivering "old-style service" in a "traditional" setting, it's "expensive" (and "not for the dieter"), but "utterly reliable", especially when you're "entertaining friends and clients."

Rye Grill & Bar *Eclectic*   18 | 20 | 18 | $38

Rye | 1 Station Plaza (on 1st St., off Purdy Ave.) | 914-967-0332 | www.ryegrill.com

"Still a handy standby", there's "something for everyone" at this "renovated" Rye Eclectic whose "beautiful" three-level digs are "large" enough to accommodate diners looking for "solid" "high-end" pub grub as well as those interested in an "attractive young bar scene"; though service can be "haphazard" and the "noise is a deal-breaker" for some, there's "never a dull moment."

Rye Roadhouse *Cajun/Creole*   18 | 12 | 18 | $33

Rye | 12 High St. (bet. Clinton & Maple Aves.) | 914-925-2668 | www.ryeroadhouse.com

You'll need a "good GPS" to track down this "deliberately seedy" Rye "roadhouse" "nestled into" a residential neighborhood and turning out "authentic" Cajun-Creole in a "laid-back" atmosphere; yes, it's "basically a bar", but the food's "a big step up from pub fare" and "friendly" staffers plus occasional live music make for a "fun night out."

Saffron *Indian*   ▽ 19 | 15 | 20 | $35

Middletown | 130 Dolson Ave. (bet. Overlook Dr. & Republic Plaza) | 845-344-0005

Middletown denizens in need of "an Indian fix" head to this "comfortable" venue that's "the only game in town" for "tasty" curries and all the usual suspects; the service is "efficient" and the rates "reasonable", especially at the "terrific daily lunch buffet", so those not hot for the "typical" decor and "strip-mall setting" simply "get takeout."

Sagi ⧄ *Italian*   23 | 19 | 23 | $40

Ridgefield | 23½ Catoonah St. (Main St.), CT | 203-431-0200 | www.sagiofridgefield.com

A mother-daughter team "welcomes everyone with open arms" at their "lovely" trattoria "nestled" off Ridgefield's main drag where chef-owner Bianca DeMasi "takes great pride" in her "well-prepared" and "well-presented" "homestyle" dishes, which can be paired with "incredibly reasonable" wines by the glass; though some report "no elbow room" in the "warm" cream-and-red interior, others find the atmosphere "relaxing" and the prices "amazing for the area."

Saigon Café *Vietnamese*   ▽ 23 | 10 | 21 | $27

Poughkeepsie | 6 Lagrange Ave. (Raymond Ave.) | 845-473-1392 | www.saigoncafe.net

"Don't be put off by the modest decor" because within this Poughkeepsie nook lies a "culinary tour of Vietnam" via "delicious" "home cooking and hospitality" from the "caring couple" who run it; all comes "value priced", and although "the menu never changes", "why tamper with a winner?"

Salsa ⓜ🚭 *Southwestern* ▽ 25 | 11 | 23 | $21

New Milford | 54 Railroad St. (Bank St.), CT | 860-350-0701

"The simple storefront" setting is "deceiving" say fans of this Southwestern specialist that's "not much in the way of decor", but a "must stop in New Milford" for "fresh, tasty" fare at "bargain prices", served in a "casual", "laid-back" environment; it offers "good value for the buck", which is why it's "often quite busy."

🆕 Salsa Fresca Mexican Grill *Mexican* – | – | – | I

Bedford Hills | 720 N. Bedford Rd. (Green Ln.) | 914-241-0900 | www.salsafrescagrill.com

Convenience is king at this family-friendly Bedford Hills Mexican with counter-style service plus online ordering with Smart Car delivery; expect the basic roundup of tacos, burritos, nachos and quesadillas spun with a Chipotle-esque eye toward fresh, healthful ingredients, with beer and margaritas to wash it down.

Sal's Pizzeria 🚭 *Pizza* 23 | 6 | 12 | $15

Mamaroneck | 316 Mamaroneck Ave. (Palmer Ave.) | 914-381-2022

The perpetual "lines" tell the story at this "authentic, gritty" "landmark" pizzeria in Mamaroneck putting out "superb", "cheesy" slices including a Sicilian slab "that will make you contemplate the meaning of life"; the "surly" service is "right out of central casting", but "that's part of the charm"; P.S. "top off your meal with gelato next door."

Sammy's Downtown *American/Continental* 22 | 21 | 22 | $50

Bronxville | 124 Pondfield Rd. (Tanglewylde Ave.) | 914-337-3200 | www.sammysbronxville.com

"It feels more like TriBeCa than Bronxville" at this "grown-up" restaurant and sib of Rosie's Bistro Italiano offering "excellent" "classic" Continental–New American cooking in a "lively" setting decked out with nude paintings ("guess it keeps the kids out"); add in "professional service" and it's generally a "winner" all around.

Sam's *Italian* 18 | 12 | 21 | $33

Dobbs Ferry | 126-128 Main St. (Oak St.) | 914-693-9724 | www.samsofdobbsferry.com

"You're bound to see your neighbors" at this "quintessential" "mom-and-pop" Italian in Dobbs Ferry that "caters to families" with "generous portions" of "good", "not great", "simple" "red-sauce" fare in an "old-time" setting; even if some are "bored just thinking about it", service is "warm" and the vibe "friendly", so folks "keep coming back."

Sam's of Gedney Way *American* 19 | 16 | 20 | $36

White Plains | 52 Gedney Way (bet. Mamaroneck Ave. & Old Mamaroneck Rd.) | 914-949-0978 | www.samsofgedneyway.com

"Lots of repeat customers" laud this "easygoing" American "old-timer" in White Plains featuring a "no-surprises" traditional menu headlined by burgers that are "hard to top"; after 80 years on the scene, perhaps the "informal" "pubby" setting could use "refreshing", but prices are moderate and service "accommodating" (especially for parties) so you "can always count on" it.

	FOOD	DECOR	SERVICE	COST

Santa Fe *Mexican/Southwestern*   17 | 15 | 18 | $33

Tarrytown | 5 Main St. (Rte. 9) | 914-332-4452 |
www.santaferestaurant.com

"You probably need a number of margaritas" to best enjoy the
"college-town" Mexican-Southwestern cooking at this Tarrytown
fallback "convenient to Town Hall" and awash in "border-cafe cli-
chés"; an "active bar" scene and low pricing mean it "works before a show", and in spite of somewhat "unexceptional" grub, it
"always seems crowded."

Santa Fe Ⓜ *Mexican*   22 | 17 | 19 | $32

Tivoli | 52 Broadway (Montgomery St.) | 845-757-4100 |
www.santafetivoli.com

"Who'd a thunk" you'd find such "tasty" Mexican eats in tiny Tivoli,
ask those preparing to "feast" on "artfully served" dishes at this
"jumping" joint; a "cheerful, colorful" setting "full of Bard students"
plus "kick-ass frozen margaritas" mean the "social buzz" can reach
high "volume", but it's "affordable" and "great fun."

Santorini Greek Restaurant *Greek*   22 | 13 | 21 | $32

Sleepy Hollow | 175 Valley St. (bet. Chestnut & Depeyster Sts.) |
914-631-4300 | www.santorinigreekrestaurant.com

For "delicious", "traditional" Greek fare in a "simple setting", try this
"cheap and cheerful" Sleepy Hollow standby putting out "huge"
helpings of grilled fish, "flavorful kebabs" and such in ample "sunwashed" digs; live music and Saturday night belly dancing make it
even more "enjoyable", especially for groups.

ⓩ Sapore *Steak*   26 | 24 | 23 | $53

Fishkill | 1108 Main St. (North St.) | 845-897-3300 |
www.saporesteakhouse.com

"Serious meat lovers" find Fishkill's "NYC-style steakhouse" "a
blessing" for its "perfect", "carefully prepared" cuts, "unusual"
choices like elk and oxtail, "well-made trimmings" and "fabulous
wine list"; prices are on the big-city side too, but an "attentive, courteous" staff and "lovely", classic chop-shop decor combine to keep
customers "coming back."

Savona's Trattoria *Italian*   ∇ 19 | 18 | 22 | $29

Kingston | 11 Broadway (W. Strand St.) | 845-339-6800 |
www.savonas.com

For "pasta dishes done right" and other "comfort food" "just like
grandma used to make", surveyors seek out this "popular" Italian in
Kingston's Rondout district serving the family recipes of second-
generation restaurateur and "engaging host" Stephen Savona; affordable tabs, a "casual" setting with big windows and sidewalk
seating all "make it easy to become a regular."

Sazan *Japanese*   24 | 15 | 18 | $44

Ardsley | 729 Saw Mill River Rd. (Center St.) | 914-674-6015
"Superb", "traditional" sushi is the bait at this "upper-end" Ardsley
Japanese where "quality" fin fare and "delicious" cooked items are

proffered by a "no-nonsense" staff; some find the "serene", "strip-mall" setting a tad "serious" (read: not "kid-friendly"), but acolytes insist it's "worth it" for an "authentic" meal.

Scalini Osteria *Italian* 21 | 21 | 19 | $54

Bronxville | 65 Pondfield Rd., lower level (bet. Garden Ave. & Park Pl.) | 914-337-4935 | www.scaliniosteria.com

Customers are "charmed" by this Bronxville "secret" serving "solid", "expensive" Tuscan cuisine on a "lovely, secluded" brick patio that's kitted out with heaters on cool nights; it can be a tight "squeeze" in the dining room, but an "accommodating" staff makes up for it.

Scaramella's *Italian* 23 | 16 | 23 | $46

Dobbs Ferry | 1 Southfield Ave. (Ashford Ave.) | 914-693-6024 | www.scaramellas.com

"Come hungry" to this Dobbs Ferry Italian "throwback" for "huge" helpings of "satisfying", "straightforward" cooking including a "laundry list" of "super specials" delivered by "refined", tuxedo-clad servers who "won't steer you wrong"; "high prices" are a sticking point for some surveyors, but the consensus is "you can't beat the food."

Scarsdale Metro Restaurant *American* 17 | 10 | 16 | $24

Scarsdale | 878 Scarsdale Ave. (off Popham Rd.) | 914-713-0309 | www.metrorestaurants.net

A "neighborhood" mainstay for over a decade, this "glorified diner" in Scarsdale is a "dependable" bet for "high-quality", "no-surprises" American fare for eat-in or takeout; while prices can feel "high", helpings are "huge" enough "for two meals", so you really can't go wrong."

Schlesinger's Steakhouse *Steak* 23 | 17 | 21 | $40

New Windsor | 475 Temple Hill Rd. (Commerce Dr.) | 845-561-1762 | www.schlesingerssteakhouse.com

This "long-established" New Windsor meatery puts out "real, honest-to-goodness" steakhouse fare like "hand-cut" filets, "hearty" sides and "homemade pickles" gratis on every table; except for a cigar shop on-site there's "not much in the way of decor" in the farmhouse-style space, but given the moderate pricing, most "would go back"; P.S. there's also live music on weekends and an outdoor entertainment space in warm weather.

☒ Schoolhouse at Cannondale ☒ *American* 27 | 23 | 24 | $59

Wilton | 34 Cannon Rd. (Seeley Rd.), CT | 203-834-9816 | www.theschoolhouseatcannondale.com

Fans would stay "after school any day of the week" to savor chef-owner Tim LaBant's "fabulous" menu of "inspired" New American cuisine featuring "locally grown produce" at his "pricey" Wilton restaurant, housed in a "charming former one-room school-house" overlooking the Norwalk River; the toque "talks with every guest" while his "friendly" staff provides "attentive" service, and

FOOD DECOR SERVICE COST

though some surveyors say they could use a hall pass from the "cramped" quarters, most give this "find" extra credit for a "delightful dining experience."

Seaside Johnnie's *Seafood* | 12 | 18 | 15 | $38 |

Rye | 94 Dearborn Ave. (Forest Ave.) | 914-921-6104 |
www.seasidejohnnies.com

The "spectacular views" of Long Island Sound are the best things going for this "shack"-like seafooder on Rye's Oakland Beach; indeed the service is "slow" and the "pricey" "deep-fried" fare and "tropical drinks" are "ordinary" at best, but somehow, "sitting out on the patio makes it all ok"; P.S. open from April–October.

Seasons American Bistro &   ▽ | 18 | 20 | 17 | $41 |
Lounge *American*

Somers | 289 Rte. 100 (Rte. 138) | 914-276-0600 |
www.seasonsatsomers.com

Whether meeting for cocktails and some nibbles, or ordering from the "varied menu" of "solid" New American cuisine, there's always "something for everyone" – even the gluten-intolerant – at this "better-than-average" Somers restaurant; "friendly" service, "nice" modern furnishings and a pondside patio enhance the "relaxing, pleasant" atmosphere.

Seasons Japanese Bistro *Japanese* | 23 | 16 | 20 | $35 |

White Plains | 105 Mamaroneck Ave. (Quarropas St.) | 914-421-1163 |
www.seasonsjapanesebistro.com

"Exceptionally fresh fish" is the hook at this storefront sushi specialist in White Plains where there are "no frills", just "solid", "fairly priced" Japanese fare; its "simple", "calming" setting and "so-so" decor may not stand out, but it's certainly convenient, and "kid-friendly" too.

ⓩ Serevan *Mediterranean* | 27 | 23 | 25 | $54 |

Amenia | 6 Autumn Ln. (Rte. 44, west of Rte. 22) | 845-373-9800 |
www.serevan.com

"A beacon amid the hayfields", this "outstanding" Amenia Mediterranean is a "gourmet paradise" where "gifted", "passionate" chef-owner Serge Madikians uses "top-quality ingredients" and "aromatic spices" to create "superb" "Middle Eastern–tinged" dishes so "scrumptious" you could "point at random" to the menu and have an "inspired" meal; slightly "pricey" tabs are trumped by the "quiet, welcoming farmhouse" setting, "polished" service and overall "convivial" experience.

Sesame Seed ⓢ *Mideastern* | 21 | 16 | 18 | $24 |

Danbury | 68 W. Wooster St. (bet. Division & Pleasant Sts.), CT |
203-743-9850 | www.sesameseedrestaurant.com

The "quirky" "knickknacks" "cluttering" this "bohemian" "Danbury institution" are a "bit dated", but the "generous helpings" of Mideast eats are "always fresh"; a "relaxed attitude" from the staff and "reasonable prices" are two more features that render it "worth the wait" when it's "crowded" (usually around lunchtime).

FOOD | DECOR | SERVICE | COST

Seven Woks *Chinese* 18 | 13 | 19 | $27

Scarsdale | Golden Horseshoe Shopping Ctr. | 1122 Wilmot Rd.
(Heathcote Rd.) | 914-472-4774 | www.shopgh.com

Though it "hasn't changed much since the '80s", this Scarsdale standby remains "remarkably consistent", turning out "better-than-average" "American-Chinese" cooking to nostalgic "locals"; decor may be "lacking", but "excellent value" and "kid-friendly" service keep it "busy", especially on Sunday nights.

Shadows on the Hudson *American* 17 | 23 | 19 | $39

Poughkeepsie | 176 Rinaldi Blvd. (bet. Church & Main Sts.) |
845-486-9500 | www.shadowsonthehudson.com

There's an "electric atmosphere" at this "enormous" riverside Poughkeepsie New American where the "phenomenal view", "flashy" dining spaces and serpentine bar with its "big-screen TV" combine to "eclipse" the "fair food"; still, the "staff is usually thoughtful" and the "diverse" menu has a "wide price range", so at least "drop anchor" to "sip a cocktail" on the deck at sunset and "enjoy the breezes."

Sherwood's *Pub Food* 20 | 12 | 16 | $27

Larchmont | 2136 Boston Post Rd. (bet. Larchmont Ave. & Manor Pl.) |
914-833-3317 | www.sherwoodsrestaurant.com

"Stick to the burgers and ribs and you won't be disappointed" at this "dark", "noisy" Larchmont tavern, a "nice neighborhood" place that's also famed for its "fine Buffalo wings"; perhaps the setting and service could use some work, but tabs are easy on the wallet, and surveyors say the casual atmosphere is especially "good for kids."

⚡ Ship Lantern Inn Ⓜ *American/Continental* 26 | 22 | 26 | $49

Milton | 1725 Rte. 9W (Old Indian Rd.) | 845-795-5400 |
www.shiplanterninn.com

"Top-notch from stem to stern", this "long-established" Milton New American–Continental stays on course with "consistently" "delicious" cooking and "impeccable", "formal" service from "professionals" "in tuxes"; add in "pleasant" seafaring decor and it's such "a flashback to the good old days" you almost "expect Bing Crosby to come and start the floor show"; P.S. the twilight menu (available 4-6 PM, Tuesday–Friday) is priced like another blast from the past.

Ship to Shore *American* 22 | 18 | 20 | $41

Kingston | 15 W. Strand St. (B'way) | 845-334-8887 |
www.shiptoshorehudsonvalley.com

An "anchor" in Kingston's Rondout district, this "cool", mid-priced New American proffers "caring chef" Samir Hrichi's "adventurous recipes" from "inventive apps" through "glorious desserts", served by an "attentive", "chatty" crew; although there's not much "elbow room" when the bar area gets busy, the back room is "inviting" and sidewalk tables in summer make the most of the "riverside atmosphere."

FOOD DECOR SERVICE COST

Shiraz ⓜ *Persian*   20 | 12 | 17 | $32

Elmsford | 81 E. Main St. (Evarts St.) | 914-345-6111

"Something exotic" is sure to grace your plate at this Elmsford Persian serving "unusual" dishes "going well beyond kebabs"; the spartan setting's "a bit grim" and service "lackadaisical", but the BYO policy makes the tabs a "terrific value."

Siam Orchid *Thai*   ▽ 20 | 15 | 18 | $30

Scarsdale | 750 Central Park Ave. (Mt. Joy Ave.) | 914-723-9131 | www.siamorchidscarsdale.com

This "pleasant", "neighborhood" Thai in Scarsdale "is a decent choice" for "solid" renditions of all the classics; the traditional setting is nothing to write home about, but low tabs and "welcoming smiles" from the staff go a long way.

Sidewalk Bistro *French*   20 | 17 | 19 | $45

Piermont | 482 Piermont Ave. (Ash St.) | 845-680-6460 | www.sidewalkbistro.com

Although a change of chef meant the French fare "faltered" for a while, this "busy" Piermont boîte still doles out "nicely done", "straightforward bistro" eats at "reasonable prices"; expect "a warm welcome", whether you choose the "relaxed" dining room, where it's "noisy, but fun" when the "lively bar crowd" gets going, the "congenial patio" in back or the namesake sidewalk seating in warm weather.

Siena ⓩ *Italian*   23 | 19 | 21 | $53

Stamford | 519 Summer St. (bet. Broad & Spring Sts.), CT | 203-351-0898 | www.sienaristorante.net

"Wonderful" Tuscan dishes are complemented by "fine" Italian wines at this moderate-to-"expensive" destination in Downtown Stamford, where "regulars" are "treated like family" by a "knowledgeable staff" (indeed, some say "it helps to be known here"); the setting is "pretty", though it would probably seem more "romantic" to more people if there weren't such a "loud", often "deafening" "noise level."

🆕 Siete Ocho Siete ❶ *Puerto Rican*   - | - | - | E

New Rochelle | 414 Pelham Rd. (Meadow Ln.) | 914-636-1229 | www.sieteochosiete.com

Clubby bottle service, frozen "Tropicaltinis" and dinners served until 1 AM on weekends are the hallmarks of this glitzy New Rochelle Puerto Rican restaurant and nightclub; look for all the Caribbean classics – pernil, mofongo and sancocho (a hearty stew) – plus live bands and happy-hour specials in the lounge; P.S. there's also patio seating overlooking the Long Island Sound in warm weather.

🆕 Sofrito *Puerto Rican*   - | - | - | M

White Plains | 175 Main St. (Renaissance Sq.) | 914-428-5500 | www.sofritowhiteplains.com

This White Plains offshoot of a Manhattan original boasts similarly vibrant Puerto Rican flavors, glittering digs and a thumping, nightclubby vibe; look for elevated takes on pernil, arroz con pollo and mofongo washed down with piña coladas and other fruity drinks.

FOOD | DECOR | SERVICE | COST

Solano's Lincoln Lounge ☒ *Italian* | - | - | - | I |

Mt. Vernon | 209 Stevens Ave. (Lincoln Ave.) | 914-664-9747
Known as Lincoln Lounge to its many regulars, this "family-run" Mt. Vernon Italian "relic" from 1950 has more recently earned a cult following for its "terrific" thin-crust pizzas, most notably the square sausage and garlic–topped pie; the pleasantly faded digs with wood paneling and Christmas lights are "old-school" all the way, and inexpensive prices complete the picture.

Solé Ristorante *Italian* | 21 | 18 | 20 | $48 |

New Canaan | 105 Elm St. (bet. Park St. & South Ave.), CT | 203-972-8887 | www.zhospitalitygroup.com
"Solid", "reliable" Northern Italian fare and "great pizzas" come via a mostly "friendly" "longtime staff" at this somewhat "pricey" New Canaan *cucina*; you can "grab a seat at the bar" overlooking the open kitchen and take part in the "lively" proceedings.

Solmar Brazilian & Portuguese Fine Cuisine *Brazilian/Portuguese* | ▽ 21 | 18 | 21 | $42 |

Tarrytown | 12 Main St. (B'way) | 914-333-0151 | www.solmartarrytown.com
"Homey" Brazilian-Portuguese dishes are the forte of this "charming" "change of pace" that's "right across the street from the Tarrytown Music Hall" offering "authentic" dishes (with lots of "fresh seafood") at relatively "reasonable" prices; a "keen-to-please" staff keeps the mood relaxed, and live jazz on Sundays is a nice touch.

☒ Sonora *Nuevo Latino* | 24 | 22 | 22 | $49 |

Port Chester | 179 Rectory St. (Willett Ave.) | 914-933-0200 | www.sonorarestaurant.net
"Like a vacation in South America", this "festive" Port Chester "favorite" from Rafael Palomino charms guests with an "innovative" mix of "refined", "artistic" Nuevo Latino plates elevated by "fabulous" cocktails "that will knock you off your barstool"; a "knowledgeable" staff shows "attention to detail", now if only they could do something about the "incredibly noisy" acoustics.

☒ Soul Dog ☒Ⓜ *Hot Dogs* | 23 | 15 | 23 | $13 |

Poughkeepsie | 107 Main St. (bet. Clover & Perry Sts.) | 845-454-3254 | www.souldog.biz
"A New Age hot-dog joint that satisfies on many levels", this affordable Poughkeepsie keeper – the Westchester/Hudson Valley Survey's No. 1 Bang for the Buck – cranks out "high-quality" beef, chicken and veggie franks with a "variety of add-ons", plus sandwiches, soups and gluten-free items washed down with sodas and beer; a "personable staff" and colorful, kid-friendly digs add yet more soul.

Southport Brewing Co. *Pub Food* | 16 | 15 | 16 | $27 |

Stamford | 131 Summer St. (Broad St.), CT | 203-327-2337 | www.southportbrewing.com
Though the pub grub is merely "routine" and the "sports-bar" decor is "nothing to get excited about", this microbrewery chain draws sudsers

with "many beers of all hues and tastes"; it's also a magnet for parents who appreciate that it's "kid-friendly" ("magic shows on Sundays"), with a "patient" staff, "good portions" and "moderate prices."

Southwest Cafe   *New Mexican* | 22 | 18 | 23 | $32 |

Ridgefield | Copps Hill Common | 109 Danbury Rd. (Farmingville Rd.), CT | 203-431-3398 | www.southwestcafe.com

Chef-owner Barbara Nevins "brings her love of Taos to your table" at this Ridgefield New Mexican where her "innovative" "take on Southwestern food" (served in small and large plates) strives for "gourmet-level" while remaining "moderately priced"; the "charming", "warm, cozy" space boasts "colorful" contemporary Navajo art and "attentive", "cheerful service", plus there's an "inviting" patio; P.S. it's a "must visit" when hatch chiles are in season.

Spaccarelli's ☒ *Italian* | 22 | 20 | 21 | $54 |

Millwood | Millwood Town Plaza | 238 Saw Mill River Rd./Rte. 100 (Rte. 133) | 914-941-0105 | www.spaccarellirestaurant.com

"Old-world charm" transcends the shopping-center locale of this "classic, white-tablecloth" Millwood Italian that "more than does the job" with "excellent" "traditional" cuisine, "cordial" service and overall "attention to detail"; "high prices" make it a "special-occasion" place for some.

☑ Spadaro ☒ *Italian* | 26 | 14 | 22 | $51 |

New Rochelle | 211 Main St. (Stephenson Blvd.) | 914-235-4595

"Arthur Avenue comes to New Rochelle" via this "impossibly tiny", "family-run" Italian where there's no menu and the kitchen sends out "delicious" "multicourse" meals that would "enchant even the most jaded diner"; never mind the "hefty" bills, "noisy" acoustics and "strip-mall" digs, "if you can get in, you'll never want to leave."

Spice Village   *Indian* | 22 | 16 | 18 | $32 |

Tuckahoe | 8 Columbus Ave. (Main St.) | 914-779-5400 | www.spicevillage.net

A "find" in Tuckahoe, this "unpretentious" Indian "satisfies cravings" with "tasty", "authentic" fare offered à la carte or in an ample lunchtime buffet; its understated decor is "typical" for the genre, though the "reasonable" prices and "attentive" service certainly stand out.

Spoon Asian Fusion Restaurant   *Asian* | 20 | 17 | 17 | $38 |

Chappaqua | 415 King St. (Bedford Rd.) | 914-238-1988 | www.spoonasianfusion.com

An "interesting" array of Asian fusion dishes plus "skillfully prepared sushi" turns up at this Chappaqua canteen inhabiting "loud", modern digs; yet despite the "right look and vibe", the food "falls short" for some, and others are irked that you "pay a premium" "for the address."

Squires of Briarcliff   *American* | 19 | 9 | 16 | $26 |

Briarcliff Manor | 94 N. State Rd. (Rte. 9A) | 914-762-3376

Regulars "rave about the burgers" at this Briarcliff Manor "haunt" that's "been there for years", turning out Traditional American

FOOD | DECOR | SERVICE | COST

eats and putting "plenty on every plate"; despite a "musty, old" "cavelike" setting and "indifferent" service, the vibe is "cozy" and it's frequently "crowded."

☑ St. Andrew's Café ☒ American

25 | 23 | 24 | $45

Hyde Park | Culinary Institute of America | 1946 Campus Dr. (off Rte. 9) | 845-471-6608 | www.ciachef.edu

"Less fancy and less expensive" than the Hyde Park cooking school's other restaurants, this New American's focus is on "heart-healthy" lunch fare, although "it looks sinfully good" and tastes so "mouthwatering", that "you'd probably never guess"; the "contemporary" setting is "cheery" and the student servers earn "an A+" for "doing their best", but even if it's a "little hit-or-miss", it's a "culinary adventure."

Stissing House ☒ French/Italian

20 | 23 | 20 | $48

Pine Plains | 7801 S. Main St./ Rte. 199 (Church St.) | 518-398-8800 | www.stissinghouse.com

"You can feel the history" at this Colonial hostelry "in the middle of cow country" (aka Pine Plains), where Michel Jean's "hearty, seasonal" French-Italian fare comes served in a "cozy" "warren of rooms" or in the "beautiful" tavern; it's a "favorite" of the "horsey set", who help create a "buzzing vibe" at the bar or do some "town-watching from the wraparound porch in summer."

Stonehenge ☒☒ Continental

22 | 23 | 22 | $59

Ridgefield | Stonehenge Inn | 35 Stonehenge Rd. (Rte. 7), CT | 203-438-6511 | www.stonehengeinn-ct.com

Since 1940, this "gorgeous old Colonial home" on many "idyllic" acres in Ridgefield has been serving "fine" Continental cuisine that's "expensive but not unreasonable" among "lovely", "elegant" adornments; some modernists "yawn" at the thought of it, but still, for a "formal" "special occasion", it "delivers."

NEW Stony Brae at Cragsmoor ☒ American

- | - | - | M

Cragsmoor | 3984 Rte. 52 (Cragsmoor Rd.) | 845-647-2108

Outdoorsy types, climbers and Cragsmoorites convene at this mountaintop tavern near Ellenville for a midpriced menu of American eats with some international accents (Thai-style chicken curry, Portuguese seafood stew); a stone fireplace, stained-glass windows and wood paneling give the renovated roadhouse digs a warm, pubby vibe, while the terrace has its own allure come summer.

Striped Bass Seafood

16 | 15 | 15 | $39

Tarrytown | Tarrytown Bow Club | 236 W. Main St. (Green St.) | 914-366-4455 | www.stripedbassny.com

"Sit outdoors, have a drink and enjoy the scenery" at this Tarrytown seafooder and cabana bar where the "beautiful river views" are the "number one reason for going"; sadly, most find the food "ordinary" and service "disappointing", although it continues to lure "boaters", "tourists" and "dates" with its "casual" vibe "on summer days."

	FOOD	DECOR	SERVICE	COST

Sukhothai *Thai*
24 | 18 | 19 | $28

Beacon | 516 Main St. (bet. North & South Sts.) | 845-440-7731 | www.sukhothainy.com

Gallerygoers in the "cool" town of Beacon are "blown way" to find "truly authentic Thai food" at this "spacious storefront" where the "gracious owner" prepares dishes "to your requested level of spiciness"; "reasonable prices" and the simple, brick-walled setting with its temple rubbings abet the feeling that "you're in Bangkok."

Sunset Cove *Continental*
16 | 18 | 17 | $40

Tarrytown | Washington Irving Boat Club | 238 Green St. (W. Main St.) | 914-366-7889 | www.sunsetcove.net

The "magical" setting "under the Tappan Zee Bridge" "surpasses" the "predictable" Continental menu at this "friendly" Tarrytown bar/restaurant where the "drop-dead" sunsets "don't get much better" or more "romantic"; perhaps the "nondescript" interior "needs a redo" but it's "reasonably priced, especially at lunch", and you "can't beat" it for "cold white wine on the terrace" in warm weather.

⛉ Sushi Mike's *Japanese*
26 | 12 | 20 | $39

Dobbs Ferry | 146 Main St. (Cedar St.) | 914-591-0054 | www.sushimikes.com

"Effusive" host and "the unofficial mayor of Dobbs Ferry", Mike Suzuki, "rules" this ultra-"popular" Japanese slicing up "outstanding", "original" (if "Americanized") sushi and specialty rolls that "don't get any fresher" at prices "on par" with the neighborhood; it's "perennially crowded" and "waits" are the norm, so fans only "wish it were bigger."

⛉ Sushi Nanase *Japanese*
29 | 15 | 23 | $72

White Plains | 522 Mamaroneck Ave. (Shapham Pl.) | 914-285-5351

He may be "a man of few words", but chef Yoshimichi Takeda is a "true master" at this "tiny" 18-seat White Plains Japanese "secret" where he fashions "pristine" fish into "truly spectacular", "delectable" creations, voted No. 1 for Food in Westchester/Hudson Valley; the setting's spare and it's certainly not cheap, but if you "put yourself in their hands" you're in for an "unforgettable" experience; P.S. "reservations are a must."

Sushi Niji *Japanese*
22 | 14 | 22 | $31

Dobbs Ferry | 71 Main St. (Chestnut St.) | 914-693-8838 | www.sushiniji.com

A "reliable" standby, especially "when the line is too long at Sushi Mike's", this Dobbs Ferry Japanese turns out "fresh", "simple" sushi and "tasty" cooked items in "peaceful" digs; "reasonable" prices including "bargain lunches" abet the overall "family-oriented" vibe.

Swaddee House of Thai Food *Thai*
21 | 12 | 20 | $27

Thornwood | 886 Franklin Ave. (Marble Ave.) | 914-769-8007 | www.swaddeehouse.com

"Behind an unassuming storefront" sits this "swell" "neighborhood Thai" in Thornwood where "charming owners" whip up "solid", "traditional" dishes from "fresh ingredients"; locals insist it works for a "fix", with "affordable" prices and an all-you-can-eat lunchtime buffet (Wednesday–Friday) ensuring their endorsement.

Sweet Grass Grill *American*   19 | 16 | 17 | $40

Tarrytown | 24 Main St. (John St.) | 914-631-0000 | www.sweetgrassgrill.com

There's "lots of local fare" on the regularly changing menu of this Tarrytown American "with an earthy feel" from David Starkey (Tomatillo) set in "appealingly casual", "rustic" digs; yet while servers "aim to please", an "unimpressed" contingent calls the cooking "uneven", even though the tabs are "reasonable."

Sweet Sue's ⊅ *American*   24 | 15 | 17 | $22

Phoenicia | 49 Main St. (bet. Church St. & Rte. 214) | 845-688-7852

"Lordy, lordy, strawberry pancakes", sigh the sated at this "cute" Phoenicia American, a breakfast and lunch "oasis" that's "celebrated" for its "countless" (actually 26) varieties of "seriously good" flapjacks so "big" "you just order one"; "delicious soups, superb sandwiches", waffles and omelets are other reasons "everyone comes" to this "*Twin Peaks*–ish" cafe, and they don't "mind waiting for a table" either.

Swiss Hütte Ⓜ *Continental/Swiss*   21 | 20 | 24 | $48

Hillsdale | Swiss Hütte Country Inn | Rte. 23 (3 mi. east of Rte. 22) | 518-325-3333 | www.swisshutte.com

The "perfect place to land" after you "ski down Catamount", this "welcoming" Columbia County inn exudes a feel of "Europe" thanks to its "beautiful views of the mountain", "hard to find", "old-world" Swiss-Continental specialties and "well-schooled service"; it's good "value" too, so the non-sporty go simply to "soak up the atmosphere" – it's "even prettier in summer" in the garden.

Swoon Kitchenbar *American*   24 | 21 | 18 | $51

Hudson | 340 Warren St. (bet. 3rd & 4th Sts.) | 518-822-8938 | www.swoonkitchenbar.com

"Talented chef" Jeffrey Gimmel is a "master" at "flavorful", "seasonal sustenance" declare those "swooning" over the "original", "locavore" cuisine at this Hudson New American, where his wife, Nina, makes the "best desserts"; "lovely surroundings top it all" ("even the flowers are fanciful"), although many surveyors find prices "a little high-end for this neck of the woods", especially given sometimes "lackluster" service.

Tabouli Grill *Mediterranean*   - | - | - | M

Stamford | 59 High Ridge Rd. (Terrace Ave.), CT | 203-504-8888 | www.tabouligrill.com

Fresh, flavorful Mediterranean cuisine reflecting Israeli, Greek, Turkish and Egyptian influences comes at moderate prices at this Stamford newcomer set in colorful, contemporary digs; look for all the classics (falafel, lamb kebabs), a full lineup of beer and wine, plus desserts like baklava and halvah ice cream.

Taiim Falafel Shack 🗷Ⓜ *Israeli* `-` `-` `-` `I`

Hastings-on-Hudson | 598 Warburton Ave. (Villard Ave.) |
914-478-0006 | www.taiimfalafelshack.com

This breezy Israeli stop in Hastings serves up falafel, kebabs and salads in a sunny-yellow storefront space with three small tables and counter seating; carryout is popular, and strong coffee and fruit juices round out the authentic Middle Eastern experience.

T&J Villaggio Trattoria Ⓜ *Italian* `21` `12` `19` `$34`

Port Chester | 223-225 Westchester Ave. (bet. Grove & Oak Sts.) |
914-937-6665

"When you don't want to shell out for Tarry Lodge", this "enjoyable" Port Chester Italian is there with "huge" helpings of "old-style" "red-sauce" fare "better than your grandma made" backed by carafes of house wine; in spite of its "shabby", "nondescript" digs adjacent to a pizzeria, supporters swear it feels "just like home."

Tandoori Taste of India *Indian* `21` `15` `18` `$33`

Port Chester | 163 N. Main St. (bet. Highland & Mill Sts.) | 914-937-2727 |
www.tandooritasteofindia.com

It's "nothing fancy", but this Port Chester Indian with a "solid lunchtime buffet" provides "reliable", "subtly flavored" takes on the classics and "the price is right" too; service is "prompt", and it doesn't hurt that it's the "only game in town" either.

Tanjore Cuisine of India *Indian* `25` `16` `18` `$29`

Fishkill | 992 Main St. (bet. Blodgett Rd. & Luyster Pl.) | 845-896-6659 |
www.tanjoreindiancuisine.com

"Don't let the strip-mall location fool you" because "absolutely delicious Indian food" lies within this Fishkill eatery, where already affordable tabs are capped by the "fabulous" lunch buffet for "cheap"; "getting the staff's attention" can be tricky, and the cheery decor is "formula", but it's the "real deal", as plenty of "South-Asian and Brit" patrons attest.

Tanzy's *American* ∇ `17` `14` `19` `$18`

Hudson | 223 Warren St. (bet. 2nd & 3rd Sts.) | 518-828-5165 |
www.tanzyshudson.com

"Homey and welcoming", this "adorable" "little" American tearoom in Hudson "oozes charm" by way of mismatched china and 1950s tablecloths forming a granny's-kitchen vibe for "a great breakfast or light lunch" of "delicious soups", sandwiches and such, served with "a big smile" from the sister owners; "relaxing" afternoon tea (reservations, please) comes with classic treats and a variety of brews.

The Tap House *American* `20` `20` `19` `$38`

Tuckahoe | 16 Depot Sq. (Main St.) | 914-337-6941 |
www.thetaphouseny.com

"Meet friends after work", "hang out all night" or partake of "inventive" "gastropub" fare at this Tuckahoe New American where the "great-looking bar" and "pretty dining room" provide a "charming, relaxed" setting further lubricated by a "terrific beer selection"; add in "well-priced" tabs and "friendly" service, and insiders insist it "never disappoints."

Tappo *Italian* <u>- | - | - | M</u>

Stamford | 51 Bank St. (Atlantic St.), CT | 203-588-9870 | www.tapporestaurant.com

This Downtown Stamford two-year-old sets a "new standard for area Italian" according to fans who claim it's the "closest you can get to Italy without flying", offering authentic, local and organic ingredient–driven favorites and Neapolitan pizzas, which are backed by an "incredible" wine list; what's more, the owner and staff "aim to please" in the hip, contemporary space with a sidewalk patio.

Taro's ⊅ *Italian/Pizza* <u>▽ 19 | 11 | 22 | $22</u>

Millerton | 18 Main St. (N. Center St.) | 518-789-6630

It's "nothing flashy", but "you feel like family" at this "welcoming" Millerton Italian dispensing "excellent New York–style pizza" and "tasty" mains that "really satisfy"; "terrific service" and "affordable" rates add to the appeal, while its "proximity to the rail trail" is handy for hikers and it's practically "a must before or after a movie."

Z Tarry Lodge *Italian* <u>24 | 23 | 22 | $53</u>

Port Chester | 18 Mill St. (Abendroth Ave.) | 914-939-3111 | www.tarrylodge.com

"An absolute winner" cheer champions of this "foodie delight" in Port Chester from Mario Batali and Joe Bastianich, where chef Andy Nusser turns out "amazing", "chichi" pizzas and "sophisticated", "wonderfully prepared" pastas in a "casually elegant" marble-clad space that feels "unique for the 'burbs'"; of course, it's "crazy crowded", "high decibel" and a "tough reservation", but the "pricey" tab is a "bargain if you choose wisely."

Tarry Tavern *American* <u>20 | 18 | 18 | $44</u>

Tarrytown | 27 Main St. (bet. Kaldenberg Pl. & Washington St.) | 914-631-7227 | www.tarrytavern.com

Fans say this moderately priced Tarrytown entry "shows promise" with rustic, locally attuned American plates that "soar above" typical "tavern fare" served in "cozy but sophisticated" cherrywood confines; the "friendly" staff is "still getting its act together", but that hasn't kept the "small space" from being "filled to capacity."

NEW Taste ● *American/Eclectic* <u>- | - | - | M</u>

Buchanan | 265 Tate Ave. (Albany Post Rd.) | 914-930-7866 | www.tasteontate.com

Eclectic is the word for this Buchanan newcomer offering specialty thin-crusted pizzettes along with Korean barbecue, burgers, lentil soup and Greek salads; hardwood floors and warm lighting accent the cozy, inviting digs, which is perhaps made even more welcoming by a dearth of other rated restaurants in the region (and the bargain-filled wine list can't hurt either).

FOOD | DECOR | SERVICE | COST

NEW Tavern at Diamond Mills *American* ‗ | ‗ | ‗ | M

Saugerties | Diamond Mills Hotel | 25 S. Partition St. (Hill St.) |
845-247-0700 | www.diamondmillshotel.com

Swank comes to Saugerties via this polished New American in a
just-built luxury hotel where a broad (and slightly pricey) menu
ranges from charcuterie and flatbreads to grilled rib-eye steak and
seafood stew, with housemade pastries, frittatas and such at
Sunday brunch; the expansive dining room has buttery walls, wood
floors, soaring ceilings and arched windows that overlook the
Esopus falls, as do tables on the terrace.

Tavern at Highlands ∇ 22 | 20 | 23 | $43
Country Club M *American*

Garrison | Highlands Country Club | 955 Rte. 9D (Lisburne Ln.) |
845-424-3254 | www.highlandscountryclub.net

"Wonderful in winter with a blazing fire" in the "intimate" tavern
room, this midpriced New American in a "memorable setting" on
the Garrison golf course offers "tasty" food along with a "good selection of beers" and wines, all caddied by an "accommodating
staff"; the terrace is newly glass-enclosed, and although some lament the loss of "one of the most beautiful outdoor dining spots",
patrons can now enjoy views of the greens year-round.

Tavern at the Beekman *American* 20 | 25 | 21 | $43

Rhinebeck | Beekman Arms Hotel | 6387 Montgomery St./Rte.9
(Rte. 308) | 845-876-1766 | www.beekmandelamaterinn.com

"Bill, Hill" and George Washington are famed visitors to this Rhinebeck
American in the "landmark" 1766 Beekman Arms inn, where "real
people and chichi weekenders" gather for "up-to-date" midpriced
fare or a "bargain lunch"; "a polite, attentive staff" serves in the
"pubby", beamed taproom, the "quaint" dining rooms with "charm
to spare" or the "pleasant" greenhouse overlooking the town.

NEW Tavern at the Gunk *American* ‗ | ‗ | ‗ | M

Ellenville | Shawangunk Country Club | 38 Country Club Rd. (Clifford St.) |
845-210-4206

Crispy chicken with smoked wild mushrooms is a fixture on the ever-
changing, farm-to-table New American menu at this newcomer to
the Shawangunk Country Club; a windowed partition divides the
lively bar from the dining room, where the green-and-white decor
has a retro appeal, while a patio overlooking the golf course and glorious mountain views has its own allure in summer.

Z Tawa *Indian* 27 | 22 | 23 | $34

Stamford | 211 Summer St. (bet. Broad & Main Sts.), CT |
203-359-8977 | www.tawaonline.com

It's "worth the vertical trek" upstairs to the second-floor fine-dining
area of this Indian in Downtown Stamford offering a "unique menu"
of dishes filled with "gorgeous flavors", including a daily lunch buffet; a subtly bejeweled setting, "solicitous staff" and "incredibly low
prices for the quality" are further draws, as is the small-plate Bread
Bar on the ground floor.

Temptations Cafe *Eclectic*

| 16 | 11 | 16 | $26 |

Nyack | 80½ Main St. (Broadway Ave.) | 845-353-3355 |
www.temptationscafe.com

True, it's "nothing fancy" but the sweet-toothed are tempted by the "luscious desserts and frozen treats" at this Nyack Eclectic "teen hangout" also offering "a nice bite" by way of "simple" sandwiches; "funky" digs and "casual service" are deemed "so-so", so "budget-conscious locals" hope the "new owners will improve" matters.

Temptation Tea House *Asian*

| 22 | 16 | 19 | $31 |

Mt. Kisco | 11A S. Moger Ave. (Main St.) | 914-666-8808

The "unique drinks" are the main enticement at this "delightfully refreshing" Mt. Kisco Pan-Asian where bubble teas and smoothies accompany a "good variety" of "little bites" on a continent-spanning menu; the "small, cute" space with a fountain and a koi pond provides a "quiet escape" along with "quality at a reasonable price."

Tengda Asian Bistro *Asian*

| 22 | 18 | 19 | $37 |

Katonah | Katonah Shopping Ctr. | 286 Katonah Ave. (Bedford Rd.) |
914-232-3900 Ⓜ

Scarsdale | 56 Garth Rd. (Popham Rd.) | 914-723-7767

Darien | Goodwives Shopping Ctr. | 25 Old Kings Hwy. N.
(Sedgewick Ave.), CT | 203-656-1688

Greenwich | 21 Field Point Rd. (bet. W. Elm St. & W. Putnam Ave.),
CT | 203-625-5338

Stamford | 235 Bedford St. (Forest St.), CT | 203-353-8005
www.asianbistrogroup.com

A "huge variety of interesting, tasty" Pan-Asian fare highlighting "tricked-up rolls" and other "inventive sushi creations" means there's "something for everyone" at this local chainlet that also mixes "awesome" cocktails; the settings swing from "soothing" to "sterile" and service is "variable" too, but prices are dependably "reasonable", making it "suitable for families, business lunches and anything in between" – and usually quite "hectic."

Ten Twenty Post *French*

| 21 | 21 | 20 | $46 |

Darien | 1020 Post Rd. (bet. Center St. & Corbin Dr.), CT |
203-655-1020 | www.tentwentypost.com

"Very Darien", this "upscale" bistro is the "most happening place in town", attracting a clientele of "preppy families and business types" with its "seafood-centric" French-American menu and "friendly" service, plus "cougars" and other "date-seeking missiles" with its "large", "loud" bar scene; critics find the noise "unbearable" and the fare "uneven", while others squirm at the "*Revolutionary Road* vibe."

Tequila Mockingbird *Mexican*

| 18 | 19 | 19 | $32 |

New Canaan | 6 Forest St. (East Ave.), CT | 203-966-2222

"Solid" "standards", "imaginative specials" and an array of "unusual tequilas" come at prices that are "reasonable" "for New Canaan" at this "enduring" Mexican restaurant with a "friendly" staff; the "lively", "kid-friendly" atmosphere features colorful folk art, but it can be "way crowded", so regulars warn to make reservations "unless you want to wait in Margaritaville"; P.S. "go late to miss the family scene."

Tequila Sunrise *Mexican* | 17 | 18 | 18 | $34 |

Larchmont | 145 Larchmont Ave. (bet. Addison St. & Boston Post Rd.) | 914-834-6378 | www.tequilasunriselarchmont.com

"Loud", "festive" and "fun", this Larchmont Mexican hosts "celebrations" galore thanks to its feel-good vibe, enhanced by weekend mariachi and "delish" margaritas; "pretty-good" prices and "family-friendly" service are perks, even if some say the "Americanized" south-of-the-border cooking leaves "much to be desired."

☑ Terrapin *American* | 24 | 23 | 23 | $43 |

Rhinebeck | 6426 Montgomery St./Rte. 9 (Livingston St.) | 845-876-3330 | www.terrapinrestaurant.com

As befits the "fabulous former church" setting, chef-owner Josh Kroner "works miracles" at this "popular" Rhinebeck New American with "a fancier", "quiet" side serving "enticing", "country-chic cuisine" and a "livelier", "laid-back" bistro offering "deals" via tapas, "design-your-own-burgers" and such; "eager to please" staffers and a porch for "people-watching" in good weather are other reasons "you'll leave happy and not much poorer."

Terra Ristorante *Italian* | 23 | 20 | 20 | $49 |

Greenwich | 156 Greenwich Ave. (bet. Elm & Lewis Sts.), CT | 203-629-5222 | www.zhospitalitygroup.com

"The smell of the wood-burning oven" draws shoppers on "super-luxe Greenwich Avenue" into this "expensive" Northern Italian where "reliable, simple", "yummy" pizzas and such are matched by "nice wines" with the aid of "friendly, knowledgeable" staffers; some feel that "loud" acoustics and "tables on top of each other" detract from the space and its "beautiful ceiling murals", so they ask for the "pleasant" patios when the weather allows.

Terra Rustica *Italian* | 19 | 17 | 20 | $40 |

Briarcliff Manor | 550 N. State Rd. (Ryder Ave.) | 914-923-8300 | www.terrarusticaristorante.com

An "extensive menu" of "hearty" Italian standards dished out in "ample portions" makes this "solid" Briarcliff Manor "standby" a down-to-earth choice "for a large group with varied tastes", be it at breakfast, lunch or dinner; the "lovely patio" is a treat in warm weather, while "fair prices" are welcome anytime.

NEW Texas de Brazil *Brazilian* | - | - | - | E |

Yonkers | Westchester's Ridge Hill | 70 Market St. (Otis Dr.) | 914-652-9660 | www.texasdebrazil.com

New to Yonkers, this upscale international chain specializes in the flag-'em-down Brazilian churrascaria format beloved by carnivores; prices are high, but it's all-you-can-eat and includes unlimited visits to a Texas-sized salad-and-sides bar; desserts, wines and signature caipirinhas are extra; P.S. children under two eat free, and under five for $5.

	FOOD	DECOR	SERVICE	COST

Thai Angels *Thai*
| 21 | 14 | 19 | $30 |

Mt. Kisco | 155 Lexington Ave. (W. Hyatt Ave.) | 914-666-0937 |
www.thaiangels.net

Diners are "delighted" by the "satisfying", "nuanced" flavors at this "reliable" Mt. Kisco Thai where BYO keeps the prices on the "cheapish" side; a "sweet, cheerful" staff plus patio seating overcome the somewhat "dreary" looks and help create a "pleasant, relaxed" vibe.

NEW Thai Elephant 2 M *Thai*
| - | - | - | M |

Patterson | 2693 Rte. 22 (S. Quaker Hill Rd.) | 845-319-6295 |
www.thaielephant2.com

Bringing a taste of Thailand to Patterson, this affordable family-run yearling dispenses curries, pad Thai and similar homey standards in a spacious setting; bright paint and Siamese accents atop the stone fireplace enliven the woodsy rooms, as do mountain views from a window table, or from the deck or garden in fair weather.

Thai Garden *Thai*
| ∇ 22 | 18 | 19 | $39 |

Orangeburg | 303 Rte. 303 (Rte. 340) | 845-680-6437 |
www.thethaigarden.com

After a move from Sleepy Hollow to Orangeburg some years back, this "inexpensive" Thai "favorite" continues to turn out "tasty", "fresh" fare – including plenty of vegetarian items – cooked to your "spice level"; "friendly" servers and golden walls warm the "intimate", onetime "college bar" setting, and when it gets "packed" to the point "you feel you're sitting on someone's lap", there's always takeout.

Thai Golden *Thai*
| ∇ 23 | 16 | 21 | $23 |

Carmel | 5 Seminary Hill Rd. (Rtes. 6 & 52) | 845-225-2722 |
www.thaigolden.net

"A much needed oasis in a culinary desert", this "little hole-in-the-wall" Thai may be Putnam County's "best-kept secret", dispensing "sincere, authentic" fare like "chicken rama that's ramadamade-licious"; a "gracious owner" "makes sure patrons are happy" in the blue-and-orange lakeside setting that has a "quirky charm" of its own, while BYO boosts prices that "can't be beat."

Thai House *Thai*
| 23 | 20 | 22 | $33 |

Ardsley | 466 Ashford Ave. (Rte. 9A) | 914-674-6633 |
www.thaihouserestaurant.com M
Nyack | 12 Park St. (bet. High Ave. & Main St.) | 845-358-9100 |
www.thaihousenyack.com

"Primo" Thai cooking "with the proper amount of spice" pops up at these "hidden gems" in equally "atmospheric" settings, one "tucked away" "up a flight of stairs" in Ardsley and the other inhabiting a "funky, old" diner space in Nyack; a "pleasant" staff in "traditional" dress and "fair prices" make these "favorites" "worth the schlep."

Thali *Indian*
| 24 | 20 | 21 | $38 |

New Canaan | 87 Main St. (bet. East & Locust Aves.), CT |
203-972-8332

(continued)

Thali

Ridgefield | Ridgefield Motor Inn | 296 Ethan Allen Hwy. (Florida Hill Rd.), CT | 203-894-1080
www.thali.com

"Sophisticated", "innovative" dishes and "generous" drinks are the specialties of these "decently priced" Indians; both branches boast "cool", "upscale" settings and "professional" service, but each offers its own distinct feature, among them an "aerial waterfall" in New Canaan and a "no-tell motel setting" in Ridgefield.

36 Main *American*   23 | 20 | 20 | $41

New Paltz | 36 Main St. (bet. Chestnut St. & Wurts Ave.) | 845-255-3636 | www.36main.com

A "regular, local crowd" convenes at this "lively" New Paltz New American for "tasty" small plates, "imaginative", "well-prepared" mains or drinks in the "popular bar"; owner "Kathy Combs makes you feel welcome" in the "relaxed", "funky"-meets-"chic" setting, while "attentive" service and a small garden where you can "enjoy a cocktail" in summer compensate for fare that's a "tad overpriced for a college town."

⚡ Thomas Henkelmann 🅂🅜 *French*   28 | 28 | 28 | $90

Greenwich | Homestead Inn | 420 Field Point Rd. (bet. Bush Ave. & Merica Ln.), CT | 203-869-7500 | www.thomashenkelmann.com

"Everything is simply exquisite" at this "destination restaurant" in a "beautiful Victorian mansion" in Greenwich, from the eponymous chef's "fabulous", "memorable" New French cuisine served by a "seasoned staff" that "treats you like royalty" to the "luxurious", "tasteful" decor; "expensive" tabs match the "formal" (ok, "a bit stuffy"), jackets-required (at dinner) atmosphere, but "for that special occasion", it's "worth it" – "you do indeed get what you pay for here."

NEW Thornwood Ale House ❶ *Pub Food*   – | – | – | M

Thornwood | 665 Commerce St. (Marietta Ave.) | 914-365-2020 | www.thornwoodalehouse.com

It's all about wings, sliders and other low-cost eats that go well with brews at this new Thornwood sports bar with a slew of suds on offer and freshly baked pretzels served on game days; look for a low-key ambiance, brick-and-golden walls and patio seating in summer; P.S. a children's menu is a plus, as is a milkshake happy hour from 3–6 PM daily.

Three Boys From Italy   ▽ 23 | 8 | 18 | $21
Brick Oven Trattoria *Pizza*

White Plains | 206 Mamaroneck Ave. (Maple Ave.) | 914-358-1500 | www.gaudiosrestaurant.com

This White Plains pizzeria supplies brick-oven slices with "fresh, unique" toppings, including an unusually large array of "crispy Sicilian" slabs that are worth "spending the calories on"; some find it "swarmed with a young crowd", so "takeout" is popular.

FOOD | DECOR | SERVICE | COST

Thyme ☒ *American*   22 | 24 | 21 | $48

Yorktown Heights | 3605 Crompond Rd. (Garden Ln.) | 914-788-8700 | www.thymerestaurant.net

"A bit of slick Manhattan" comes to Yorktown Heights via this "posh" spot offering an "ambitious" New American menu "beautifully served" in a "chic, comfortable" room enlivened by an open kitchen; some surveyors find the food "not memorable" enough for the "expensive" tab, although the "upscale" atmosphere "like nothing else around" has made it "popular" from the outset.

NEW Toad Holly Pub ☒ *American*   - | - | - | M

Tillson | 713 Rte. 32 (River Rd.) | 845-658-2097 | www.toadhollypub.com

Tillson denizens trot into this new tavern for a menu of fairly priced American comfort eats, from burgers to seafood, along with a few Asian flourishes like pad Thai and shrimp lo mein; the Tudor-esque building houses a buzzing bar on one side and a calmer dining room decorated in reds and yellows with Tiffany-style lamps on the other.

Tomatillo ☒ *Mexican*   22 | 13 | 17 | $24

Dobbs Ferry | 13 Cedar St. (Rte. 9) | 914-478-2300 | www.mexchester.com

"Everything tastes fresh" at this "cheerful" Dobbs Ferry Mexican where the "crazy-good" "overstuffed burritos", "homemade chips" and such are prepared with "local, farm-fresh ingredients" and served up with a "terrific" array of microbrews; it can be "crowded and noisy", but "quick" service that's "on top of it" and "cheap" tabs make it a "standby for families with kids."

Tombolino's ☒ *Italian*   23 | 19 | 24 | $46

Yonkers | 356 Kimball Ave. (Yonkers Ave.) | 914-237-1266 | www.tombolinoristorante.com

"Something of a time warp", this circa-1977 Yonkers Italian is a find for "genuine", "homestyle" cooking that's "a cut above" dished out in "ample" portions; a "tuxedo-clad" staff adds another "classic" touch, although it's a tad too "expensive" for some.

Tony's Woodridge Family   - | - | - | I
Restaurant *Eclectic*

Woodridge | 22 Green Ave. (bet. Dairyland Rd. & Greenfield Rd.) | 845-434-4073

Hungry travelers in the hinterlands of Sullivan County will find hearty helpings at this budget-friendly, family-run Woodridge Eclectic serving three squares a day; the wide-ranging eats run the gamut from Middle Eastern standards to stuffed cabbage and pizza, all dished up in cheery blue-and-orange digs overlooking a dining terrace and garden; just remember, it's BYO.

Torches on The Hudson *American*   17 | 23 | 17 | $41

Newburgh | 120 Front St. (4th St.) | 845-568-0100 | www.torchesonthehudson.com

"If you're hungry for a view" this "flashy", "festive" Newburgh American in a "prime location" on the waterfront supplies several, with "stunning river and mountain" vistas, a "gorgeous" 30-ft. saltwater aquarium behind the bar and a passel of "look-at-me" singles; it's "expensive" considering the food is only "fair" and the service "mediocre", yet it gets "mobbed", especially on the deck in summer.

Toro 🈂 *Japanese/Korean* ▽ 20 | 15 | 21 | $31

Fishkill | 1004 Main St. (Cary Ave.) | 845-897-9691 | www.toronewyork.com

"Good sushi is hard to come by" in Fishkill, so "avid" afishionados satisfy their "cravings" at this spot also turning out hot Japanese fare along with "authentic Korean dishes", from bibimbop to BBQ; chef Kevin Park presides over the narrow, strip-mall setting, where booths and paper lanterns help create a "nice, neighborhood" vibe.

Toscana *Italian* 22 | 22 | 20 | $47

Ridgefield | 43 Danbury Rd. (bet. Grove St. & Mountain View Ave.), CT | 203-894-8995 | www.toscanaridgefield.com

"Scrumptious" Tuscan dishes are served alongside "excellent" wines in "delightful", upscale-casual, mural-bedecked surroundings at this "high-end Ridgefield Italian"; a few complain that the fees are too "pricey" and the acoustics "too loud", but with a "welcoming" chef-owner and "pleasant" staff thrown into the mix, it's hard not to have an "enjoyable evening" here.

Town Dock Tavern *American* 19 | 14 | 20 | $32

Rye | 15 Purdy Ave. (bet. 1st & 2nd Sts.) | 914-967-2497

Rye folks rely on this "trusty neighborhood spot", a "great place to fall into" for American "comfort" food with a "New England" spin (think burgers and chowder); expect "dark", "divey" seafaring digs, a "cheerful" staff and prices that "won't break the bank."

Toyo Sushi *Japanese* 21 | 16 | 18 | $34

Mamaroneck | 253 Mamaroneck Ave. (bet. Palmer & Prospect Aves.) | 914-777-8696 | www.toyosushi.com

Considered a "staple" for families, this "solid, but not remarkable", Japanese on Mamaroneck's "sushi row" slices up an "extensive" array of "fresh" fish in spare, modern surroundings; its popularity makes for "loud" acoustics and "officiously efficient" service, and some guests gripe "they're always rushing you out."

Traditions 118 *American/Italian* 21 | 20 | 21 | $44

Somers | 11 Old Tomahawk St. (Rte. 202/Tomahawk St.) | 914-248-7200 | www.traditions118restaurant.com

A "favorite neighborhood place" in Somers, this "comfortable", mid-priced Traditional American–Italian purveys "imaginative" dishes crafted from "simple, quality" ingredients along with a "great martini" selection; there's a "romantic feel" to the "lovely" room, "especially in winter" near the "beautiful" stone fireplace.

Tramonto *Italian* 19 | 18 | 21 | $43

Hawthorne | 27 Saw Mill River Rd. (Saw Mill River Pkwy. N., exit 25) | 914-347-8220 | www.tramontos.com

"Lazy weeknight dinners", "business lunches" and post-multiplex meals are well served by this "low-key" Hawthorne Italian deemed a "good choice" for a "reliable", midpriced bite in "homey" surroundings; although a number note that food "can be up and down", the "warm, friendly" service is a constant.

Trattoria Vivolo *Italian*   25 | 17 | 25 | $42

Harrison | 301 Halstead Ave. (bet. Parsons & Purdy Sts.) | 914-835-6199 | www.trattorlavivolo.com

Though it "looks like an old-fashioned diner" from the outside, this Harrisonite is a "delightful surprise" dispensing "top-notch" Italian fare "lovingly" crafted by chef-owner Dean Vivolo and his "warm" staff; prices are deemed "fair for the quality", while the "elegantly refurbished" space is strung with "twinkle lights", and equally suited for jeans or a "dress-up" night on the town.

Travelers Rest 🅼 *German*   19 | 20 | 21 | $49

Ossining | Rte. 100 (Rte. 134) | 914-941-7744 | www.thetravelersrest.com

"One of the few German restaurants left" in the area, this "charming" Ossining vet in a former stagecoach stop is "popular" for "special occasions" thanks to its "pleasant country setting" with "manicured lawns" and "festive holiday decorations" plus an "accommodating" staff that "handles groups well"; the "hearty" menu of schnitzel, sauerbraten and Continental classics feels a tad "outdated" to some, but the "value" pricing suits its "older" fans just fine.

Tre Angelina *Italian*   21 | 18 | 23 | $49

White Plains | 478 Mamaroneck Ave. (bet. Marion & Shapham Pls.) | 914-686-0617 🅢
Monroe | 355 Rte. 17M (Orchard Dr.) | 845-238-5721 🅼
www.treangelinany.com

Deemed a "cut above" the usual Italian, this Downtown White Plains trattoria with a Monroe sibling rolls out "fine, Northern-style" specialties in "cozy" quarters chock-full of "politicos"; a "genteel" staff "aims to please" ("they'll make you anything you like") and may account for the "pricey" bills.

Trevi Ristorante 🅼 *Italian*   ▽ 23 | 20 | 19 | $46

West Harrison | 11 Taylor Sq. (Harrison Blvd.) | 914-949-5810 | www.treviofharrison.com

"A neighborhood joint with a New York City price tag", this West Harrison Italian doles out "old-time" favorites, pizzas plus a handful of "gluten-free options" that "hit the spot"; "attentive" service and a handsome strip-mall space in view of Silver Lake complete the package.

Trinity Grill & Bar *American*   20 | 16 | 20 | $34

Harrison | 7-9 Purdy St. (Halstead Ave.) | 914-835-5920 | www.trinitygrill.net

"A pleasant local option", this "family-oriented" Harrison tavern delivers "dependable" American fare (not unlike an "upscale diner") in roomy digs with a "welcoming" bar up front; some say the "food could be better", but nevertheless it's a "quiet", "comfortable" place where "you always feel well cared for."

| | FOOD | DECOR | SERVICE | COST |

Tsuru *Japanese*

23 | 13 | 21 | $37

Hartsdale | Westchester Square Mall | 259 N. Central Ave. (bet. Jane St. & Lakeview Ave.) | 914-761-0057 | www.tsurusushibar.com

Purists praise this "no-pretence" Hartsdale Japanese that channels "Toyko" with "impeccably fresh" sushi served up in an utterly "no-frills" "hole-in-the-wall" setting; "budget-conscious" pricing is a plus, as is attentive treatment, especially if you "sit at the bar" and "ask the chef what's good."

Turkish Cuisine Westchester *Turkish*

21 | 8 | 18 | $25

White Plains | 116 Mamaroneck Ave. (Quarropas St.) | 914-683-6111 | www.turkishcuisineny.com

"What a find!" marvel fans of this "quick-bite" Turk in White Plains offering "huge helpings" of "simple", "authentic" cooking in a "di-minutive" storefront setting; perhaps the "drab" atmosphere's not unlike "eating in a lunchroom", but at least service is "caring" and "BYO keeps the price low."

Turkish Meze *Turkish*

23 | 16 | 21 | $37

Mamaroneck | 409 Mt. Pleasant Ave. (Stanley Ave.) | 914-777-3042 | www.turkishmeze.com

"Always packed", this "boisterous" Mamaroneck eatery is the place for "sensational", "exotic" Turkish cooking – from "soul-warming moussaka" and "incredible grilled fish" to "plentiful" meze – backed by "hard-to-find" beers and wines; a "genuinely friendly" staff keeps the mood "pleasant", and it "isn't too expensive" either.

Turquoise *Mediterranean/Turkish*

21 | 18 | 20 | $39

Larchmont | 1895 Palmer Ave. (bet. Chatsworth Ave. & Depot Way W.) | 914-834-9888 | www.turqmed.com

"Istanbul meets the suburbs" at this Larchmont Med-Turkish "trans-porting" diners with "fresh", "authentic" cuisine including "excellent grilled meats" and "tasty" meze "you can make a meal of"; although it's not cheap, service is "warm and welcoming" and the atmospheric setting with lanterns throughout is especially "fun for groups."

Tuscan Oven Trattoria *Italian*

20 | 18 | 19 | $39

Mt. Kisco | 360 N. Bedford Rd. (bet. Foxwood Circle & Park Dr.) | 914-666-7711 | www.tuscanoven.com

This "reliable" Northern Italian "may not knock your socks off", but it provides "homemade pastas", "crisp pizzas" and other "serviceably cooked" standards to its Mt. Kisco clientele; with a "surprisingly cute" setting (indoors and alfresco on the patio), "cordial" service and "reasonably priced" tabs, it's "ideal for large, impromptu gatherings."

Tuthill House *American*

- | - | - | M

Gardiner | 20 Gristmill Ln. (Tuthilltown Rd.) | 845-255-4151 | www.tuthillhouse.com

Atmospheric as all get-out, this dining room in Gardiner's gussied-up 1788 grist mill offers midpriced American tavern eats ranging from steaks and burgers to dressier dishes like duck breast in port and cherries; the beautifully renovated landmark building retains

	FOOD	DECOR	SERVICE	COST

the original plank floors, with crystal chandeliers and a deck overlooking the stream and waterwheel as a warm-weather bonus.

TuttaBella Trattoria *Italian* ▽ 23 | 20 | 24 | $49

Scarsdale | 754 White Plains Rd. (New Wilmot Rd.) | 914-725-0566 | www.tuttabellatrattoria.com

A sib of Valbella in Connecticut, this sleek Scarsdale Italian is "not your usual red-sauce joint", with "first-rate" Northern-style cuisine and a 200-bottle wine list offered at "four-star prices"; service that makes you feel "most welcome" is an added perk, and if the contemporary dining room can be "noisy", insiders insist "upstairs is quieter."

12 Grapes Music & 21 | 20 | 21 | $39
Wine Bar Ⓜ *American*

Peekskill | 12 N. Division St. (Union Ave.) | 914-737-6624 | www.12grapes.com

A "destination" for a "night out" in Downtown Peekskill, this "delightful" New American wine bar and music venue provides "excellent" by-the-glass vino and food that's "enjoyable" enough, even if "the entertainment is the bigger draw"; with its "inviting environment", "pleasant" staff and "decent prices", this "cool" spot has "settled into a nice groove"; P.S. live bands Thursday–Sunday.

Twisted Soul Ⓔ *Eclectic* ▽ 24 | 19 | 19 | $18

Poughkeepsie | 47 Raymond Ave. (Fulton Ave.) | 845-454-2770 | www.twistedsoulconcepts.com

Poughkeepsie locals "love, love, love" this "fabulous" little Eclectic "find" near Vassar for its "wide array" of "wordly", "flavorful" street food, like Argentinean empanadas, "terrific goat-cheese arepas", dumplings and "noodle bowls", all mixed and matched by "creative" chef-owner Ira Lee; the narrow storefront is "pretty tight", but it's "good for a quick bite" and the price is right too.

Two Spear Street Ⓜ *American* 22 | 24 | 24 | $61

Nyack | Nyack Seaport | 2 Spear St. (Piermont Ave.) | 845-353-7733 | www.2spearstreet.com

"Huge windows" "overlook the harbor" at this "classy" riverside American in Nyack, where the "lights of the Tappan Zee Bridge twinkling in the distance" combine with the room's "beautiful decor" to create an "unrushed", "romantic" mood for "gourmet" fare and "excellent service"; it's a tad "pricey" so "don't go expecting a bargain", but a "pleasant evening is almost guaranteed."

NEW 2Taste Food & - | - | - | M
Wine Bar Ⓔ *American*

Hyde Park | 4290 Albany Post Rd./Rte. 9 (Pine Woods Rd.) | 845-233-5647 | www.2tastefoodandwinebar.com

Located in the strip-mall spot that once housed Twist, this Hyde Park New American newcomer offers a midpriced menu of dressed-up bistro favorites like truffle-and-porcini mac 'n' cheese, braised lamb shank, applejack duck breast and bouillabaisse; patrons in the tile-and-tan room can opt for a table, a booth with a chalkboard to record their thoughts, or a perch at the chef's bar overlooking the kitchen.

FOOD | DECOR | SERVICE | COST

Tyrynda Thai Ⓜ *Thai* ▽ 23 | 20 | 24 | $30

Sleepy Hollow | 128 Cortlandt St. (College Ave.) | 914-524-5003 | www.tyryndathai.com

The "charming owners" "aim to please" at this "lovely", "tucked away" Sleepy Hollow Thai where the "spicy" fare is "not dumbed down for Western palates"; expect "good-sized portions" and good-value pricing, especially in its "bargain" of a lunch special.

Ümami Café *Eclectic* 21 | 13 | 19 | $34

Croton-on-Hudson | 325 S. Riverside Ave. (Oneida Ave.) | 914-271-5555 | www.umamicafe.com

"Warm homemade potato chips" and truffled mac 'n' cheese "like mom never made" are some of the "bright spots" at this "neighborhood favorite" in Croton where "out-of-the-ordinary" seasonal Eclectic eats are served in "Park Slope–esque" surroundings "crowded" with kids; though some suggest its "once-innovative" "fusion" shtick is getting "old", many return for "reasonable" tabs and to "eat outside" on the patio in summer months.

NEW Umami Sushi Bar *Japanese* – | – | – | M

Ardsley | 724 Saw Mill River Rd. (Ashford Ave.) | 914-231-9444 | www.umamisushibar.com

Neighborhood types are already filling up this modest new Japanese in Ardsley boasting a vast list of sushi rolls plus all the classics, from teriyaki to soba noodles; modest prices match the low-key space.

Underhills Crossing *American* 21 | 20 | 19 | $47

Bronxville | 74½ Pondfield Rd. (bet. Garden Ave. & Park Pl.) | 914-337-1200 | www.underhillscrossing.com

"Always hopping", this "stylish", "upscale" Bronxville bistro delivers a "Manhattan"-caliber experience with "tasty", "artfully presented" New American fare and a "lively bar scene" filled with "yuppies galore"; "annoyingly loud" acoustics and occasionally "inattentive" service can be downsides, but on the whole it's "tough to go wrong", especially if you snag a table "outside in warm weather."

Union Restaurant & Bar Latino Ⓜ *American/Pan-Latin* 24 | 22 | 23 | $49

Haverstraw | 22-24 New Main St. (bet. B'way & Maple Ave.) | 845-429-4354 | www.unionrestaurant.net

Foodies find it's "worth schlepping to Haverstraw" to visit this "outstanding" New American eatery where "Peter Kelly protégés" turn out "terrific, confident" cooking "with Latin overtones"; expect an "enthusiastic" staff working the "appealing", hacienda-style space, and although it's "a little pricey for the area", it's such a "congenial" "hot spot" even the "noise level" is "part of the charm."

Valbella Ⓩ *Italian* 25 | 23 | 25 | $74

Riverside | 1309 E. Putnam Ave. (Sound Beach Ave.), CT | 203-637-1155 | www.valbellact.com

"Porsche Turbos in the parking lot" and celebrities like "Regis or Frank Gifford" in the dining room generate a "glow" at this "way up-

FOOD DECOR SERVICE COST

scale" Italian in Riverside, a "posh playground" for a "chic crowd", where "exquisitely prepared" dishes and an "extensive wine list" are served by an "expert" staff in an "elegant" space that includes a "romantic" wine cellar; sure, the bill will "burn a hole in your pocket", but many say it's "worth it" for a "truly memorable evening."

Valentina's ▯ *Italian*   - | - | - | M

Carmel | 4 Church St. (Rte. 6) | 845-228-9655 |
www.valentinasrestaurant.weebly.com

"Hearty, unpretentious Italian" matches the "casual", "homey setting" at this "oasis" in Carmel that aims to please with classics from pizza and pasta to seafood and tastes for the tykes; add a staff that "cares" plus a BYO policy that abets reasonable tabs and "what more could you want?"

Valentino's *Italian*   24 | 13 | 22 | $40

Yonkers | 132 Bronx River Rd. (bet. New Pl. & Wakefield Ave.) |
914-776-6731 | www.valentinositalianrestaurant.com

"If you've never had an Italian grandmother", this timeworn Yonkers Italian "will fill the bill" with "Hungryman-sized" platters of "delicious", "honest" fare set down in a "comfortable" space that "evokes Little Italy"; a "welcoming" staff provides "extremely professional" service (and there's quite the "fanfare" around birthdays too) and helps distract from the "premium" prices.

Valhalla Crossing *American*   16 | 16 | 17 | $26

Valhalla | 2 Cleveland St. (B'way) | 914-682-4076 |
www.valhallacrossing.com

"Sit right on the tracks and watch the choo choos go by" at this Valhalla venue dishing out "decent" American "comfort" grub in a "unique" setting fashioned from an old train caboose; perhaps it's "nothing to write home about", but "kids love" the digs, and live music on Saturdays is a plus for grown-ups.

Valley Restaurant   ▽ 23 | 25 | 23 | $61
at The Garrison ▯ *American*

Garrison | The Garrison | 2015 Rte. 9 (Coleman Rd.) | 845-424-2339 |
www.thegarrison.com

"It's always a treat" say those enjoying the "fine" New American cuisine, "beautiful setting" and "stunning views" of the Hudson Highlands at this "wonderful" spot at The Garrison resort; service can be "inconsistent" and prices suggest "special occasion", but most still "wish it were open all winter" instead of just March–December; P.S. open for dinner on Thursday–Saturday, and brunch on Sunday.

NEW Vanderbilt House   - | - | - | M
Restaurant ▯ *American*

Philmont | Vanderbilt House Hotel | 161 Main St. (Railroad Ave.) |
518-672-9993 | www.vanderbilt-house.com

Set in a handsomely renovated circa-1860 hotel, this Philmont newcomer near the Taconic dispenses elevated American fare (prime rib, duckling, calf's liver) in a spiffy dining room with original tin ceilings, deep-red walls and buttery beadboard wainscoting; casual

| | FOOD | DECOR | SERVICE | COST |

Vega *Mexican*   21 | 21 | 18 | $34

Hartsdale | 187-189 E. Hartsdale Ave. (Rockledge Rd.) | 914-723-0010 | www.vegamexican.com

This "classy" Hartsdale canteen ensconced in "cool, contemporary" quarters with a "neat" bar delivers "modern" takes on Mexican cuisine, including "fresh, homemade tortillas"; it's "hipper than anything" the area's seen for a while, so most are willing to overlook "service issues" and somewhat "steep" pricing.

Velo Bistro & Wine Bar 🅱🅼 *American*   24 | 22 | 23 | $53

Nyack | 12 N. Broadway (New St.) | 845-353-7667 | www.velonyack.com

Chef-owner Anthony DeVanzo "loves his job and it shows" at this "cute" Nyack American sending out "consistently" "delicious, interesting", "market-fresh" plates at "terrific value"; an "efficient" staff bops around the "intimate" brick-walled space with its "tiny bar" and bicycle motif, so even though the "tables are a little tight" and the "acoustics make conversation difficult", it's a "great local scene."

Versailles *Bakery/French*   24 | 22 | 19 | $37

Greenwich | 339 Greenwich Ave. (Arch St.), CT | 203-661-6634 | www.versaillesgreenwich.com

This "institution" has been "revitalized" with a move to a "beautiful" new location "just a wee bit down Greenwich Avenue" and the addition of "sublime" seasonal French bistro dinners (in a "charming back area") to its roster of lunch and bakery fare, the latter starring "beautifully crafted" desserts; best of all, prices are "affordable", a welcome surprise considering the level of "sophistication."

Via Vanti! *Italian*   23 | 21 | 22 | $35

Mt. Kisco | Mt. Kisco Train Station | 2 Kirby Plaza (Main St.) | 914-666-6400 | www.viavanti.com

"It's not your typical pasta and meatball experience" at this "quirky all-day Italian "tucked inside the train station" in Mt. Kisco turning out "fab pizzettes", "trendy small plates" and "amazing gelato" among other "palate-pleasing" plates and "unusual" wines; "prompt" service, a "hip", "Euro-pop vibe" and "moderate pricing" keep it on track.

Vico *Italian*   ▽ 19 | 18 | 18 | $45

Hudson | 136 Warren St. (bet. 1st & 2nd Sts.) | 518-828-6529 | www.vico-restaurant.com

"Always good" for "a nice plate of pasta" and "tasty" Tuscan eats, this "cozy" Hudson venue is manned by a "lovely staff" that "makes everyone feel at home"; amber walls, a "warm fireplace" and a garden in back create "an inviting atmosphere", while "fair prices" are another welcome touch, and the $29 three-course prix fixe is particularly "good value."

	FOOD	DECOR	SERVICE	COST

The Village *Pub Food*   20 | 15 | 20 | $32

Litchfield | 25 West St. (bet. Meadow St. & Rte. 63), CT | 860-567-8307 |
www.village-litchfield.com

Fans say "every neighborhood needs" a "local hangout" like this
Litchfield "tradition", which offers "dependable", "hearty" American
pub grub and "more ambitious", "upscale" dishes in a "hopping bar
area" and "cozy dining room"; the staff "tries hard to please", and
while some critics find the surroundings a bit "boring", defenders insist the "fair fare at fair prices" makes up for "what it lacks in decor."

Village Social Kitchen & Bar *American*   - | - | - | E

Mt. Kisco | 251 E. Main St. (bet. Gregory & Hyatt Aves.) | 914-241-6260 |
www.villagesocialkb.com

Comfort grub gets some sprucing up at this hip Mt. Kisco entry offering upper-end New American–Med selections like Sriracha
chicken wings, braised short ribs and designer wood-fired pizzas
topped with artisanal cheeses and meats; exposed duct work and
weathered-wood walls create a rustic-industrial look, with a bustling bar that's quite the area hot spot.

Village Square Bagels ✏ *Bakery*   ▽ 18 | 3 | 11 | $12

Larchmont | 1262 Boston Post Rd. (Weaver St.) | 914-834-6969 |
www.villagesquarebagel.com

"Basically a take-out place with just a few bare tables", this Larchmont
bakery is the scene of "morning lines" for "great" bagels (hot all day
long) and the usual "kosher" nosherie of lox, spreads and salads; service "can be slow", but it's satisfactory "if they get your order right."

Village TeaRoom Ⓜ *American*   25 | 20 | 21 | $34

New Paltz | 10 Plattekill Ave. (bet. Lookout Ave. & Main St.) |
845-255-3434 | www.thevillagetearoom.com

Those "yearning for comfort food" find "remarkable" renditions at
this "adorable" New Paltz all-organic American serving not just tea-
time treats, but "scrumptious" fare for breakfast, lunch and dinner
too; the "quaint, cozy" 1833 beamed building "wins the cutesy
award" with "lovely patio dining" come summer, while service is "always good", tabs are "worth it" and "oh my – the cream puffs."

Vinny's Backyard ⬤ *Pizza/Pub Food*   ▽ 20 | 11 | 17 | $21

Stamford | Springdale Shopping Ctr. | 1078 Hope St. (bet. Camp Ave. &
Mulberry St.), CT | 203-461-9003 | www.vinnysbackyard.com

Catch the game on 10 large-screen TVs while noshing on "home-run"
pizzas, ribs, wings and other "great" grub at this "down-to-earth"
Stamford strip-mall sports pub and pizzeria; "away from the bar",
there's a dining room whose "reasonable prices" and "kid-friendly"
service make it appropriate for a "totally casual" family meal.

NEW Vintage 1891 ☒ *American*   - | - | - | E

Larchmont | 2098 Boston Post Rd. (bet. Chatsworth & Larchmont Aves.) |
914-834-9463 | www.vintage1891.com

This new Larchmont sophisticate is both a chic wine bar – with
slouchy seating and scores of by-the-glass picks dispensed by a

FOOD | DECOR | SERVICE | COST

Cruvinet – as well as a full-service restaurant with a darker, moodier dining room done up in slate gray with white banquettes; its upmarket American menu is divided by food-delivery utensil: toothpick (tapas), fork (salads and apps), knife (steaks, fowl and other proteins) and spoon (desserts).

Vinum Café ☒ *American*   - | - | - | M

Washingtonville | Brotherhood Winery | 84 Brotherhood Plaza Dr. (Ahern Blvd.) | 845-496-9001 | www.vinumcafe.com

Occupying an 1839 building at Washington's vintage winery, this unaffiliated venture from chef-owner Christian Pierrel (of the defunct Ile de France in Goshen) offers French-accented American fare with a long wine list to match; foie gras, duck magret and lobster Newburg are dinnertime favorites in the brick-walled and burgundy dining room, while fancy burgers and such are served in the more casual and affordable cafe, which is also open for lunch.

Violette *American*   ▽ 20 | 20 | 20 | $42

Woodstock | 85 Mill Hill Rd./Rte. 212 (Playhouse Ln.) | 845-679-5300 | www.violettewoodstock.com

This "delightful bistro on the edge of Woodstock" is "a pleasant surprise" for those discovering the "tasty" French-accented American country-style cooking by the mother-and-son chef-owners; "reasonable prices" and "accommodating service" are a plus, while the casual, Provençal-style setting has "a lovely atmosphere", whether in winter when the "beautiful fireplace" is ablaze, or on the patio in summer.

Virgo's Sip N Soul Cafe ☒ *Soul Food*   - | - | - | M

Beacon | 469 Fishkill Ave. (State St.) | 845-831-1543 | www.virgossipnsoul.com

Some come to this Beacon boîte for the "great soul food" (think po' boys, ribs, fried chicken and such, plus nibbles for the tots), while others amble in for music and nightlife in the lounge (Thursday–Saturday and a "super jam session on Sundays"); either way, the relaxed setting and affordable prices suit families and scenesters alike.

Vox ☒ *American/French*   21 | 20 | 20 | $55

North Salem | 721 Titicus Rd. (bet. Rtes. 116 & 121) | 914-669-5450 | www.voxnorthsalem.com

A "highly enjoyable" oasis of "Gallic charm" "in the middle of nowhere", this "lovely" North Salem bistro serves a "clever" mix of French–New American dishes, from burgers to lamb shanks, with a "warm greeting" and "professional" attention; take your pick of a "spacious dining room" or, weather permitting, a patio with "beautiful views" that most believe is "worth the trip" and the "high prices."

☒ Walter's ⊅ *Hot Dogs*   22 | 9 | 13 | $10

Mamaroneck | 937 Palmer Ave. (bet. Fulton & Richbell Rds.) | no phone | www.waltershotdogs.com

The "cars are double parked" all the way down the block at this "iconic" Mamaroneck hot dog stand set in a circa-1928 "art deco" pagoda turning out "decadent" butter-griddled franks, "thick, creamy shakes" and "curly fries with a nice zing"; there are only a

FOOD | DECOR | SERVICE | COST

few picnic tables and "you'll need patience" for the "lines", but it's a "national treasure" that "shouldn't be missed on a warm day."

Ward's Bridge Inn Ⓜ *American* ▽ 19 | 18 | 19 | $43

Montgomery | 135 Ward St./Rte. 17K (Wallkill Ave.) | 845-457-1300 | www.wardsbridgeinn.com

Housed in "a great old building" in Montgomery, this American offers a broad, modestly priced menu of "above-average" Traditional American eats; patrons enjoy "a nice experience", whether in the sunroom, the atmospheric tavern or joining in at the bar scene.

Wasabi *Japanese* ▽ 18 | 15 | 20 | $34

Hudson | 807 Warren St. (bet. 8th St. & Prospect Ave.) | 518-822-1888 | www.wasabiyummy.com

Hudson residents "hankering for sushi" head for this "cute" Japanese that's admittedly "the only game in town", but offers "fresh, well-prepared" fish along with "an extensive menu" of hot dishes and "interesting daily specials"; a "young" staff in traditional garb tends the "pleasant", simple space, and "reasonable" rates add to the appeal.

☑ Wasabi *Japanese* 26 | 21 | 22 | $49

Nyack | 110 Main St. (bet. Cedar & Park Sts.) | 845-358-7977

☑ Wasabi Grill *Japanese*

New City | Town Plaza | 195 S. Main St. (3rd St.) | 845-638-2202 www.wasabichi.com

Rockland County residents are "hooked" on this "happening" twosome that "redefines Japanese cuisine" with "exceptional food" and "exciting sushi", plus hibachi at the "smaller", more-affordable New City sibling; the "SoHo"-esque spaces are "packed wall-to-wall on weekends", with "good-looking" servers adding to the "chic" "scene", so although all this "swank" "isn't cheap", it's "worth every penny."

Watercolor Cafe ❶ *American* 18 | 16 | 18 | $39

Larchmont | 2094 Boston Post Rd. (bet. Chatsworth & Larchmont Aves.) | 914-834-2213 | www.watercolorcafe.net

"Live music" fans are "in for a treat" at this "arty" "little hideaway" in Larchmont whose "cozy" digs provide an "intimate setting" for "high-caliber" jazz, pop and folk; service is "attentive" and the American fare is "more than good enough", but it's really about the "scene."

Watermoon *Asian* 23 | 19 | 18 | $39

Rye | 66 Purchase St. (bet. Elm Pl. & W. Purdy Ave.) | 914-921-8880 | www.watermoonrye.com

An "ample" array of "fresh-tasting" Pan-Asian offerings – from sushi to pad Thai – is served at this "chic" canteen "in the heart" of Rye boasting an indoor waterfall; moderate prices are a perk, although service can be "slow" and locals lament "if only it weren't so noisy."

Waters Edge at Giovanni's *Italian/Steak* 19 | 17 | 19 | $45

Darien | 2748 Boston Post Rd. (I-95, exit 9), CT | 203-325-9979 | www.watersedgeatgiovannis.com

"Great bang for the buck" is found in the prix fixes available at this "old-fashioned" Italian steakhouse in Darien, and though tabs can be a bit "pricey" if you go à la carte, "huge portions" ensure there's "always enough for leftovers"; a renovation in late 2011 (which may not be fully reflected in the Decor score) helps ameliorate the "tired catering hall" feel, while "great" service and "beautiful" water views (from the banquet room) are added inducements.

Westchester Burger Co. *Burgers* | 20 | 15 | 17 | $25 |

NEW Mt. Kisco | 353 N. Bedford Rd. (Park Dr.) | no phone
NEW Rye Brook | 275 S. Ridge St. (Garibaldi Pl.) | 914-305-6095
White Plains | 106 Westchester Ave. (Bloomingdale Rd.) | 914-358-9399
www.westchesterburger.com

"Damn-good" burgers "to satisfy just about every hankering" await at this "impressive" White Plains grill (and its newer offshoots) featuring 20 different "juicy" versions as well as offering "vegetarian alternatives" on its "inventive" American menu; though the "boring" brick-lined setting's akin to an "upscale Applebee's" and "service issues" still need to be worked out, it's "always crowded" with a "nice bar for drinks" while you wait.

West Street Grill *American* | 24 | 21 | 23 | $57 |

Litchfield | 43 West St. (North St.), CT | 860-567-3885 |
www.weststreetgrill.com

Mixing "upscale dining with relaxed Connecticut countryside" "works very well" for this "iconic" Litchfield New American that offers "inventive", "high-quality" fare and an "excellent" wine list in a "lovely" setting, garnering a "loyal following" that includes "locals and celebs"; while the service is "top-notch" and the owners "pay attention that all goes well", a few are put off by the "'in' crowd" vibe.

When Pigs Fly 🕸 *BBQ* | ∇ 21 | 16 | 19 | $26 |

Mabbettsville | 3826 Rte. 44 (Crescent Rd.) | 847-677-4735 |
www.hudsonvalleybbq.com

At this BBQ joint in Mabbettsville focusing on takeout, "accomplished chef" Bennett Chinn "explores his passion for Southern cooking", incorporating Texas, North Carolina and St. Louis styles, as well as organic meats and local produce, into his "finger-licking" fare; catering is popular, so is their soft-serve ice cream.

The Wherehouse *American* | - | - | - | I |

Newburgh | 119 Liberty St. (Ann St.) | 845-561-7240 |
www.thewherehouserestaurant.com

"Contributing to Newburgh's renaissance" by "bringing nightlife and music" to the neighborhood, this "funky" American mixes "large portions" of "typical" pub grub with samosas, pierogi and potstickers, then caps it with BBQ and "veg-friendly" offerings; prices are "good", the '60s "retro" setting is "fun" and the "beer selection is one of the best", so overall, "it's a gem."

Whistling Willie's *American* | ∇ 19 | 14 | 18 | $28 |

Cold Spring | 184 Main St. (Rte. 9D) | 845-265-2012 |
www.whistlingwillies.com

"Big burgers" and beer – that's what this affordable Cold Spring tavern is about, although the "standard American fare" runs the gamut from sandwiches to salmon; the vintage brick setting's on the "dingy" side, but add sidewalk seating, "a bartender who's a stitch", plus music most nights and you're not just whistling Dixie.

White Horse Country Pub   *Pub Food*   19 | 23 | 20 | $32

New Preston | 258 New Milford Tpke. (Findley Rd.), CT | 860-868-1496 | www.whitehorsecountrypub.com

"Snuggle up near the fireplace" or "get a seat on the patio overlooking the river" at this "quintessential country pub" in New Preston, housed in a "tastefully updated" building decorated with "historical pieces from England", where the "congenial" owner and "friendly" staff foster an atmosphere that encourages "hanging around"; critics find the fare merely "average", but others point out that "on this stretch of 202, there ain't many choices."

White Wolf   *American*   - | - | - | M

Napanoch | 7400 Rte. 209 (Old Rte. 209) | 845-647-4200 | www.whitewolfdining.com

A "wide-ranging menu" of American eats suits those wolfing down "more-than-ample portions" at this "neighborhood" outpost in rural Napanoch; prices are "good" and service likewise, and if the spacious mahogany-paneled dining rooms feel "somewhat formal", you can join the "crowd" in the cozier bar.

Wildfire Grill   *Eclectic*   ▽ 19 | 19 | 20 | $43

Montgomery | 74 Clinton St. (bet. Bridge & Union Sts.) | 845-457-3770

"Sophisticated and homey at the same time", this Montgomery Eclectic offers chef Krista Wild's midpriced menu with "new choices regularly added", including some for vegetarians; the "low-key" decor mixes rural America with an African motif, so even if a "Led Zep" soundtrack seems out of whack, somehow it adds up to a "nice local atmosphere."

Wild Ginger   *Asian*   20 | 17 | 19 | $33

Bronxville | 10 Park Pl. (Kraft Ave.) | 914-337-2198 | www.wildgingerbronxville.com

A "mishmash" of "modern" Pan-Asian plates – from "creative" takes on sushi to General Tso's chicken – characterizes this "good-value" Bronxville canteen that's a "solid choice" for a "quick bite"; given the "crowded", "casual" digs and "rushed service", carryout is also appealing.

Wild Hive Farm,   ▽ 20 | 13 | 19 | $21
Bakery & Cafe   Ⓜ *American*

Clinton Corners | 2411 Salt Point Tpke. (Clinton Corners Rd.) | 845-266-5863 | www.wildhivefarm.com

Like a "New England country store transported to the Hudson Valley", this "homespun, wholesome" Clinton Corners American cafe whips up "tasty" breakfasts, lunches and baked goods from "immaculately sourced" ingredients and also vends "first-rate, farm-fresh" groceries; a "cozy, country setting" and staff that's "nice as can be" complete the picture; P.S. family-style dinners are served on Thursday nights.

FOOD | DECOR | SERVICE | COST

Willett House *Steak*   24 | 21 | 23 | $67

Port Chester | 20 Willett Ave. (Abendroth Ave.) | 914-939-7500 |
www.thewilletthouse.com

Dubbed "the Peter Luger of Westchester" by its devotees, this "expensive" Port Chester "warhorse" set in a "historic" turn-of-the-century grain building channels the "old-school" chophouses of yore with "superior" cuts and "wonderful" sides "all done right" and ferried by an "experienced", "top-notch" staff; detractors declare it a little "tired", but "there's a reason it's been here so long."

Winvian ⓜ *American*   ▽ 27 | 28 | 26 | $87

Litchfield | Winvian Resort | 155 Alain White Rd. (bet. County &
E. Shore Rds.), CT | 860-393-3004 | www.winvian.com

"Feel like landed gentry" in what seems like "your own private 18th-century dining room" on an "idyllic" country estate in the Litchfield Hills that specializes in seasonal, locally driven American cuisine; the "innovative" menu is a "delight to the senses" and the service is "sophisticated" (i.e. "attentive but not intrusive"), but "cash in your stocks before going" and consider trying to "stay the night in one of the very special cottages" on this Relais & Châteaux property, which many agree is also "out of this world."

Wobble Café ⓜ *Eclectic*   21 | 13 | 18 | $24

Ossining | 21 Campwoods Rd. (Croton Ave.) | 914-762-3459 |
www.wobblecafe.com

"Breakfast is a delight" at this "homey little cafe" in Ossining turning out "smart", affordable Eclectic eats like migas and brioche French toast with "inventive" dinner choices (Thursday–Saturday) drawn from "all over the map"; the setup is a "comfortable" jumble of "funky" "garage-sale" furniture with a play area for "fidgety toddlers", while a "helpful" staff abets the overall "family-friendly" feel.

The Woodland ⓜ *American/Continental*   22 | 19 | 22 | $45

Lakeville | 192 Sharon Rd. (bet. Lake & Wells Hill Rds.), CT |
860-435-0578 | www.thewoodlandrestaurant.com

"Something for everyone and then some" is found on the "unbelievably varied" American-Continental menu at this "lively" Lakeville "old faithful" where even the "yummy sushi" is doled out in "large portions", and for "fair" prices too; the "wonderful, rustic" setting "feels like home" to its droves of devotees, who further appreciate the many wine "values", "big bar scene" and "efficient" service; P.S. "don't think of going without a reservation, even in the dead of winter."

Woody's All Natural *Burgers*   ▽ 18 | 14 | 15 | $19

Cornwall | 30 Quaker Ave. (Oak St.) | 845-534-1111 |
www.woodysallnatural.com

"Sustainable fast food" is the theme at this "terrific, farm-to-table" Cornwall burger joint also turning out "tasty" sandwiches and hot dogs along with craft beers and "delicious milkshakes" in "unusual flavors" ("try the lavender"); counter service adds to the "informal" vibe in the vintage yellow building, though noshers usually head to the deck when it's warm.

FOOD | DECOR | SERVICE | COST

Woody's Parkside Grill ⓜ Eclectic   ▽ 19 | 14 | 18 | $42

Sparkill | 623 Main St. (Sparkhill Ave.) | 845-680-6169 |
www.woodysparksidegrill.com

The "congenial host" establishes a "warm, welcoming" tone at this
Sparkill Eclectic, a "local hangout" dispensing "homestyle cooking"
from a broad "seasonal menu"; service is "willing, but not always efficient" and the "bar scene overshadows the restaurant", yet "the
word is out" about the "good value."

The Would ⓩⓜ American   22 | 17 | 20 | $42

Highland | Inn at Applewood | 120 North Rd. (Rte. 9W) | 845-691-9883 |
www.thewould.com

Yes, "it's a strange name" and "a most unlikely setting" amid "out-
of-the-way" orchards in Highland, yet this "terrific" New American
keeps 'em coming with an "interesting menu" (think grilled tuna and
short ribs) served by a staff that's hard to "faze"; patrons pick one of
two "comfortable" rooms, sip a "skillfully prepared cocktail" in the
bar or head to the patio in summertime.

ⓩ Xaviars at Piermont ⓜ American   28 | 25 | 27 | $82

Piermont | 506 Piermont Ave. (Ash St.) | 845-359-7007 |
www.xaviars.com

"Foodies" "feel pampered" at Peter Kelly's "jewel box of a restaurant"
in Piermont, thanks to "memorable", "marvelous" New American
fare, "well-chosen wines", "on-point", practically "flawless service"
and a "quietly elegant", "intimate" room with "beautiful flower ar-
rangements" and "lovely" china; you need "deep pockets", whether
you choose an "exemplary tasting menu" or go à la carte, but "treat
yourself" – it's "heaven sent" for a "celebratory meal."

ⓩ X2O Xaviars on the Hudson ⓜ American   27 | 28 | 26 | $68

Yonkers | Historic Yonkers Pier | 71 Water Grant St. (Main St.) |
914-965-1111 | www.xaviars.com

"Nothing short of spectacular" swoon fans of Peter Kelly's "splurge-
worthy" New American "showcase" – once again voted Westchester/
Hudson Valley's Most Popular – set in a "strikingly beautiful" "glass
cube" on the Yonkers pier with "majestic views of the Hudson, even
from the restrooms"; "superb" food "that inspires 'oohs' from neigh-
boring tables" and a "deep wine list" plus "exceptional, but not at all
stuffy" service (including tableside visits from the chef himself) add
up to an experience that's "worth every penny"; P.S. the prix fixe
lunch and "free-flowing champagne brunch" are "easier on the wallet", or try nibbles at the bar.

Yama Fuji Sushi Japanese   24 | 13 | 21 | $33

Briarcliff Manor | 1914 Pleasantville Rd. (Old Briarcliff Rd.) |
914-941-3100 | www.myyamafujisushi.com

"Reliably delicious" sushi and "well-prepared" cooked specialties
"more than make up" for the "less-than-inviting" setting at this
"postage stamp–sized" Briarcliff Manor Japanese; service is
"prompt", though sometimes "surly", and "delivery" is "speedy"

too, but it's the bento box lunch and overall "reasonable" prices that inspire return visits.

NEW Yard House ● *American* — — — M

Yonkers | Westchester's Ridge Hill | 237 Market St. (Archer St.) | 914-375-9273 | www.yardhouse.com

Bigger is apparently better at this new Yonkers branch of a vast chain whose outlets boast 150-plus beers on tap, which are fed via conspicuous refrigerated lines that constitute a ceiling design feature; look for blasting classic rock and a democratic American menu with Hawaiian poke and Korean tacos alongside the usual burger-wings-fries pub fare; P.S. parents, take note: there is a children's menu, plus gluten-free picks too.

Yobo *Asian* 21 21 21 $31

Newburgh | 1297 Rte. 300 (Rte. 84, exit 7B) | 845-564-3848 | www.yoborestaurant.com

Those near Newburgh with a yen for "delicious" Korean barbecue or looking to "satisfy the sushi craving" appreciate the "terrific blend" of affordable Pan-Asian fare at this "consistent" stalwart; the staff is "accommodating" and the "unique" decor "has lots of character" with a brook coursing through the dining room to create a "kitschy" but pleasant atmosphere.

Yum Yum Noodle Bar *Asian* ▽ 19 15 16 $19

NEW Kingston | 275 Fair St. (bet. John & Main Sts.) | 845-338-1400 🗷
Woodstock | 4 Rock City Rd. (Mill Hill Rd.) | 845-679-7992
www.yumyumnoodlebar.com

An Asian outpost from the folks who own Oriole 9 across the street in Woodstock, this "much-needed" eatery offers (you guessed it) "great noodles" along with "light" takes on street food like pork buns, chicken satay and such; "utilitarian" digs with "limited seating" and "slow service" are trumped by "cheap" tabs and a "friendly" feel; P.S. the colorful, roomier new Kingston branch has a full bar.

ZaZa *Italian* 16 21 18 $35

Scarsdale | 753 Central Park Ave. (bet. Mt. Joy Ave. & Sentry Pl.) | 914-472-4005 | www.zazarestaurant.com

"A budget version of Rustico", which it replaced, this Scarsdale Italian focuses primarily on "authentic" Neopolitan pizzas pumped out of a wood-burning oven; its "hip", "updated" look with a red marble bar and "cool lighting" earns kudos, although locals find they're "still getting the kinks out" with food and service.

NEW ZaZa *Italian* — — — M

Stamford | 122 Broad St. (Bedford St.), CT | 203-348-2300 | www.zazagastrobar.com

This retro 1950s Rome-meets–New York Italian in Downtown Stamford is sister to Molto Wine Bar in Fairfield and shares its lively (noisy) popularity and midpriced menu of small plates and brick-oven pizzas in a striking setting with red leather banquettes, a white marble bar and big, black-and-white vintage photos; expect a cosmopolitan vibe and clientele.

	FOOD	DECOR	SERVICE	COST

ⓩ Zephs' Ⓜ American/Eclectic

25 | 19 | 25 | $54

Peekskill | 638 Central Ave. (bet. Briarcliff-Peekskill Pkwy. & Washington St.) | 914-736-2159 | www.zephsrestaurant.com

"Always on the mark", this "sophisticated" Peekskill "favorite" from chef Victoria Zeph "excels" with an "imaginative" New American-Eclectic menu that "changes with the seasons" and is served with "gracious aplomb"; never mind that some say the "simple", white-tablecloth setting's overly "conservative" and it's a bit of a "schlep", because "there's real value" in the pricing, and overall it's a "treat."

Zitoune Moroccan

19 | 21 | 19 | $42

Mamaroneck | 1127 W. Boston Post Rd. (Richbell Rd.) | 914-835-8350 | www.zitounerestaurant.com

"Lovely for a date", this "dark, mysterious" Moroccan in Mamaroneck "transports you to Marrakesh" with "nicely spiced" tagines and couscous served by an "attentive" staff in an "exotic" pillow-strewn setting; it can be "expensive", although the early-bird special offers "great value."

Zuppa Restaurant & Lounge Italian

23 | 22 | 22 | $49

Yonkers | 59 Main St. (bet. Hawthorne & Warburton Aves.) | 914-376-6500 | www.zupparestaurant.com

There's a "lively" vibe at this "trendy" Italian and "date-night" standby set in the turn-of-the-century Gazette building in the heart of the "burgeoning waterfront" district in Yonkers; "creative" "but unfussy" Northern-style cooking focusing on "pizza, pasta and prime meats" and a "gracious", "pro" staff mean it "exceeds expectations" for most, even if the bills can feel "a bit pricey"; P.S. free valet parking is "a plus."

WESTCHESTER/ HUDSON VALLEY WITH NEARBY CONNECTICUT TOWNS INDEXES

Cuisines 180
Locations 193
Special Features 206

Cuisines

Includes names, locations and Food ratings.

AMERICAN

Adrienne	New Milford	25
AJ's Burgers	New Roch	20
ⓩ American Bounty	Hyde Pk	26
American Pie	Sherman	22
ⓩ An American Bistro	Tuck	23
Another Fork	Milan	22
Aroma Thyme	Ellenville	23
ⓩ Artist's Palate	Poughkp	26
@ the Corner	Litchfield	20
Aux Délices	multi.	24
Babette's Kitchen	Millbrook	20
Babycakes Cafe	Poughkp	-
ⓩ Back Yard	Montgomery	26
Bailey's	Ridgefield	21
NEW Bangall Whaling	Stanfordville	-
Beach Hse. Café	Old Greenwich	18
Bear Cafe	Woodstock	24
ⓩ Bedford Post/Barn	Bedford	23
ⓩ Bedford Post/Farm	Bedford	25
Beech Tree Grill	Poughkp	22
Beehive	Armonk	21
Belvedere	Staatsburg	20
Bird & Bottle Inn	Garrison	22
ⓩ Birdsall Hse.	Peekskill	24
Bistro/Commons	Highland	-
Bistro Lilly	Goshen	-
Bistro Z	Tarrytown	20
ⓩ Blue Hill	Poc Hills	28
Blue Plate	Chatham	20
Boathouse	Lakeville	17
Boathouse	Ossining	18
Bobby Valentine	Stamford	15
Boitson's	Kingston	-
Brazen Fox	White Pl	17
Briar's	Briarcliff Manor	17
Bridge View	Sleepy Hollow	22
Bruynswyck Inn	Wallkill	-
Bull's Bridge	Kent	16
Bull's Head	Campbell Hall	18
Byrne & Hanrahan	Yonkers	-
Bywater	Rosendale	23
Cabin	Greenburgh	15
Café Amarcord	Beacon	24
Café Barcel	Nyack	25
Cafe Mio	Gardiner	-
Café of Love	Mt. Kisco	22
Cafe Tamayo	Saugerties	25
Caffé Azzurri	Hartsdale	22
Calico	Rhinebeck	25
Camillo's	Montgomery	18
Catamount	Mt. Tremper	17
Catherine's	Goshen	23
Catskill Rose	Mt. Tremper	-
NEW Cedar St.	Dobbs Ferry	-
Chat	multi.	18
ⓩ Cheesecake Fac.	multi.	17
Chef Luis	New Canaan	25
NEW Club Car	Mamaro	-
Cobble Stone	Purchase	15
NEW Comfort	Hastings/Hud	-
Commissary	Tappan	-
Community Table	Washington	27
Country Bistro	Salisbury	-
ⓩ Crabtree's	Chappaqua	25
NEW Craftsman Ale	Harrison	-
Crave	Poughkp	25
DABA	Hudson	21
Daily Planet	LaGrangeville	17
Damon Baehrel	Earlton	29
NEW Darien Social	Darien	-
Division St. Grill	Peekskill	20
Dutch Ale	Saugerties	-
Egg's Nest	High Falls	19
808 Bistro	Scarsdale	22
Eleven 11	Fishkill	22
NEW Elm	New Canaan	-
Emma's Ale House	White Pl	18
ⓩ Equus	Tarrytown	25
F.A.B.	Mt. Kisco	19
Farmer's Wife	Ancramdale	21
NEW Farm to Table	Fishkill	-
Fife 'n Drum	Kent	18
Fifty Coins	Ridgefield	16
59 Bank	New Milford	19
Flatiron	Red Hook	23
ⓩ 42	White Pl	22

☑ Freelance Cafe | **Piermont**	28
Gilded Otter | **New Paltz**	16
Ginger Man | **Greenwich**	18
☑ Glenmere | **Chester**	24
Gnarly Vine | **New Roch**	17
Goose | **Darien**	-
Grandma's | **Yorktown Hts**	15
Greens | **Copake**	23
Greenwich Tav. | **Old Greenwich**	21
G.W. Tavern | **Wash Depot**	20
Half Moon | **Dobbs Ferry**	19
Halstead Ave. | **Harrison**	20
Harper's | **Dobbs Ferry**	-
Harrys/Hartsdale | **Hartsdale**	20
Harvest Café | **New Paltz**	23
☑ Harvest Supper | **New Canaan**	27
Haven | **P'ville**	24
Henry's/Buttermilk | **Milton**	-
Homespun | **Beacon**	28
Horse & Hound | **S Salem**	19
Horsefeathers | **Tarrytown**	18
Horseman | **Sleepy Hollow**	19
NEW Hudson | **Briarcliff Manor**	-
Hudson Grille | **White Pl**	20
NEW Hudson Hil's | **Cold Spring**	-
Hudson Hse. Inn | **Cold Spring**	22
Hudson Hse. Nyack | **Nyack**	23
Hudson St. | **Cornwall/Hud**	-
Hudson Water | **W Haverstraw**	18
Infinity Hall/Bistro | **Norfolk**	20
Inn/Stone Ridge | **Stone Ridge**	21
Iron Forge Inn | **Warwick**	24
☑ Iron Horse Grill | **P'ville**	27
Julianna's | **Cortlandt Man**	24
Juniper | **Hastings/Hud**	-
Justin Thyme | **Croton/Hud**	17
NEW Karma Lounge | **Poughkp**	-
Kelly's Corner | **Brewster**	17
Kona Grill | **Stamford**	17
Kraft Bistro | **Bronxville**	21
Landmark Inn | **Warwick**	20
Larchmont Tav. | **Larch**	17
Last Chance | **Tanners**	22
Le Chambord Restaurant | **Hopewell Jct**	-
Lexington Sq. Café | **Mt. Kisco**	21
NEW Liberty Public | **Rhinebeck**	-
Litchfield Saltwater | **Litchfield**	20

Local | **Rhinebeck**	-
Local 111 | **Philmont**	23
NEW Local/Ice Cream | **Chappaqua**	-
Lodge | **Wingdale**	-
Long Ridge Tav. | **Stamford**	14
Louie's/Ave. | **Pearl River**	21
Madalin's Table | **Tivoli**	19
Maggie's Krooked | **Tanners**	-
Mickey/Molly Spill. | **multi.**	15
Main Course | **New Paltz**	25
Marco | **Lake Mahopac**	21
Maud's Tavern | **Hastings/Hud**	16
Mayflower Inn | **Washington**	24
☑ McKinney/Doyle | **Pawling**	25
Meetinghouse | **Bedford Vill**	20
Me-Oh-My | **Red Hook**	25
Meritage | **Scarsdale**	23
Michael's Tavern | **P'ville**	17
Millstone Café | **Kent**	-
Miss Lucy's | **Saugerties**	22
NEW MOD | **Hudson**	-
☑ Moderne Barn | **Armonk**	22
Mohonk Mtn. Hse. | **New Paltz**	18
Napa & Co. | **Stamford**	24
New World | **Saugerties**	22
☑ No. 9 | **Millerton**	27
Northern Spy | **High Falls**	18
North Star | **Pound Ridge**	20
Oakhurst Diner | **Millerton**	16
Olde Stone Mill | **Tuck**	17
Old '76 House | **Tappan**	18
☑ 121 Rest. | **N Salem**	22
On the Way Café | **Rye**	-
Opus 465 | **Armonk**	18
Palmer's Crossing | **Larch**	21
Pantry | **Wash Depot**	24
NEW Park 143 | **Bronxville**	-
Peekamoose | **Big Indian**	24
Peekskill Brew | **Peekskill**	19
Peter Pratt's | **Yorktown**	25
Pete's Saloon | **Elmsford**	18
Phoenix | **Mt. Tremper**	-
Pine Social | **New Canaan**	23
Piper's Kilt | **Eastchester**	22
☑ Plates | **Larch**	25
Plumbush Inn | **Cold Spring**	21
Pony Express | **P'ville**	22

Porter Hse. | **White Pl**	19
Post Rd. Ale | **New Roch**	-
Pumpernickel | **Ardsley**	15
Raccoon Saloon | **Marlboro**	21
Rainwater | **Hastings/Hud**	16
Z Rebeccas | **Greenwich**	26
Red Brick Tav. | **Rosendale**	20
Red Devon | **Bangall**	23
Red Dot | **Hudson**	17
Z Red Hat | **Irvington**	23
Red Onion | **Saugerties**	23
Z Rest. North | **Armonk**	26
Z Rest. X/Bully | **Congers**	27
River City Grille | **Irvington**	19
River Club | **Nyack**	14
River Grill | **Newburgh**	20
Riverview | **Cold Spring**	24
Roasted Peppers | **Mamaro**	21
NEW Rock and Rye | **New Paltz**	-
Route 100 | **Yonkers**	22
Sammy's | **Bronxville**	22
Sam's/Gedney | **White Pl**	19
Scarsdale Metro | **Scarsdale**	17
Z Schoolhouse | **Wilton**	27
Seasons American | **Somers**	18
Shadows | **Poughkp**	17
Z Ship Lantern | **Milton**	26
Ship to Shore | **Kingston**	22
Z Soul Dog | **Poughkp**	23
Southport Brew. | **Stamford**	16
Squires | **Briarcliff Manor**	19
Z St. Andrew's | **Hyde Pk**	25
NEW Stony Brae | **Cragsmoor**	-
Sweet Grass | **Tarrytown**	19
Sweet Sue's | **Phoenicia**	24
Swoon | **Hudson**	24
Tanzy's | **Hudson**	17
Tap House | **Tuck**	20
Tarry Tavern | **Tarrytown**	20
NEW Taste | **Buchanan**	-
NEW Tavern/Diamond | **Saugerties**	-
Tavern/Highlands | **Garrison**	22
Tavern/Beekman | **Rhinebeck**	20
NEW Tavern/Gunk | **Ellenville**	-
Z Terrapin | **Rhinebeck**	24
36 Main | **New Paltz**	23
Thyme | **Yorktown Hts**	22

NEW Toad Holly | **Tillson**	-
Torches/Hudson | **Newburgh**	17
Town Dock Tavern | **Rye**	19
Traditions 118 | **Somers**	21
Trinity Grill | **Harrison**	20
Tuthill House | **Gardiner**	-
12 Grapes | **Peekskill**	21
Two Spear St. | **Nyack**	22
NEW 2Taste | **Hyde Pk**	-
Underhills | **Bronxville**	21
Union | **Haverstraw**	24
Valhalla Crossing | **Valhalla**	16
Valley/Garrison | **Garrison**	23
NEW Vanderbilt House Restaurant | **Philmont**	-
Velo | **Nyack**	24
Village | **Litchfield**	20
Village Social | **Mt. Kisco**	-
Village Tea. | **New Paltz**	25
NEW Vintage 1891 | **Larch**	-
Violette | **Woodstock**	20
Vox | **N Salem**	21
Ward's Bridge | **Montgomery**	19
Watercolor Cafe | **Larch**	18
Westchester Burger | **multi.**	20
West St. Grill | **Litchfield**	24
Wherehouse | **Newburgh**	-
Whistling Willie's | **Cold Spring**	19
White Wolf | **Napanoch**	-
Wild Hive | **Clinton Corners**	20
Winvian | **Litchfield**	27
Woodland | **Lakeville**	22
Would | **Highland**	22
Z Xaviars | **Piermont**	28
Z X2O Xaviars | **Yonkers**	27
NEW Yard House | **Yonkers**	-
Z Zephs' | **Peekskill**	25

ARGENTINEAN

Milonga | **N White Plains**	22

ASIAN

Asiana Cafe | **Greenwich**	21
Asian Tempt. | **White Pl**	20
Baang Cafe | **Riverside**	23
Bambou | **Greenwich**	21
Blue Asian | **Mt. Kisco**	19
Blue Finn | **Middletown**	21
Bull & Buddha | **Poughkp**	19
Ching's/Wild Ginger | **multi.**	24

Euro Asian	**Port Chester**	17
Ginban Asian	**Mamaro**	23
Golden Rod	**New Roch**	18
Lucky Buddha	**Thornwood**	24
Neo World	**Mt. Kisco**	23
Penang Grill	**Greenwich**	22
Red Plum	**Mamaro**	21
Spoon	**Chappaqua**	20
Temptation Tea	**Mt. Kisco**	22
Watermoon	**Rye**	23
Wild Ginger	**Bronxville**	20

AUSTRIAN

Hopkins Inn	**Warren**	19

BAKERIES

American Pie	**Sherman**	22
☑ Apple Pie	**Hyde Pk**	26
Babette's Kitchen	**Millbrook**	20
☑ Bedford Post/Barn	**Bedford**	23
Bread Alone	**multi.**	22
NEW Cafe Le Perche	**Hudson**	–
Calico	**Rhinebeck**	25
☑ Chiboust	**Tarrytown**	24
Corner Bakery	**Pawling**	23
Culinary Creations	**Pine Bush**	–
Homespun	**Beacon**	28
Jean Claude's	**multi.**	25
Me-Oh-My	**Red Hook**	25
Millstone Café	**Kent**	–
Versailles	**Greenwich**	24
Village Sq. Bagels	**Larch**	18
Village Tea.	**New Paltz**	25

BARBECUE

Barnstormer	**Ft Montgomery**	21
☑ Big W's	**Wingdale**	26
Boatyard/Smokey Joe's	**Stamford**	19
Cookhouse	**New Milford**	22
Hickory BBQ	**Kingston**	18
Holy Smoke	**Mahopac**	22
Max's Memphis	**Red Hook**	21
Memphis Mae's	**Croton/Hud**	19
Q Rest.	**Port Chester**	22
When Pigs Fly	**Mabbettsville**	21

BRAZILIAN

Aquario	**W Harrison**	23
Caravela	**Tarrytown**	22
Copacabana	**Port Chester**	21
Solmar	**Tarrytown**	21
NEW Texas de Brazil	**Yonkers**	–

BURGERS

AJ's Burgers	**New Roch**	20
Antoine McGuire	**Haverstraw**	24
Beech Tree Grill	**Poughkp**	22
Blazer Pub	**Purdys**	22
Briar's	**Briarcliff Manor**	17
Burgers/Shakes	**multi.**	22
Bywater	**Rosendale**	23
Candlelight Inn	**Scarsdale**	22
Clamp's	**New Milford**	–
Cobble Stone	**Purchase**	15
Croton Creek	**Crot Falls**	20
Flatiron	**Red Hook**	23
Horsefeathers	**Tarrytown**	18
Larchmont Tav.	**Larch**	17
Lucky's	**Stamford**	18
Meetinghouse	**Bedford Vill**	20
Oakhurst Diner	**Millerton**	16
Piper's Kilt	**Eastchester**	22
Pony Express	**P'ville**	22
Poppy's	**Beacon**	24
Porter Hse.	**White Pl**	19
Raccoon Saloon	**Marlboro**	21
Red Onion	**Saugerties**	23
☑ Red Rooster	**Brewster**	18
Route 22	**Armonk**	14
Sam's/Gedney	**White Pl**	19
Sherwood's	**Larch**	20
Squires	**Briarcliff Manor**	19
Sweet Grass	**Tarrytown**	19
☑ Terrapin	**Rhinebeck**	24
Town Dock Tavern	**Rye**	19
Westchester Burger	**multi.**	20
Whistling Willie's	**C old Spring**	19
Woody's All Natural	**Cornwall**	18

CAJUN

Bayou	**Mt. Vernon**	19
Rye Roadhse.	**Rye**	18

CALIFORNIAN

Gates	**New Canaan**	19

CARIBBEAN

Alvin/Friends	**New Roch**	26

CHINESE

(* dim sum specialist)

Aberdeen* | **White Pl**	23
Bao's | **White Pl**	20
China Rose | **Rhinecliff**	21
NEW China White | **multi.**	-
David Chen | **Armonk**	18
East Harbor | **Yonkers**	21
Empire | **Yorktown Hts**	20
Golden House | **Jeff Valley**	22
Hunan Larchmont | **Larch**	17
Imperial | **N White Plains**	17
Isamu | **Beacon**	25
Mill House Panda | **multi.**	19
Pagoda* | **Scarsdale**	17
P.F. Chang's | **multi.**	18
Ray's Cafe | **Larch**	19
Seven Woks | **Scarsdale**	18
Yobo | **Newburgh**	21

COFFEEHOUSES

Cafe Mozart | **Mamaro**	17
Irving Farm | **Millerton**	19

COFFEE SHOPS/ DINERS

Bread Alone | **multi.**	22
Z City Limits | **multi.**	19
Daily Planet | **LaGrangeville**	17
Eveready Diner | **multi.**	20
Lucky's | **Stamford**	18
Martindale Chief | **Craryville**	11
Nautilus | **Mamaro**	16
Oakhurst Diner | **Millerton**	16
Orem's Diner | **Wilton**	15
Scarsdale Metro | **Scarsdale**	17

CONTINENTAL

Bruynswyck Inn | **Wallkill**	-
Canterbury | **Cornwall/Hud**	23
Chateau Hathorn | **Warwick**	23
Friends & Family | **Accord**	22
Grande Centrale | **Congers**	19
Hoffman Hse. | **Kingston**	23
Hopkins Inn | **Warren**	19
Jennifer's | **Yorktown Hts**	23
Le Chambord Restaurant | **Hopewell Jct**	-
Mt. Ivy Cafe | **Pomona**	18
Pond Rest. | **Ancramdale**	14

Roger Sherman | **New Canaan**	24
Sammy's | **Bronxville**	22
Z Ship Lantern | **Milton**	26
Stonehenge | **Ridgefield**	22
Sunset Cove | **Tarrytown**	16
Swiss Hütte | **Hillsdale**	21
Travelers | **Ossining**	19
Woodland | **Lakeville**	22

CREOLE

Bayou | **Mt. Vernon**	19
Rye Roadhse. | **Rye**	18

CUBAN

Karamba | **White Pl**	22
NEW La Bella Havana | **Yonkers**	-

DELIS

Z Bagels & More | **Hartsdale**	21
Epstein's Deli | **multi.**	19
Kisco Kosher | **White Pl**	17
Lange's Deli | **Scarsdale**	20

DESSERT

American Pie | **Sherman**	22
Z Apple Pie | **Hyde Pk**	26
Aux Délices | **multi.**	24
Cafe Mozart | **Mamaro**	17
Calico | **Rhinebeck**	25
Z Cheesecake Fac. | **multi.**	17
Z City Limits | **multi.**	19
Corner Bakery | **Pawling**	23
Grandma's | **Yorktown Hts**	15
Jean Claude's | **multi.**	25
Z McKinney/Doyle | **Pawling**	25
Me-Oh-My | **Red Hook**	25
Pantry | **Wash Depot**	24
Temptations Cafe | **Nyack**	16
Versailles | **Greenwich**	24
Via Vanti! | **Mt. Kisco**	23
Village Tea. | **New Paltz**	25

ECLECTIC

Z Arch | **Brewster**	27
Bank St. Tavern | **New Milford**	18
Beehive | **Armonk**	21
Café Mezzaluna | **Saugerties**	23
Cafe Mirage | **Port Chester**	22
Calico | **Rhinebeck**	25
Crew | **Poughkp**	22
Culinary Creations | **Pine Bush**	-

Division St. Grill | **Peekskill**	20
Dragonfly | **Stamford**	17
Earth Foods | **Hudson**	21
Global Palate | **W Park**	26
Lakeview Hse. | **Newburgh**	21
Luna 61 | **Tivoli**	20
Maggie's Krooked | **Tanners**	–
Manna Dew | **Millerton**	22
New World | **Saugerties**	22
Nina | **Middletown**	25
Painted Bistro | **Red Hook**	18
Painter's | **Cornwall/Hud**	19
Reality Bites | **Nyack**	20
Red Dot | **Hudson**	17
River City Grille | **Irvington**	19
Rye Grill | **Rye**	18
NEW Taste | **Buchanan**	–
Temptations Cafe | **Nyack**	16
Tony's | **Woodridge**	–
Twisted Soul | **Poughkp**	24
Ümami Café | **Croton/Hud**	21
Wildfire Grill | **Montgomery**	19
Wobble Café | **Ossining**	21
Woody's Parkside | **Sparkill**	19
Z Zephs' | **Peekskill**	25

ETHIOPIAN

Lalibela | **Mt. Kisco**	–

EUROPEAN

Charlotte's | **Millbrook**	21
On the Way Café | **Rye**	–
Oriole 9 | **Woodstock**	20
Rhinecliff Hotel Bar | **Rhinecliff**	19

FONDUE

Brasserie Swiss | **Ossining**	19
Last Chance | **Tanners**	22
Melting Pot | **multi.**	17

FRENCH

Aux Délices | **multi.**	24
Z Bernard's | **Ridgefield**	27
NEW Brasserie 292 | **Poughkp**	–
Z Buffet/Gare | **Hastings/Hud**	28
Café of Love | **Mt. Kisco**	22
Z Equus | **Tarrytown**	25
Z Escoffier | **Hyde Pk**	27
Harrys/Hartsdale | **Hartsdale**	20
Z Jean-Louis | **Greenwich**	28

La Bretagne | **Stamford**	24
Z La Crémaillère | **Bedford**	27
La Duchesse | **Mt. Tremper**	19
Z La Panetière | **Rye**	27
Le Bouchon | **Cold Spring**	21
Z Le Château | **S Salem**	25
L'Escale | **Greenwich**	23
Madalin's Table | **Tivoli**	19
Meli-Melo | **Greenwich**	25
Z Ondine | **Danbury**	26
Stissing Hse. | **Pine Plains**	20
Z Thomas Henkelmann | **Greenwich**	28
Vinum Cafe | **Washingtonville**	–
Violette | **Woodstock**	20
Vox | **N Salem**	21

FRENCH (BISTRO)

NEW Alain's | **Nyack**	–
Antoine McGuire | **Haverstraw**	24
Bistro Bonne Nuit | **New Canaan**	25
Bistro Brie | **Windham**	21
Bistro Rollin | **Pelham**	23
NEW Cafe Le Perche | **Hudson**	–
Café Les Baux | **Millbrook**	24
Chez Jean-Pierre | **Stamford**	24
Z Chiboust | **Tarrytown**	24
Country Bistro | **Salisbury**	–
Encore Bistro | **Larch**	23
F.A.B. | **Mt. Kisco**	19
Jackie's Bistro | **Eastchester**	22
Le Canard | **Kingston**	23
NEW Le Express | **Poughkp**	–
Le Gamin | **Hudson**	19
Le Jardin du Roi | **Chappaqua**	21
Le Petit Bistro | **Rhinebeck**	25
Z Le Provençal | **Mamaro**	23
Luc's Café | **Ridgefield**	24
Pascal's | **Larch**	23
Pastorale | **Lakeville**	23
Z Red Hat | **Irvington**	23
Rue/Crêpes | **Harrison**	19
Sidewalk Bistro | **Piermont**	20
Ten Twenty Post | **Darien**	21
Versailles | **Greenwich**	24

GASTROPUB

Z Birdsall Hse. | Amer. | **Peekskill**	24
NEW Growlers | Amer. | **Tuck**	–

Gunk Haus | German | **Highland** 24

Rhinecliff Hotel Bar | Euro. | 19
   Rhinecliff

GERMAN

Gunk Haus | **Highland** 24

Jennifer's | **Yorktown Hts** 23

Mountain Brauhaus | **Gardiner** 24

Travelers | **Ossining** 19

GREEK

Elia Taverna | **Bronxville** 23

Eos Greek | **Stamford** 24

🆕 Ionian | **New Roch** -

🇿 Lefteris Gyro | **multi.** 21

🆕 Mythos | **Thornwood** -

🆕 Nemea | **Mamaro** -

Niko's Greek | **White Pl** 20

Post Corner Pizza | **Darien** 20

Santorini | **Sleepy Hollow** 22

HEALTH FOOD

(See also Vegetarian)

Aroma Thyme | **Ellenville** 23

HOT DOGS

Lubins-N-Links | **Tarrytown** 24

Pony Express | **P'ville** 22

🇿 Red Rooster | **Brewster** 18

🇿 Soul Dog | **Poughkp** 23

🇿 Walter's | **Mamaro** 22

INDIAN

Bollywood | **P'ville** 20

Chutney | **Irvington** 23

🆕 Cinnamon | **Rhinebeck** -

🇿 Coromandel | **multi.** 25

India Hse. | **Montrose** 22

Jaipore Indian | **Brewster** 23

Little Kabab | **Mt. Kisco** -

Malabar Hill | **Elmsford** 21

Masala Kraft | **Hartsdale** 22

Mughal Palace | **Valhalla** 25

Orissa | **Dobbs Ferry** 24

Passage to India | **Mt. Kisco** 22

Priya | **Suffern** 19

Rani Mahal | **Mamaro** 23

Red Hook Curry | **Red Hook** 21

Royal Palace | **White Pl** 20

Saffron | **Middletown** 19

Spice Vill. | **Tuck** 22

Tandoori Taste | **Port Chester** 21

Tanjore | **Fishkill** 25

🇿 Tawa | **Stamford** 27

Thali | **multi.** 24

IRISH

Antoine McGuire | **Haverstraw** 24

Mickey/Molly Spill. | **multi.** 15

🆕 Rambler's Rest | **multi.** -

ISRAELI

Taiim Falafel | **Hastings/Hud** -

ITALIAN

(N=Northern; S=Southern)

Abatino's | **N White Plains** 20

Abruzzi Tratt. | **Patterson** 21

Agriturismo | **Pine Plains** 23

Alba's | N | **Port Chester** 23

Amalfi | **Briarcliff Manor** 19

A' Mangiare/Ianella | S | **multi.** 20

Angelina's | **Tuck** 21

Anna Maria's | **Larch** 21

🇿 Aroma Osteria | S | **Wapp Falls** 26

Arrivederci | N | **Sherman** -

Arrosto | **Port Chester** 23

🆕 A Tavola | **New Paltz** -

Aurora | N | **Rye** 21

Aversano's | **Brewster** 21

Bacco | **Poughkp** 21

Bacio Tratt. | **Cross River** 23

Bar Rosso | **Stamford** -

Bellizzi | **multi.** 15

Bertucci's | **multi.** 16

Blue Dolphin | S | **Katonah** 23

Brothers Tratt. | **Beacon** 25

Buon Amici | **White Pl** 22

Cafe Giulia | **Lakeville** 22

Cafe Livorno | N | **Rye** 19

Café/Green | N | **Danbury** 22

Cafe Portofino | **Piermont** 23

🇿 Cafe Silvium | **Stamford** 26

Caffé Macchiato | **Newburgh** -

Ca'Mea | N | **Hudson** 22

Casa Rina | **Thornwood** 18

🇿 Caterina/Medici | **Hyde Pk** 27

Cathryn's | N | **Cold Spring** 23

Cava Wine | N | **New Canaan** 22

Cena 2000 | N | **Newburgh** 23

Centro | N | **Greenwich** 20

Chef Antonio | S | **Mamaro** 20

Ciao! | **Eastchester** 19

Columbus Park | **Stamford** 25

🔁 Cookery | **Dobbs Ferry** 26

Cosimo's Brick | **multi.** 20

Cosimo's Tratt. | **Poughkp** 19

Cucina | **Woodstock** 25

DaCapo Italiano Ristorante | **Litchfield** 19

Da Giorgio | **New Roch** 25

DiNardo's | **Pound Ridge** 19

Doc's Tratt. | **Kent** 19

NEW Don Tommaso's | **Yorktown Hts** -

Eclisse | N | **Stamford** 21

808 Bistro | **Scarsdale** 22

Emilio Rist. | **Harrison** 25

Enzo's | **Mamaro** 20

Ferrante | N | **Stamford** 20

59 Bank | **New Milford** 19

Finalmente | **Sleepy Hollow** 24

Francesca's | **Rhinebeck** 21

Frank Guido's | **Kingston** 21

Fratelli | **New Roch** 19

Gabriele's | **Greenwich** -

Gaudio's | **Yorktown Hts** 18

Gavi | **Armonk** 19

Gianna's | **Yonkers** 22

🔁 Gigi Tratt. | **Rhinebeck** 24

Giulio's/Harvest | **Tappan** -

Grande Centrale | **Congers** 19

Graziella's | **White Pl** 19

Halstead Ave. | **Harrison** 20

🔁 Harvest/Hudson | **Hastings/Hud** 22

Il Bacio Tratt. | **Bronxville** 20

🔁 Il Barilotto | **Fishkill** 27

Il Castello | **Mamaro** 24

🔁 Il Cenàcolo | N | **Newburgh** 28

Il Forno | **Somers** 21

Il Portico | N | **Tappan** 23

Il Sogno | **Port Chester** 24

Il Sorriso | **Irvington** 21

Il Tesoro | N | **Goshen** 25

Isabella Italian | **Tarrytown** 15

La Bocca | **White Pl** 23

La Fontanella | N | **Pelham** 24

La Lanterna | **Yonkers** 22

La Manda's | **White Pl** 19

Lanterna Tuscan | N | **Nyack** 24

La Piccola Casa | N | **Mamaro** 21

La Riserva | N | **Larch** 21

La Stazione | **New Paltz** 21

La Villetta | **Larch** 24

Le Fontane | S | **Katonah** 22

Little Sorrento | **Cortlandt** 20

Louie & Johnnies' | **Yonkers** 22

🔁 Luca Rist. | **Wilton** 26

🔁 Lusardi's | **Larch** 24

Madonia | **Stamford** -

Maestro's | **New Roch** 20

Mamma Assunta | S | **Tuck** 20

🔁 Marcello's | **Suffern** 26

Marianacci's | **Port Chester** 21

NEW Mario's Tratt. | **Kingston** -

Massa' | **Scarsdale** -

Mediterraneo | **P'ville** 20

Mercato | **Red Hook** 25

Meritage | **Scarsdale** 23

Milonga | **N White Plains** 22

🔁 Mima | **Irvington** 25

Modern Rest. | S | **New Roch** 22

Morello | **Greenwich** 22

Moscato | **Scarsdale** 23

🔁 Mulino's | **White Pl** 24

Nanuet Hotel | **Nanuet** 21

Nessa | **Port Chester** 21

Nino's | **S Salem** 20

Nino's | **Bedford Hills** 21

Osteria Applausi | **Old Greenwich** 24

Pasta Cucina | **multi.** 18

Pasta Vera | **Greenwich** 20

Pas-Tina's | **Hartsdale** 19

Pellicci's | **Stamford** 19

Peppino's | N | **Katonah** 20

Piatto Grill | N | **Yorktown Hts** 20

Piero's | **Port Chester** 24

Pinocchio | **Eastchester** 21

NEW Polpettina | **Eastchester** -

Polpo | **Greenwich** 24

Portofino Pizza | **Goldens Br** 22

Portofino Rist. | **Staatsburg** 23

Posto 22 | **New Roch** 21

NEW Pranzi | **White Pl** -

WEST/HV/CT

CUISINES

Primavera | N | **Crot Falls** — 24

Puccini | **Rhinebeck** — -

Quattro Pazzi | **Stamford** — 23

NEW RéNapoli | **Old Greenwich** — -

Rigatoni | **Pelham** — 21

Risotto | **Thornwood** — 21

Rist. Buona Sera | **Mt. Vernon** — 22

Ristorante Lucia | **Bedford** — 18

NEW Rizzuto's | **Stamford** — 20

Roma | **Tuck** — 18

Rosa's La Scarbitta | **Mamaro** — -

Z Rosie's Bistro | **Bronxville** — 23

Z Rraci | **Brewster** — 26

Sagi | **Ridgefield** — 23

Sam's | **Dobbs Ferry** — 18

Savona's Trattoria | **Kingston** — 19

Scalini | N | **Bronxville** — 21

Scaramella's | **Dobbs Ferry** — 23

Siena | N | **Stamford** — 23

Solano's | **Mt. Vernon** — -

Solé Rist. | N | **New Canaan** — 21

Spaccarelli's | **Millwood** — 22

Z Spadaro | **New Roch** — 26

Stissing Hse. | **Pine Plains** — 20

T&J Villaggio | **Port Chester** — 21

Tappo | **Stamford** — -

Taro's | **Millerton** — 19

Z Tarry Lodge | **Port Chester** — 24

Terra Rist. | N | **Greenwich** — 23

Terra Rustica | **Briarcliff Manor** — 19

Tombolino's | **Yonkers** — 23

Toscana | N | **Ridgefield** — 22

Traditions 118 | **Somers** — 21

Tramonto | **Hawthorne** — 19

Tratt. Vivolo | **Harrison** — 25

Tre Angelina | N | **multi.** — 21

Trevi Ristorante | **W Harrison** — 23

Tuscan Oven | N | **Mt. Kisco** — 20

TuttaBella | N | **Scarsdale** — 23

Valbella | **Riverside** — 25

Valentina's | **Carmel** — -

Valentino's | **Yonkers** — 24

Via Vanti! | **Mt. Kisco** — 23

Vico | N | **Hudson** — 19

Waters Edge | **Darien** — 19

ZaZa | **Scarsdale** — 16

NEW ZaZa | **Stamford** — -

Zuppa | N | **Yonkers** — 23

JAPANESE
(* sushi specialist)

Abis* | **multi.** — 19

Azuma Sushi* | **Hartsdale** — 25

East Harbor* | **Yonkers** — 21

Edo | **multi.** — 20

Empire* | **Yorktown Hts** — 20

Fin/Fin II* | **Stamford** — 23

Fuji Mtn. | **Larch** — 15

Gasho of Japan | **multi.** — 18

Gomen-Kudasai | **New Paltz** — -

Z Haiku* | **multi.** — 22

Z Hajime* | **Harrison** — 25

Hanada Sushi* | **P'ville** — 19

Hokkaido* | **New Paltz** — 27

Hunan Larchmont | **Larch** — 17

Ichi Riki* | **Elmsford** — 19

Imperial | **N White Plains** — 17

NEW Impulse Hibachi | **White Pl** — -

Isamu* | **Beacon** — 25

Japan Inn* | **Bronxville** — 24

Karuta* | **New Roch** — 18

Kira* | **Armonk** — 23

Kirari* | **Scarsdale** — 20

Kona Grill* | **Stamford** — 17

Koo* | **multi.** — 23

Kotobuki* | **Stamford** — 24

Kujaku* | **Stamford** — 18

NEW KYO Sushi* | **Hartsdale** — -

Kyoto Sushi* | **Kingston** — 21

Made In Asia* | **Armonk** — 21

Magoya* | **Chester** — 23

Momiji* | **multi.** — 24

Mount Fuji | **Hillburn** — 19

Murasaki* | **Nyack** — 22

Neko Sushi* | **multi.** — 21

Noda's Steak* | **White Pl** — 19

Norimaki* | **Washington** — -

Okinawa* | **multi.** — 20

Oriental Hse.* | **Pine Bush** — -

Osaka* | **multi.** — 22

Plum Tree* | **New Canaan** — 20

Sazan* | **Ardsley** — 24

Seasons Japanese* | **White Pl** — 23

Z Sushi Mike's* | **Dobbs Ferry** — 26

Z Sushi Nanase* | **White Pl** — 29

Sushi Niji* | **Dobbs Ferry** — 22

Tengda* | **multi.** — 22

Toro*	**Fishkill**	20
Toyo Sushi*	**Mamaro**	21
Tsuru*	**Hartsdale**	23
NEW Umami Sushi	**Ardsley**	–
Wasabi*	**Hudson**	18
Z Wasabi/Grill*	**multi.**	26
Yama Fuji*	**Briarcliff Manor**	24

KOREAN

(* barbecue specialist)

Kalbi Hse.*	**White Pl**	19
Kang Suh*	**Yonkers**	21
Oriental Hse.	**Pine Bush**	–
Toro*	**Fishkill**	20

KOSHER/ KOSHER-STYLE

Epstein's Deli	**multi.**	19
Kisco Kosher	**White Pl**	17
Village Sq. Bagels	**Larch**	18

LEBANESE

| Layla's Falafel | **Stamford** | 22 |

MEDITERRANEAN

Arielle	**Rhinebeck**	22
Aurelia	**Millbrook**	19
Bacio Tratt.	**Cross River**	23
Café d'Azur	**Darien**	–
Centro	**Greenwich**	20
Z Chiboust	**Tarrytown**	24
Dolphin	**Yonkers**	21
Douro	**Greenwich**	–
Fez	**Stamford**	20
Fig & Olive	**Scarsdale**	–
Gates	**New Canaan**	19
Z Gigi Tratt.	**Rhinebeck**	24
Z Harvest/Hudson	**Hastings/Hud**	22
Il Sogno	**Port Chester**	24
Kraft Bistro	**Bronxville**	21
Z Lusardi's	**Larch**	24
Mediterraneo	**Greenwich**	21
NEW Mint Premium	**Tarrytown**	–
Moscato	**Scarsdale**	23
NEW NoMa Social	**New Roch**	–
Oliva Cafe	**New Preston**	24
Primavera	**Crot Falls**	24
Z Serevan	**Amenia**	27
Turquoise	**Larch**	21
Village Social	**Mt. Kisco**	–

MEXICAN

Avocado	**Cornwall**	22
Bartaco	**multi.**	–
Blue Moon	**Bronxville**	17
NEW Cactus Rose	**Wilton**	–
Cafe Maya/Maya	**multi.**	22
Coyote Flaco	**multi.**	23
Don Juan	**P'ville**	–
El Tio	**multi.**	18
Gaby's Cafe	**multi.**	–
Guadalajara	**Briarcliff Manor**	19
Gusano Loco	**Mamaro**	21
Gypsy Wolf	**Woodstock**	19
La Herradura	**multi.**	18
La Puerta Azul	**Salt Pt**	23
Little Mex. Cafe	**New Roch**	21
Lolita	**Greenwich**	22
Los Abuelos	**Ossining**	18
Mexican Radio	**Hudson**	18
Olé Molé	**Stamford**	19
Que Chula	**Sleepy Hollow**	23
NEW Salsa Fresca	**Bedford Hills**	–
Santa Fe	**Tarrytown**	17
Santa Fe	**Tivoli**	22
Tequila Mock.	**New Canaan**	18
Tequila Sunrise	**Larch**	17
Tomatillo	**Dobbs Ferry**	22
Vega	**Hartsdale**	21

MIDDLE EASTERN

NEW Hash-O-Nash	**Mamaro**	–
Sesame Seed	**Danbury**	21
Tabouli Grill	**Stamford**	–

MOROCCAN

| Fez | **Stamford** | 20 |
| Zitoune | **Mamaro** | 19 |

NEW MEXICAN

| Southwest Cafe | **Ridgefield** | 22 |

NOODLE SHOPS

| Gomen-Kudasai | **New Paltz** | – |
| Yum Yum | **multi.** | 19 |

NUEVO LATINO

Cienega	**New Roch**	–
NEW Ramiro's 954 Latin Bistro	**Mahopac**	–
Z Sonora	**Port Chester**	24

PAN-LATIN

NEW Bistro Latino | **Tuck**	–
Brasitas | **Stamford**	25
Karamba | **White Pl**	22
Mango Café | **Mt. Kisco**	18
Union | **Haverstraw**	24

PERSIAN

Shiraz | **Elmsford**	20

PERUVIAN

NEW Hudson Hil's | **Cold Spring**	–
Machu Picchu | **Newburgh**	–

PIZZA

Abatino's | **N White Plains**	20
A' Mangiare/Ianella | **multi.**	20
Amedeos | **LaGrangeville**	21
Angelina's | **Tuck**	21
Anthony's Pizza | **White Pl**	22
Aurora | **Rye**	21
Baba Louie's | **Hudson**	24
Bellizzi | **multi.**	15
Bertucci's | **multi.**	16
Brothers Tratt. | **Beacon**	25
NEW Burrata | **Eastchester**	–
California Pizza | **multi.**	17
Ciao! | **Eastchester**	19
Colony Grill | **Stamford**	24
Cosimo's Brick | **multi.**	20
Cosimo's Tratt. | **Poughkp**	19
Cucina | **Woodstock**	25
DiNardo's | **Pound Ridge**	19
Doc's Tratt. | **Kent**	19
Francesca's | **Rhinebeck**	21
Frankie/Fanucci's | **multi.**	21
Z Frank Pepe | **multi.**	24
Gaudio's | **Yorktown Hts**	18
Grimaldi's | **New Paltz**	21
Horseman | **Sleepy Hollow**	19
Il Bacio Tratt. | **Bronxville**	20
Il Forno | **Somers**	21
Johnny's | **Mt. Vernon**	25
La Manda's | **White Pl**	19
Maestro's | **New Roch**	20
Modern Rest. | **New Roch**	22
Nanuet Hotel | **Nanuet**	21
Nino's | **S Salem**	20
Nino's | **Bedford Hills**	21
Portofino Pizza | **Goldens Br**	22

Post Corner Pizza | **Darien**	20
NEW RéNapoli | **Old Greenwich**	–
Rigatoni | **Pelham**	21
Riverview | **Cold Spring**	24
NEW Rizzuto's | **Stamford**	20
Roma | **Tuck**	18
Sal's Pizzeria | **Mamaro**	23
Taro's | **Millerton**	19
Z Tarry Lodge | **Port Chester**	24
Terra Rist. | **Greenwich**	23
3 Boys From Italy | **White Pl**	23
Vinny's | **Stamford**	20

PORTUGUESE

Aquario | **W Harrison**	23
Caravela | **Tarrytown**	22
Docas | **Ossining**	21
Douro | **Greenwich**	–
Piri-Q | **Mamaro**	20
Quinta Steak | **Pearl River**	21
Solmar | **Tarrytown**	21

PUB FOOD

NEW Bangall Whaling | **Stanfordville**	–
Blazer Pub | **Purdys**	22
Brazen Fox | **White Pl**	17
Bridge View | **Sleepy Hollow**	22
Candlelight Inn | **Scarsdale**	22
Dutch Ale | **Saugerties**	–
Egg's Nest | **High Falls**	19
Emma's Ale House | **White Pl**	18
Garth Road Inn | **Scarsdale**	15
Gilded Otter | **New Paltz**	16
Ginger Man | **Greenwich**	18
Goose | **Darien**	–
Kelly's Corner | **Brewster**	17
Larchmont Tav. | **Larch**	17
Lazy Boy Saloon | **White Pl**	19
Little Pub | **Ridgefield**	23
Mackenzie's | **Old Greenwich**	16
Michael's Tavern | **P'ville**	17
Peekskill Brew | **Peekskill**	19
Piper's Kilt | **Eastchester**	22
Pumpernickel | **Ardsley**	15
Raccoon Saloon | **Marlboro**	21
Ron Blacks | **White Pl**	16
Route 22 | **Armonk**	14
Sherwood's | **Larch**	20
Southport Brew. | **Stamford**	16

NEW Thornwood Ale | **Thornwood** ⌐⌐

Valhalla Crossing | **Valhalla** 16

Village | **Litchfield** 20

Vinny's | **Stamford** 20

White Horse | **New Preston** 19

PUERTO RICAN

Don Coqui | **New Roch** 23

NEW Siete Ocho Siete | **New Roch** ⌐⌐

NEW Sofrito | **White Pl** ⌐⌐

SANDWICHES

(See also Delis)

Z Apple Pie | **Hyde Pk** 26

Z Bagels & More | **Hartsdale** 21

Bread Alone | **multi.** 22

NEW Cafe Le Perche | **Hudson** ⌐⌐

Corner Bakery | **Pawling** 23

Così | **multi.** 16

Epstein's Deli | **multi.** 19

Harney/Sons | **Millerton** 21

NEW Hudson Hil's | **Cold Spring** ⌐⌐

Irving Farm | **Millerton** 19

Kisco Kosher | **White Pl** 17

Lange's Deli | **Scarsdale** 20

Pantry | **Wash Depot** 24

Sweet Sue's | **Phoenicia** 24

Temptations Cafe | **Nyack** 16

SCANDINAVIAN

DABA | **Hudson** 21

SEAFOOD

Aquario | **W Harrison** 23

Boatyard/Smokey Joe's | **Stamford** 19

Caffe Regatta | **Pelham** 22

Conte's Fishmkt. | **Mt. Kisco** 22

Dolphin | **Yonkers** 21

Z Eastchester Fish | **Scarsdale** 25

80 West | **White Pl** 19

Elm St. Oyster | **Greenwich** 24

Gadaleto's | **New Paltz** 21

Goldfish | **Ossining** 21

Gus's Franklin Pk. | **Harrison** 21

Hudson's Ribs | **Fishkill** 19

Hudson Water | **W Haverstraw** 18

Legal Sea Foods | **White Pl** 19

Litchfield Saltwater | **Litchfield** 20

Morgans Fish | **Rye** 21

Z Ocean Hse. | **Croton/Hud** 27

Ruby's Oyster | **Rye** 23

Seaside Johnnie's | **Rye** 12

Striped Bass | **Tarrytown** 16

Ten Twenty Post | **Darien** 21

Town Dock Tavern | **Rye** 19

SMALL PLATES

(See also Spanish tapas specialist)

Bar Rosso | Italian | **Stamford** ⌐⌐

Bull & Buddha | Asian | **Poughkp** 19

Douro | Portug. | **Greenwich** ⌐⌐

Dragonfly | Eclectic | **Stamford** 17

Fez | Med./Moroccan | **Stamford** 20

Fig & Olive | Med. | **Scarsdale** ⌐⌐

Gnarly Vine | Amer. | **New Roch** 17

Inn/Stone Ridge | Amer. | **Stone Ridge** 21

NEW Karma Lounge | Amer. | **Poughkp** ⌐⌐

Milonga | Argent./Italian | **N White Plains** 22

Z Mima | Italian | **Irvington** 25

NEW Park 143 | Amer. | **Bronxville** ⌐⌐

Reality Bites | Amer. | **Nyack** 20

Southwest Cafe | New Mex. | **Ridgefield** 22

Temptation Tea | Asian | **Mt. Kisco** 22

36 Main | Amer. | **New Paltz** 23

Velo | Amer. | **Nyack** 24

Via Vanti! | Italian | **Mt. Kisco** 23

SOUL FOOD

Virgo's Sip N Soul Cafe | **Beacon** ⌐⌐

SOUTHERN

Alvin/Friends | **New Roch** 26

CB Kitchen Bar | **New City** ⌐⌐

Memphis Mae's | **Croton/Hud** 19

SOUTHWESTERN

Armadillo B&G | **Kingston** 25

Boxcar Cantina | **Greenwich** 21

NEW Cactus Rose | **Wilton** ⌐⌐

Salsa | **New Milford** 25

Santa Fe | **Tarrytown** 17

SPANISH

(* tapas specialist)

Barcelona* | **multi.** 24

Bellota/42* | **White Pl** ⌐⌐

WEST/HV/CT

CUISINES

Elephant* | **Kingston** 24
España* | **Larch** 20
La Camelia* | **Mt. Kisco** 23
NEW Mezon | **Danbury** -
Olive Mkt.* | **Georgetown** 24
NEW Panzur | **Tivoli** -
(P.M.) Wine Bar* | **Hudson** -

SRI LANKAN

NEW Cinnamon | **Rhinebeck** -

STEAKHOUSES

Benjamin Steak | **White Pl** 24
Z BLT Steak | **White Pl** 23
Byrne & Hanrahan | **Yonkers** -
Capital Grille | **Stamford** 25
Chuck's Steak | **multi.** 18
Croton Creek | **Crot Falls** 20
Edo | **multi.** 20
Flames Steak | **Briarcliff Manor** 22
Flatiron | **Red Hook** 23
Frankie/Johnnie's | **Rye** 24
Gabriele's | **Greenwich** -
Grande Centrale | **Congers** 19
Hudson's Ribs | **Fishkill** 19
Louie's/Ave. | **Pearl River** 21
Marc Charles | **Armonk** 20
Morton's | **multi.** 24
Mount Fuji | **Hillburn** 19
Okinawa | **Mt. Kisco** 20
Olde Stone Mill | **Tuck** 17
Outback Steak | **multi.** 17
Quinta Steak | **Pearl River** 21
Ruth's Chris | **Tarrytown** 25
Z Sapore | **Fishkill** 26
Schlesinger's | **New Windsor** 23
Waters Edge | **Darien** 19
Willett House | **Port Chester** 24

SWISS

Brasserie Swiss | **Ossining** 19
Canterbury | **Cornwall/Hud** 23
Swiss Hütte | **Hillsdale** 21

TEAROOMS

Chaiwalla | **Salisbury** 25
Harney/Sons | **Millerton** 21

Tanzy's | **Hudson** 17
Village Tea. | **New Paltz** 25

TEX-MEX

Mary Ann's | **multi.** 15

THAI

Aroi Thai | **Rhinebeck** 22
Bangkok Spice | **Shrub Oak** 23
D Thai | **Thornwood** -
Full Moon | **White Pl** 24
King & I | **Nyack** 17
Kit's Thai | **Stamford** 21
Little Thai/Buddha | **multi.** 23
Red Lotus | **New Roch** 21
Reka's | **White Pl** 19
Siam Orchid | **Scarsdale** 20
Sukhothai | **Beacon** 24
Swaddee Hse. | **Thornwood** 21
Thai Angels | **Mt. Kisco** 21
NEW Thai Elephant | **Patterson** -
Thai Garden | **Orangeburg** 22
Thai Golden | **Carmel** 23
Thai Hse. | **multi.** 23
Tyrynda | **Sleepy Hollow** 23

TURKISH

NEW Bosphorus | **Hartsdale** -
Turkish Cuisine | **White Pl** 21
Turkish Meze | **Mamaro** 23
Turquoise | **Larch** 21

VEGETARIAN

(* vegan)
Earth Foods | **Hudson** 21
Garden Café* | **Woodstock** 26
Luna 61* | **Tivoli** 20
Masala Kraft | **Hartsdale** 22
Northern Spy | **High Falls** 18
Rosendale Cafe* | **Rosendale** 15
Z Soul Dog | **Poughkp** 23
Z Tawa | **Stamford** 27
Thai Garden | **Orangeburg** 22
Thali | **multi.** 24
Village Tea.* | **New Paltz** 25

VIETNAMESE

Saigon Café | **Poughkp** 23

Locations

Includes names, cuisines and Food ratings.

Westchester County

ARDSLEY

Pumpernickel | *Pub*   15
Sazan | *Japanese*   24
Thai Hse. | *Thai*   23
NEW Umami Sushi | *Japanese*   —

ARMONK

Beehive | *Amer./Eclectic*   21
David Chen | *Chinese*   18
Gavi | *Italian*   19
Kira | *Japanese*   23
Made In Asia | *Asian*   21
Marc Charles | *Steak*   20
Z Moderne Barn | *Amer.*   22
Opus 465 | *Amer.*   18
Z Rest. North | *Amer.*   26
Route 22 | *Pub*   14

BEDFORD

Z Bedford Post/Barn | *Amer.*   23
Z Bedford Post/Farm | *Amer.*   25
Z La Crémaillère | *French*   27
Ristorante Lucia | *Italian*   18

BEDFORD HILLS

Nino's | *Italian*   21
NEW Salsa Fresca | *Mex.*   —

BEDFORD VILLAGE

Meetinghouse | *Amer.*   20

BRIARCLIFF MANOR

Amalfi | *Italian*   19
Briar's | *Amer.*   17
Flames Steak | *Steak*   22
Guadalajara | *Mex.*   19
NEW Hudson | *Amer.*   —
Squires | *Amer.*   19
Terra Rustica | *Italian*   19
Yama Fuji | *Japanese*   24

BRONXVILLE

A' Mangiare/Ianella | *Italian*   20
Blue Moon | *Mex.*   17

Elia Taverna | *Greek*   23
Z Haiku | *Asian*   22
Il Bacio Tratt. | *Italian*   20
Japan Inn | *Japanese*   24
Kraft Bistro | *Amer./Med.*   21
NEW Park 143 | *Amer.*   —
Z Rosie's Bistro | *Italian*   23
Sammy's | *Amer./Continental*   22
Scalini | *Italian*   21
Underhills | *Amer.*   21
Wild Ginger | *Asian*   20

BUCHANAN

NEW Taste | *Amer./Eclectic*   —

CHAPPAQUA

Z Crabtree's | *Amer.*   25
Le Jardin du Roi | *French*   21
NEW Local/Ice Cream | —
   Amer./Ice Cream
Spoon | *Asian*   20

CORTLANDT

Little Sorrento | *Italian*   20

CORTLANDT MANOR

Julianna's | *Amer.*   24

CROSS RIVER

Bacio Tratt. | *Italian/Med.*   23
Z Haiku | *Asian*   22

CROTON FALLS

Croton Creek | *Steak*   20
Primavera | *Italian*   24

CROTON-ON-HUDSON

Justin Thyme | *Amer.*   17
Memphis Mae's | *BBQ*   19
Z Ocean Hse. | *Seafood*   27
Ümami Café | *Eclectic*   21

DOBBS FERRY

NEW Cedar St. | *Amer.*   —
Z Cookery | *Italian*   26
Half Moon | *Amer.*   19
Harper's | *Amer.*   —

Orissa | *Indian*	24
Sam's | *Italian*	18
Scaramella's | *Italian*	23
Z Sushi Mike's | *Japanese*	26
Sushi Niji | *Japanese*	22
Tomatillo | *Mex.*	22

EASTCHESTER

NEW Burrata | *Pizza*	-
Ciao! | *Italian/Pizza*	19
Jackie's Bistro | *French*	22
Mickey/Molly Spill. | *Pub*	15
Pinocchio | *Italian*	21
Piper's Kilt | *Pub*	22
NEW Polpettina | *Italian*	-

ELMSFORD

A' Mangiare/Ianella | *Italian*	20
Ichi Riki | *Japanese*	19
Malabar Hill | *Indian*	21
Pete's Saloon | *Amer.*	18
Shiraz | *Persian*	20

GOLDENS BRIDGE

Portofino Pizza | *Italian/Pizza*	22

GREENBURGH

Cabin | *Amer.*	15

HARRISON/ W. HARRISON

Aquario | *Brazilian/Portug.*	23
NEW Craftsman Ale | *Amer.*	-
Emilio Rist. | *Italian*	25
Gus's Franklin Pk. | *Seafood*	21
Z Hajime | *Japanese*	25
Halstead Ave. | *Amer.*	20
Rue/Crêpes | *French*	19
Tratt. Vivolo | *Italian*	25
Trevi Ristorante | *Italian*	23
Trinity Grill | *Amer.*	20

HARTSDALE

Azuma Sushi | *Japanese*	25
Z Bagels & More | *Deli*	21
NEW Bosphorus | *Turkish*	-
Caffé Azzurri | *Amer.*	22
Epstein's Deli | *Deli*	19
Frankie/Fanucci's | *Pizza*	21
Harrys/Hartsdale | *Amer./French*	20

NEW KYO Sushi | *Japanese*	-
Masala Kraft | *Indian/Veg.*	22
Pas-Tina's | *Italian*	19
Tsuru | *Japanese*	23
Vega | *Mex.*	21

HASTINGS-ON-HUDSON

Z Buffet/Gare | *French*	28
NEW Comfort | *Amer.*	-
Z Harvest/Hudson | *Italian/Med.*	22
Juniper | *Amer.*	-
Maud's Tavern | *Amer.*	16
Rainwater | *Amer.*	16
Taiim Falafel | *Israeli*	-

HAWTHORNE

Gasho of Japan | *Japanese*	18
Tramonto | *Italian*	19

IRVINGTON

Chutney | *Indian*	23
Il Sorriso | *Italian*	21
Z Mima | *Italian*	25
Z Red Hat | *Amer.*	23
River City Grille | *Amer./Eclectic*	19

JEFFERSON VALLEY

Golden House | *Chinese*	22

KATONAH

Blue Dolphin | *Italian*	23
Le Fontane | *Italian*	22
Peppino's | *Italian*	20
Tengda | *Asian*	22

LARCHMONT

Anna Maria's | *Italian*	21
Bellizzi | *Italian*	15
Chat | *Amer.*	18
Così | *Sandwiches*	16
Encore Bistro | *French*	23
España | *Spanish*	20
Fuji Mtn. | *Japanese*	15
Hunan Larchmont | *Chinese/Japanese*	17
Larchmont Tav. | *Amer.*	17
La Riserva | *Italian*	21
La Villetta | *Italian*	24
Z Lusardi's | *Italian*	24

Palmer's Crossing | *Amer.* 21
Pascal's | *French* 23
ꝫ Plates | *Amer.* 25
Ray's Cafe | *Chinese* 19
Sherwood's | *Pub* 20
Tequila Sunrise | *Mex.* 17
Turquoise | *Med./Turkish* 21
Village Sq. Bagels | *Bakery* 18
NEW Vintage 1891 | *Amer.* -1
Watercolor Cafe | *Amer.* 18

MAMARONECK

Cafe Mozart | *Coffee* 17
Chef Antonio | *Italian* 20
NEW Club Car | *Amer.* -1
Enzo's | *Italian* 20
Frankie/Fanucci's | *Pizza* 21
Ginban Asian | *Asian* 23
Gusano Loco | *Mex.* 21
ꝫ Haiku | *Asian* 22
NEW Hash-O-Nash | *Mideast.* -1
Il Castello | *Italian* 24
La Herradura | *Mex.* 18
La Piccola Casa | *Italian* 21
ꝫ Le Provençal | *French* 23
Mickey/Molly Spill. | *Pub* 15
Nautilus | *Diner* 16
NEW Nemea | *Greek* -1
Piri-Q | *Portug.* 20
Rani Mahal | *Indian* 23
Red Plum | *Asian* 21
Roasted Peppers | *Amer.* 21
Rosa's La Scarbitta | *Italian* -1
Sal's Pizzeria | *Pizza* 23
Toyo Sushi | *Japanese* 21
Turkish Meze | *Turkish* 23
ꝫ Walter's | *Hot Dogs* 22
Zitoune | *Moroccan* 19

MILLWOOD

Spaccarelli's | *Italian* 22

MONTROSE

India Hse. | *Indian* 22

MT. KISCO

Bellizzi | *Italian* 15
Blue Asian | *Asian* 19
Café of Love | *Amer./French* 22

Conte's Fishmkt. | *Seafood* 22
Così | *Sandwiches* 16
F.A.B. | *Amer./French* 19
La Camelia | *Spanish* 23
Lalibela | *Ethiopian* -1
ꝫ Lefteris Gyro | *Greek* 21
Lexington Sq. Café | *Amer.* 21
Little Kabab | *Indian* -1
Mango Café | *Pan-Latin* 18
Neo World | *Asian* 23
Okinawa | *Japanese* 20
Passage to India | *Indian* 22
Temptation Tea | *Asian* 22
Thai Angels | *Thai* 21
Tuscan Oven | *Italian* 20
Via Vanti! | *Italian* 23
Village Social | *Amer.* -1
Westchester Burger | *Burgers* 20

MT. VERNON

Bayou | *Cajun/Creole* 19
Johnny's | *Pizza* 25
Mickey/Molly Spill. | *Pub* 15
Rist. Buona Sera | *Italian* 22
Solano's | *Italian* -1

NEW ROCHELLE

AJ's Burgers | *Amer.* 20
Alvin/Friends | *Carib./Southern* 26
Cienega | *Nuevo Latino* -1
ꝫ Coromandel | *Indian* 25
Così | *Sandwiches* 16
Coyote Flaco | *Mex.* 23
Da Giorgio | *Italian* 25
Don Coqui | *Puerto Rican* 23
El Tio | *Mex.* 18
Fratelli | *Italian* 19
Gnarly Vine | *Amer.* 17
Golden Rod | *Asian* 18
NEW Ionian | *Greek* -1
Karuta | *Japanese* 18
La Herradura | *Mex.* 18
Little Mex. Cafe | *Mex.* 21
Maestro's | *Italian* 20
Modern Rest. | *Italian* 22
NEW NoMa Social | *Med.* -1
Posto 22 | *Italian* 21
Post Rd. Ale | *Amer.* -1

Red Lotus | *Thai* — 21

NEW Siete Ocho Siete | *Puerto Rican* — –

Z Spadaro | *Italian* — 26

NORTH SALEM

Z 121 Rest. | *Amer.* — 22

Vox | *Amer./French* — 21

OSSINING

Boathouse | *Amer.* — 18

Brasserie Swiss | *Swiss* — 19

Docas | *Portug.* — 21

Goldfish | *Seafood* — 21

Los Abuelos | *Mex.* — 18

Okinawa | *Japanese* — 20

Travelers | *German* — 19

Wobble Café | *Eclectic* — 21

PEEKSKILL

Z Birdsall Hse. | *Amer.* — 24

Division St. Grill | *Amer./Eclectic* — 20

Peekskill Brew | *Amer.* — 19

12 Grapes | *Amer.* — 21

Z Zephs' | *Amer./Eclectic* — 25

PELHAM

Bistro Rollin | *French* — 23

Caffe Regatta | *Seafood* — 22

Edo | *Japanese/Steak* — 20

La Fontanella | *Italian* — 24

Rigatoni | *Italian* — 21

PLEASANTVILLE

A' Mangiare/Ianella | *Italian* — 20

Bollywood | *Indian* — 20

Don Juan | *Mex.* — –

Hanada Sushi | *Japanese* — 19

Haven | *Amer.* — 24

Z Iron Horse Grill | *Amer.* — 27

Mediterraneo | *Italian* — 20

Michael's Tavern | *Pub* — 17

Pony Express | *Amer.* — 22

POCANTICO HILLS

Z Blue Hill | *Amer.* — 28

PORT CHESTER

Alba's | *Italian* — 23

Arrosto | *Italian* — 23

Bartaco | *Mex.* — –

Cafe Mirage | *Eclectic* — 22

NEW Coals | *Pizza* — –

Copacabana | *Brazilian* — 21

Coyote Flaco | *Mex.* — 23

Edo | *Japanese/Steak* — 20

El Tio | *Mex.* — 18

Euro Asian | *Asian* — 17

Il Sogno | *Italian/Med.* — 24

Marianacci's | *Italian* — 21

Mary Ann's | *Tex-Mex* — 15

Nessa | *Italian* — 21

Piero's | *Italian* — 24

Q Rest. | *BBQ* — 22

Z Sonora | *Nuevo Latino* — 24

T&J Villaggio | *Italian* — 21

Tandoori Taste | *Indian* — 21

Z Tarry Lodge | *Italian* — 24

Willett House | *Steak* — 24

POUND RIDGE

DiNardo's | *Italian* — 19

North Star | *Amer.* — 20

PURCHASE

NEW China White | *Chinese* — –

Cobble Stone | *Amer.* — 15

PURDYS

Blazer Pub | *Pub* — 22

RYE

Aurora | *Italian* — 21

Cafe Livorno | *Italian* — 19

Così | *Sandwiches* — 16

Frankie/Johnnie's | *Steak* — 24

Koo | *Japanese* — 23

Z La Panetière | *French* — 27

Morgans Fish | *Seafood* — 21

On the Way Café | *Amer./Euro.* — –

Ruby's Oyster | *Seafood* — 23

Rye Grill | *Eclectic* — 18

Rye Roadhse. | *Cajun/Creole* — 18

Seaside Johnnie's | *Seafood* — 12

Town Dock Tavern | *Amer.* — 19

Watermoon | *Asian* — 23

RYE BROOK

Westchester Burger | *Burgers* — 20

SCARSDALE

California Pizza	*Pizza*	17
Candlelight Inn	*Pub*	22
Chat	*Amer.*	18
☑ Eastchester Fish	*Seafood*	25
808 Bistro	*Amer.*	22
Fig & Olive	*Med.*	–
Garth Road Inn	*Pub*	15
Kirari	*Japanese*	20
Lange's Deli	*Deli*	20
Massa'	*Italian*	–
Meritage	*Amer./Italian*	23
Moscato	*Italian/Med.*	23
Pagoda	*Chinese*	17
Scarsdale Metro	*Amer.*	17
Seven Woks	*Chinese*	18
Siam Orchid	*Thai*	20
Tengda	*Asian*	22
TuttaBella	*Italian*	23
ZaZa	*Italian*	16

SHRUB OAK

Bangkok Spice	*Thai*	23

SLEEPY HOLLOW

Bridge View	*Pub*	22
Finalmente	*Italian*	24
Horseman	*Amer./Pizza*	19
Que Chula	*Mex.*	23
Santorini	*Greek*	22
Tyrynda	*Thai*	23

SOMERS

Il Forno	*Italian*	21
Seasons American	*Amer.*	18
Traditions 118	*Amer./Italian*	21

SOUTH SALEM

Horse & Hound	*Amer.*	19
☑ Le Château	*French*	25
Nino's	*Italian*	20

TARRYTOWN

Bistro Z	*Amer.*	20
Caravela	*Brazilian/Portug.*	22
☑ Chiboust	*French/Med.*	24
☑ Equus	*Amer./French*	25
Horsefeathers	*Amer.*	18
Isabella Italian	*Italian*	15
☑ Lefteris Gyro	*Greek*	21

Lubins-N-Links	*Hot Dogs*	24
NEW Mint Premium	*Med.*	–
Ruth's Chris	*Steak*	25
Santa Fe	*Mex./SW*	17
Solmar	*Brazilian/Portug.*	21
Striped Bass	*Seafood*	16
Sunset Cove	*Continental*	16
Sweet Grass	*Amer.*	19
Tarry Tavern	*Amer.*	20

THORNWOOD

Abis	*Japanese*	19
Casa Rina	*Italian*	18
D Thai	*Thai*	–
Lucky Buddha	*Asian*	24
NEW Mythos	*Greek*	–
Risotto	*Italian*	21
Swaddee Hse.	*Thai*	21
NEW Thornwood Ale	*Pub Food*	–

TUCKAHOE

☑ An American Bistro	*Amer.*	23
Angelina's	*Italian*	21
NEW Bistro Latino	*Pan-Latin*	–
NEW Growlers	*Amer.*	–
Mamma Assunta	*Italian*	20
Olde Stone Mill	*Amer.*	17
Roma	*Pizza*	18
Spice Vill.	*Indian*	22
Tap House	*Amer.*	20

VALHALLA

Mughal Palace	*Indian*	25
Valhalla Crossing	*American*	16

WHITE PLAINS/ N. WHITE PLAINS

Abatino's	*Italian*	20
Aberdeen	*Chinese*	23
Anthony's Pizza	*Pizza*	22
Asian Tempt.	*Asian*	20
Bao's	*Chinese*	20
Bellota/42	*Spanish*	–
Benjamin Steak	*Steak*	24
☑ BLT Steak	*Steak*	23
Brazen Fox	*Pub*	17
Buon Amici	*Italian*	22
☑ Cheesecake Fac.	*Amer.*	17
☑ City Limits	*Diner*	19

80 West	*Seafood*	19
Emma's Ale House	*Pub*	18
☑ 42	*Amer.*	22
Full Moon	*Thai*	24
Graziella's	*Italian*	19
☑ Haiku	*Asian*	22
Hudson Grille	*Amer.*	20
Imperial	*Chinese/Japanese*	17
NEW Impulse Hibachi	*Japanese*	-
Kalbi Hse.	*Korean*	19
Karamba	*Cuban/Pan-Latin*	22
Kisco Kosher	*Deli*	17
La Bocca	*Italian*	23
La Manda's	*Italian*	19
Lazy Boy Saloon	*Pub*	19
Legal Sea Foods	*Seafood*	19
Melting Pot	*Fondue*	17
Milonga	*Argent./Italian*	22
Morton's	*Steak*	24
☑ Mulino's	*Italian*	24
Niko's Greek	*Greek*	20
Noda's Steak	*Japanese*	19
Outback Steak	*Steak*	17
P.F. Chang's	*Chinese*	18
Porter Hse.	*Amer./Pub*	19
NEW Pranzi	*Italian*	-
Reka's	*Thai*	19
Ron Blacks	*Pub*	16
Royal Palace	*Indian*	20
Sam's/Gedney	*Amer.*	19
Seasons Japanese	*Japanese*	23
NEW Sofrito	*Puerto Rican*	-
☑ Sushi Nanase	*Japanese*	29
3 Boys From Italy	*Pizza*	23
Tre Angelina	*Italian*	21
Turkish Cuisine	*Turkish*	21
Westchester Burger	*Burgers*	20

YONKERS

Byrne & Hanrahan	*Amer./Steak*	-
Dolphin	*Seafood*	21
East Harbor	*Chinese/Japanese*	21
Epstein's Deli	*Deli*	19
☑ Frank Pepe	*Pizza*	24
Gianna's	*Italian*	22
Kang Suh	*Korean*	21
NEW La Bella Havana	*Cuban*	-
La Lanterna	*Italian*	22

☑ Lefteris Gyro	*Greek*	21
Louie & Johnnies'	*Italian*	22
Outback Steak	*Steak*	17
Route 100	*Amer.*	22
NEW Texas de Brazil	*Brazilian*	-
Tombolino's	*Italian*	23
Valentino's	*Italian*	24
☑ X2O Xaviars	*Amer.*	27
NEW Yard House	*Amer.*	-
Zuppa	*Italian*	23

YORKTOWN

Peter Pratt's	*Amer.*	25

YORKTOWN HEIGHTS

NEW Don Tommaso's	*Italian*	-
Empire	*Chinese/Japanese*	20
Gaudio's	*Italian*	18
Grandma's	*Amer.*	15
Jennifer's	*Continental/German*	23
Piatto Grill	*Italian*	20
Thyme	*Amer.*	22

Hudson Valley

ACCORD

Friends & Family	*Continental*	22

AMENIA

☑ Serevan	*Med.*	27

ANCRAMDALE

Farmer's Wife	*Amer.*	21
Pond Rest.	*Continental*	14

BANGALL

Red Devon	*Amer.*	23

BEACON

Brothers Tratt.	*Italian*	25
Café Amarcord	*Amer.*	24
Homespun	*Amer./Bakery*	28
Isamu	*Chinese/Japanese*	25
Poppy's	*Burgers*	24
Sukhothai	*Thai*	24
Virgo's Sip N Soul Cafe	*Soul*	-

BIG INDIAN

Peekamoose	*Amer.*	24

BOICEVILLE

Bread Alone | *Bakery/Coffee* 22

BREWSTER

Z Arch | *Eclectic* 27
Aversano's | *Italian* 21
Eveready Diner | *Diner* 20
Jaipore Indian | *Indian* 23
Kelly's Corner | *Pub* 17
Z Red Rooster | *Burgers* 18
Z Rraci | *Italian* 26

CAMPBELL HALL

Bull's Head | *Amer.* 18

CARMEL

Thai Golden | *Thai* 23
Valentina's | *Italian* -

CENTRAL VALLEY

Cosimo's Brick | *Italian* 20
Gasho of Japan | *Japanese* 18

CHATHAM

Blue Plate | *Amer.* 20

CHESTER

Z Glenmere | *Amer.* 24
Magoya | *Japanese* 23

CLINTON CORNERS

Wild Hive | *Amer.* 20

COLD SPRING

Cathryn's | *Italian* 23
NEW Hudson Hil's | *Amer.* -
Hudson Hse. Inn | *Amer.* 22
Le Bouchon | *French* 21
Plumbush Inn | *Amer.* 21
Riverview | *Amer.* 24
Whistling Willie's | *Amer.* 19

CONGERS

Grande Centrale | *Continental/Italian* 19
Z Rest. X/Bully | *Amer.* 27

COPAKE

Greens | *Amer.* 23

CORNWALL/ CORNWALL-ON-HUDSON

Avocado | *Mex.* 22
Canterbury | *Continental/Swiss* 23
Hudson St. | *Amer.* -
Painter's | *Eclectic* 19
Woody's All Natural | *Burgers* 18

CRAGSMOOR

NEW Stony Brae | *Amer.* -

CRARYVILLE

Martindale Chief | *Diner* 11

EARLTON

Damon Baehrel | *Amer.* 29

ELLENVILLE

Aroma Thyme | *Amer./Health* 23
Gaby's Cafe | *Mex.* -
NEW Tavern/Gunk | *Amer.* -

FISHKILL

Cafe Maya/Maya | *Mex.* 22
Eleven 11 | *Amer.* 22
NEW Farm to Table | *Amer.* -
Hudson's Ribs | *Seafood/Steak* 19
Z Il Barilotto | *Italian* 27
Z Sapore | *Steak* 26
Tanjore | *Indian* 25
Toro | *Japanese/Korean* 20

FORT MONTGOMERY

Barnstormer | *BBQ* 21

GARDINER

Cafe Mio | *Amer.* -
Mountain Brauhaus | *German* 24
Tuthill House | *Amer.* -

GARRISON

Bird & Bottle Inn | *Amer.* 22
Tavern/Highlands | *Amer.* 22
Valley/Garrison | *Amer.* 23

GOSHEN

Bistro Lilly | *Amer.* -
Catherine's | *Amer.* 23
Il Tesoro | *Italian* 25

GREENWOOD LAKE
Jean Claude's | Dessert | 25

HAVERSTRAW
Antoine McGuire | French/Irish | 24
Union | Amer./Pan-Latin | 24

HIGH FALLS
Egg's Nest | Pub | 19
Northern Spy | Amer. | 18

HIGHLAND
Bistro/Commons | Amer. | -
Gunk Haus | German | 24
Would | Amer. | 22

HILLBURN
Mount Fuji | Japanese/Steak | 19

HILLSDALE
Swiss Hütte | Continental/Swiss | 21

HOPEWELL JUNCTION
Le Chambord Restaurant | Amer./Continental | -

HUDSON
Baba Louie's | Pizza | 24
NEW Cafe Le Perche | French | -
Ca'Mea | Italian | 22
DABA | Amer./Scan. | 21
Earth Foods | Eclectic | 21
Le Gamin | French | 19
Mexican Radio | Mex. | 18
NEW MOD | Amer. | -
(P.M.) Wine Bar | Spanish | -
Red Dot | Eclectic | 17
Swoon | Amer. | 24
Tanzy's | Amer. | 17
Vico | Italian | 19
Wasabi | Japanese | 18

HYDE PARK
Z American Bounty | Amer. | 26
Z Apple Pie | Bakery/Sandwiches | 26
Z Caterina/Medici | Italian | 27
Z Escoffier | French | 27
Eveready Diner | Diner | 20
Z St. Andrew's | Amer. | 25
NEW 2Taste | Amer. | -

KINGSTON
Armadillo B&G | SW | 25
Boitson's | Amer. | -
Elephant | Spanish | 24
Frank Guido's | Italian | 21
Hickory BBQ | BBQ | 18
Hoffman Hse. | Continental | 23
Kyoto Sushi | Japanese | 21
Le Canard | French | 23
NEW Mario's Tratt. | Italian | -
Savona's Trattoria | Italian | 19
Ship to Shore | Amer. | 22
Yum Yum | Asian | 19

LAGRANGEVILLE
Amedeos | Pizza | 21
Daily Planet | Diner | 17

LAKE MAHOPAC
Marco | Amer. | 21

MABBETTSVILLE
When Pigs Fly | BBQ | 21

MAHOPAC
Holy Smoke | BBQ | 22
NEW Ramiro's 954 Latin Bistro | Nuevo Latino | -

MARLBORO
Raccoon Saloon | Pub | 21

MIDDLETOWN
Blue Finn | Asian | 21
Cosimo's Brick | Italian | 20
Nina | Eclectic | 25
Saffron | Indian | 19

MILAN
Another Fork | Amer. | 22

MILLBROOK
Aurelia | Med. | 19
Babette's Kitchen | Amer. | 20
Café Les Baux | French | 24
Charlotte's | Euro. | 21

MILLERTON
Harney/Sons | Tea | 21
Irving Farm | Coffee/Sandwiches | 19
Manna Dew | Eclectic | 22

Z No. 9 | *Amer.* 27

Oakhurst Diner | *Diner* 16

Taro's | *Italian/Pizza* 19

MILTON

Henry's/Buttermilk | *Amer.* –

Z Ship Lantern | 26
Amer./Continental

MONROE

NEW Rambler's Rest | *Irish* –

Tre Angelina | *Italian* 21

MONTGOMERY

Z Back Yard | *Amer.* 26

Camillo's | *Amer.* 18

Ward's Bridge | *Amer.* 19

Wildfire Grill | *Eclectic* 19

MT. TREMPER

Catamount | *Amer.* 17

Catskill Rose | *Amer.* –

La Duchesse | *French* 19

Phoenix | *Amer.* –

NANUET

Nanuet Hotel | *Italian* 21

NAPANOCH

White Wolf | *Amer.* –

NEWBURGH

Caffé Macchiato | *Italian* –

Cena 2000 | *Italian* 23

Cosimo's Brick | *Italian* 20

Z Il Cenàcolo | *Italian* 28

Lakeview Hse. | *Eclectic* 21

Machu Picchu | *Peruvian* –

River Grill | *Amer.* 20

Torches/Hudson | *Amer.* 17

Wherehouse | *Amer.* –

Yobo | *Asian* 21

NEW CITY

CB Kitchen Bar | *Southern* –

Z Wasabi/Grill | *Japanese* 26

NEW PALTZ

NEW A Tavola | *Italian* –

Gadaleto's | *Seafood* 21

Gilded Otter | *Pub* 16

Gomen-Kudasai | –
Japanese/Noodles

Grimaldi's | *Pizza* 21

Harvest Café | *Amer.* 23

Hokkaido | *Japanese* 27

La Stazione | *Italian* 21

Main Course | *Amer.* 25

Mohonk Mtn. Hse. | *Amer.* 18

Neko Sushi | *Japanese* 21

NEW Rock and Rye | *Amer.* –

36 Main | *Amer.* 23

Village Tea. | *Amer.* 25

NEW WINDSOR

Schlesinger's | *Steak* 23

NYACK

NEW Alain's | *French* –

Café Barcel | *Amer.* 25

Hudson Hse. Nyack | *Amer.* 23

King & I | *Thai* 17

Lanterna Tuscan | *Italian* 24

Murasaki | *Japanese* 22

Reality Bites | *Eclectic* 20

River Club | *Amer.* 14

Temptations Cafe | *Eclectic* 16

Thai Hse. | *Thai* 23

Two Spear St. | *Amer.* 22

Velo | *Amer.* 24

Z Wasabi/Grill | *Japanese* 26

ORANGEBURG

Thai Garden | *Thai* 22

PATTERSON

Abruzzi Tratt. | *Italian* 21

NEW Thai Elephant | *Thai* –

PAWLING

Corner Bakery | *Bakery* 23

Z McKinney/Doyle | *Amer.* 25

PEARL RIVER

Louie's/Ave. | *Amer./Steak* 21

Quinta Steak | *Portug./Steak* 21

PHILMONT

Local 111 | *Amer.* 23

NEW Vanderbilt House –
Restaurant | *Amer.*

PHOENICIA

Sweet Sue's | *Amer.* — 24

PIERMONT

Cafe Portofino | *Italian* — 23
Z Freelance Cafe | *Amer.* — 28
Sidewalk Bistro | *French* — 20
Z Xaviars | *Amer.* — 28

PINE BUSH

Culinary Creations | *Bakery/Eclectic* — -
Oriental Hse. | — -
  Japanese/Korean

PINE PLAINS

Agriturismo | *Italian* — 23
Stissing Hse. | *French/Italian* — 20

POMONA

Mt. Ivy Cafe | *Continental* — 18

POUGHKEEPSIE

Z Artist's Palate | *Amer.* — 26
Babycakes Cafe | *Amer.* — -
Bacco | *Italian* — 21
Beech Tree Grill | *Amer.* — 22
NEW Brasserie 292 | *French* — -
Bull & Buddha | *Asian* — 19
Cosimo's Tratt. | *Italian* — 19
Crave | *Amer.* — 25
Crew | *Eclectic* — 22
NEW Karma Lounge | *Amer.* — -
NEW Le Express | *French* — -
Melting Pot | *Fondue* — 17
Mill House Panda | *Chinese* — 19
Saigon Café | *Viet.* — 23
Shadows | *Amer.* — 17
Z Soul Dog | *Hot Dogs* — 23
Twisted Soul | *Eclectic* — 24

POUGHQUAG

NEW Rambler's Rest | *Irish* — -

RED HOOK

Flatiron | *Amer./Steak* — 23
Max's Memphis | *BBQ* — 21
Me-Oh-My | *Amer.* — 25
Mercato | *Italian* — 25
Painted Bistro | *Eclectic* — 18
Red Hook Curry | *Indian* — 21

RHINEBECK

Arielle | *Med.* — 22
Aroi Thai | *Thai* — 22
Bread Alone | *Bakery/Coffee* — 22
Calico | *Amer./Eclectic* — 25
NEW Cinnamon | *Indian* — -
Francesca's | *Italian/Pizza* — 21
Gaby's Cafe | *Mex.* — -
Z Gigi Tratt. | *Italian/Med.* — 24
Le Petit Bistro | *French* — 25
NEW Liberty Public | *Amer.* — -
Local | *Amer.* — -
Mill House Panda | *Chinese* — 19
Momiji | *Japanese* — 24
Osaka | *Japanese* — 22
Puccini | *Italian* — -
Tavern/Beekman | *Amer.* — 20
Z Terrapin | *Amer.* — 24

RHINECLIFF

China Rose | *Chinese* — 21
Rhinecliff Hotel Bar | *Euro.* — 19

ROSENDALE

Bywater | *Amer.* — 23
Red Brick Tav. | *Amer.* — 20
Rosendale Cafe | *Veg.* — 15

SALT POINT

La Puerta Azul | *Mex.* — 23

SAUGERTIES

Café Mezzaluna | *Eclectic* — 23
Cafe Tamayo | *Amer.* — 25
Dutch Ale | *Amer.* — -
Miss Lucy's | *Amer.* — 22
New World | *Amer./Eclectic* — 22
Red Onion | *Amer.* — 23
NEW Tavern/Diamond | *Amer.* — -

SPARKILL

Woody's Parkside | *Eclectic* — 19

STAATSBURG

Belvedere | *Amer.* — 20
Portofino Rist. | *Italian* — 23

STANFORDVILLE

NEW Bangall Whaling | *Amer.* — -

STONE RIDGE

Inn/Stone Ridge | *Amer.* — 21
Momiji | *Japanese* — 24

STONY POINT

Pasta Cucina | *Italian* — 18

SUFFERN

Z Marcello's | *Italian* — 26
Pasta Cucina | *Italian* — 18
Priya | *Indian* — 19

TANNERSVILLE

Last Chance | *Amer.* — 22
Maggie's Krooked | *Amer.* — -

TAPPAN

Commissary | *Amer.* — -
Giulio's/Harvest | *Italian* — -
Il Portico | *Italian* — 23
Old '76 House | *Amer.* — 18

TILLSON

NEW Toad Holly | *Amer.* — -

TIVOLI

Luna 61 | *Eclectic/Veg.* — 20
Madalin's Table | *Amer.* — 19
Osaka | *Japanese* — 22
NEW Panzur | *Spanish* — -
Santa Fe | *Mex.* — 22

WALLKILL

Bruynswyck Inn | *Amer./Continental* — -

WAPPINGERS FALLS

Z Aroma Osteria | *Italian* — 26
Cafe Maya/Maya | *Mex.* — 22
Neko Sushi | *Japanese* — 21

WARWICK

Chateau Hathorn | *Continental* — 23
Iron Forge Inn | *Amer.* — 24
Jean Claude's | *Dessert* — 25
Landmark Inn | *Amer.* — 20

WASHINGTONVILLE

Vinum Cafe | *Amer.* — -

WEST HAVERSTRAW

Hudson Water | *Amer.* — 18

WEST NYACK

Z Cheesecake Fac. | *Amer.* — 17

WEST PARK

Global Palate | *Eclectic* — 26

WINDHAM

Bistro Brie | *French* — 21

WINGDALE

Z Big W's | *BBQ* — 26
Lodge | *Amer.* — -

WOODRIDGE

Tony's | *Eclectic* — -

WOODSTOCK

(Including Bearsville)
Bear Cafe | *Amer.* — 24
Bread Alone | *Bakery/Coffee* — 22
Cucina | *Italian* — 25
Garden Café | *Veg.* — 26
Gypsy Wolf | *Mex.* — 19
Oriole 9 | *Euro.* — 20
Violette | *Amer.* — 20
Yum Yum | *Asian* — 19

Connecticut

DANBURY

Bertucci's | *Italian* — 16
Café/Green | *Italian* — 22
Chuck's Steak | *Steak* — 18
Z Frank Pepe | *Pizza* — 24
Koo | *Japanese* — 23
NEW Mezon | *Spanish* — -
Z Ondine | *French* — 26
Outback Steak | *Steak* — 17
Sesame Seed | *Mideast.* — 21

DARIEN

Aux Délices | *Amer./French* — 24
Bertucci's | *Italian* — 16
Burgers/Shakes | *Burgers* — 22
Café d'Azur | *Med.* — -
Ching's/Wild Ginger | *Asian* — 24
Chuck's Steak | *Steak* — 18
Z Coromandel | *Indian* — 25
NEW Darien Social | *Amer.* — -
Goose | *Amer.* — -

Little Thai/Buddha	*Thai*	23	Pastorale	*French*	23
Melting Pot	*Fondue*	17	Woodland	*Amer./Continental*	22
Post Corner Pizza	*Pizza*	20		
Tengda	*Asian*	22		

GEORGETOWN

Olive Mkt.	*Spanish*	24

GREENWICH

Abis	*Japanese*	19
Asiana Cafe	*Asian*	21
Aux Délices	*Amer./French*	24
Bambou	*Asian*	21
Barcelona	*Spanish*	24
Boxcar Cantina	*SW*	21
Burgers/Shakes	*Burgers*	22
Centro	*Italian/Med.*	20
NEW China White	*Chinese*	-
Così	*Sandwiches*	16
Douro	*Portug.*	-
Elm St. Oyster	*Seafood*	24
Gabriele's	*Italian/Steak*	-
Ginger Man	*Pub*	18
Z Jean-Louis	*French*	28
L'Escale	*French*	23
Little Thai/Buddha	*Thai*	23
Lolita	*Mex.*	22
Mediterraneo	*Med.*	21
Meli-Melo	*French*	25
Morello	*Italian*	22
Pasta Vera	*Italian*	20
Penang Grill	*Asian*	22
Polpo	*Italian*	24
Z Rebeccas	*Amer.*	26
Tengda	*Asian*	22
Terra Rist.	*Italian*	23
Z Thomas Henkelmann	*French*	28
Versailles	*Bakery/French*	24

KENT

Bull's Bridge	*Amer.*	16
Doc's Tratt.	*Italian*	19
Fife 'n Drum	*Amer.*	18
Millstone Café	*Amer.*	-

LAKEVILLE

Boathouse	*Amer.*	17
Cafe Giulia	*Italian*	22

LITCHFIELD

@ the Corner	*Amer.*	20
DaCapo Italiano Ristorante	*Italian*	19
Litchfield Saltwater	*Amer./Seafood*	20
Village	*Pub*	20
West St. Grill	*Amer.*	24
Winvian	*Amer.*	27

NEW CANAAN

Bistro Bonne Nuit	*French*	25
Cava Wine	*Italian*	22
Chef Luis	*Amer.*	25
Ching's/Wild Ginger	*Asian*	24
NEW Elm	*Amer.*	-
Gates	*Calif./Med.*	19
Z Harvest Supper	*Amer.*	27
Pine Social	*Amer.*	23
Plum Tree	*Japanese*	20
Roger Sherman	*Continental*	24
Solé Rist.	*Italian*	21
Tequila Mock.	*Mex.*	18
Thali	*Indian*	24

NEW MILFORD

Adrienne	*Amer.*	25
Bank St. Tavern	*Eclectic*	18
Clamp's	*Burgers*	-
Cookhouse	*BBQ*	22
59 Bank	*Amer.*	19
Salsa	*SW*	25

NEW PRESTON

Oliva Cafe	*Med.*	24
White Horse	*Pub*	19

NORFOLK

Infinity Hall/Bistro	*Amer.*	20

OLD GREENWICH

Beach Hse. Café	*Amer.*	18
Greenwich Tav.	*Amer.*	21
Mackenzie's	*Pub*	16
Osteria Applausi	*Italian*	24
NEW RéNapoli	*Pizza*	-

RIDGEFIELD

Bailey's	*Amer.*	21
Z Bernard's	*French*	27

Fifty Coins | *Amer.* 16
Little Pub | *Pub* 23
Luc's Café | *French* 24
Sagi | *Italian* 23
Southwest Cafe | *New Mex.* 22
Stonehenge | *Continental* 22
Thali | *Indian* 24
Toscana | *Italian* 22

RIVERSIDE

Aux Délices | *Amer./French* 24
Baang Cafe | *Asian* 23
Valbella | *Italian* 25

SALISBURY

Chaiwalla | *Tea* 25
Country Bistro | *Amer./French* -

SHERMAN

American Pie | *Amer.* 22
Arrivederci | *Italian* -

STAMFORD

Barcelona | *Spanish* 24
Bar Rosso | *Italian* -
Bartaco | *Mex.* -
Boatyard/Smokey Joe's | *BBQ/Seafood* 19
Bobby Valentine | *Amer.* 15
Brasitas | *Pan-Latin* 25
🄑 Cafe Silvium | *Italian* 26
California Pizza | *Pizza* 17
Capital Grille | *Steak* 25
Chez Jean-Pierre | *French* 24
🄑 City Limits | *Diner* 19
Colony Grill | *Pizza* 24
Columbus Park | *Italian* 25
🄑 Coromandel | *Indian* 25
Così | *Sandwiches* 16
Dragonfly | *Eclectic* 17
Eclisse | *Italian* 21
Eos Greek | *Greek* 24
Ferrante | *Italian* 20
Fez | *Med./Moroccan* 20

Fin/Fin II | *Japanese* 23
Kit's Thai | *Thai* 21
Kona Grill | *Amer./Asian* 17
Kotobuki | *Japanese* 24
Kujaku | *Japanese* 18
La Bretagne | *French* 24
Layla's Falafel | *Lebanese* 22
Little Thai/Buddha | *Thai* 23
Long Ridge Tav. | *Amer.* 14
Lucky's | *Diner* 18
Madonia | *Italian* -
Mary Ann's | *Tex-Mex* 15
Morton's | *Steak* 24
Napa & Co. | *Amer.* 24
Olé Molé | *Mex.* 19
Pellicci's | *Italian* 19
P.F. Chang's | *Chinese* 18
Quattro Pazzi | *Italian* 23
🆕 Rizzuto's | *Italian* 20
Siena | *Italian* 23
Southport Brew. | *Pub* 16
Tabouli Grill | *Med.* -
Tappo | *Italian* -
🄑 Tawa | *Indian* 27
Tengda | *Asian* 22
Vinny's | *Pizza/Pub* 20
🆕 ZaZa | *Italian* -

WARREN

Hopkins Inn | *Austrian/Continental* 19

WASHINGTON

Community Table | *Amer.* 27
G.W. Tavern | *Amer.* 20
Mayflower Inn | *Amer.* 24
Norimaki | *Japanese* -
Pantry | *Amer.* 24

WILTON

🆕 Cactus Rose | *SW* -
🄑 Luca Rist. | *Italian* 26
Orem's Diner | *Diner* 15
Outback Steak | *Steak* 17
🄑 Schoolhouse | *Amer.* 27

Special Features

Listings cover the best in each category and include names, locations and Food ratings. Multi-location restaurants' features may vary by branch.

ADDITIONS

(Properties added since the last edition of the book)

Alain's | **Nyack** ⌐⌐
Arrivederci | **Sherman** ⌐⌐
A Tavola | **New Paltz** ⌐⌐
Babycakes Cafe | **Poughkp** ⌐⌐
Bangall Whaling | **Stanfordville** ⌐⌐
Bistro Latino | **Tuck** ⌐⌐
Bosphorus | **Hartsdale** ⌐⌐
Brasserie 292 | **Poughkp** ⌐⌐
Bruynswyck Inn | **Wallkill** ⌐⌐
Burrata | **Eastchester** ⌐⌐
Byrne & Hanrahan | **Yonkers** ⌐⌐
Cactus Rose | **Wilton** ⌐⌐
Cafe Le Perche | **Hudson** ⌐⌐
Cedar St. | **Dobbs Ferry** ⌐⌐
China White | **multi.** ⌐⌐
Cinnamon | **Rhinebeck** ⌐⌐
Club Car | **Mamaro** ⌐⌐
Coals | **Port Chester** ⌐⌐
Comfort | **Hastings/Hud** ⌐⌐
Craftsman Ale | **Harrison** ⌐⌐
Darien Social | **Darien** ⌐⌐
Don Tommaso's | **Yorktown Hts** ⌐⌐
Dutch Ale | **Saugerties** ⌐⌐
Elm | **New Canaan** ⌐⌐
Farm to Table | **Fishkill** ⌐⌐
Growlers | **Tuck** ⌐⌐
Hash-O-Nash | **Mamaro** ⌐⌐
Hudson | **Briarcliff Manor** ⌐⌐
Hudson Hil's | **Cold Spring** ⌐⌐
Impulse Hibachi | **White Pl** ⌐⌐
Ionian | **New Roch** ⌐⌐
Karma Lounge | **Poughkp** ⌐⌐
KYO Sushi | **Hartsdale** ⌐⌐
La Bella Havana | **Yonkers** ⌐⌐
Le Express | **Poughkp** ⌐⌐
Liberty Public | **Rhinebeck** ⌐⌐
Local/Ice Cream | **Chappaqua** ⌐⌐
Lodge | **Wingdale** ⌐⌐
Machu Picchu | **Newburgh** ⌐⌐
Madonia | **Stamford** ⌐⌐
Mario's Tratt. | **Kingston** ⌐⌐

Mezon | **Danbury** ⌐⌐
Mint Premium | **Tarrytown** ⌐⌐
MOD | **Hudson** ⌐⌐
Mythos | **Thornwood** ⌐⌐
Nemea | **Mamaro** ⌐⌐
NoMa Social | **New Roch** ⌐⌐
Panzur | **Tivoli** ⌐⌐
Park 143 | **Bronxville** ⌐⌐
Polpettina | **Eastchester** ⌐⌐
Pranzi | **White Pl** ⌐⌐
Rambler's Rest | **multi.** ⌐⌐
Ramiro's 954 Latin Bistro | **Mahopac** ⌐⌐
RéNapoli | **Old Greenwich** ⌐⌐
Rock and Rye | **New Paltz** ⌐⌐
Salsa Fresca | **Bedford Hills** ⌐⌐
Siete Ocho Siete | **New Roch** ⌐⌐
Sofrito | **White Pl** ⌐⌐
Stony Brae | **Cragsmoor** ⌐⌐
Tabouli Grill | **Stamford** ⌐⌐
Taste | **Buchanan** ⌐⌐
Tavern/Diamond | **Saugerties** ⌐⌐
Tavern/Gunk | **Ellenville** ⌐⌐
Texas de Brazil | **Yonkers** ⌐⌐
Thai Elephant | **Patterson** ⌐⌐
Thornwood Ale | **Thornwood** ⌐⌐
Toad Holly | **Tillson** ⌐⌐
2Taste | **Hyde Pk** ⌐⌐
Umami Sushi | **Ardsley** ⌐⌐
Vanderbilt House Restaurant | **Philmont** ⌐⌐
Vintage 1891 | **Larch** ⌐⌐
Vinum Cafe | **Washingtonville** ⌐⌐
Yard House | **Yonkers** ⌐⌐
ZaZa | **Stamford** ⌐⌐

BREAKFAST

(See also Hotel Dining)

American Pie | **Sherman** 22
Another Fork | **Milan** 22
☑ Apple Pie | **Hyde Pk** 26
Aux Délices | **multi.** 24
Babette's Kitchen | **Millbrook** 20
Babycakes Cafe | **Poughkp** ⌐⌐
Bread Alone | **multi.** 22

NEW Cafe Le Perche | **Hudson** ⏌
Cafe Mio | **Gardiner** ⏌
Cafe Mozart | **Mamaro** 17⏌
Calico | **Rhinebeck** 25⏌
Z City Limits | **White Pl** 19⏌
Corner Bakery | **Pawling** 23⏌
Così | **multi.** 16⏌
Z Equus | **Tarrytown** 25⏌
Garden Café | **Woodstock** 26⏌
Grandma's | **Yorktown Hts** 15⏌
NEW Hudson Hil's | **Cold Spring** ⏌
Hudson St. | **Cornwall/Hud** ⏌
Irving Farm | **Millerton** 19⏌
Karamba | **White Pl** 22⏌
Le Jardin du Roi | **Chappaqua** 21⏌
Maggie's Krooked | **Tanners** ⏌
Meli-Melo | **Greenwich** 25⏌
Oakhurst Diner | **Millerton** 16⏌
Orem's Diner | **Wilton** 15⏌
Pantry | **Wash Depot** 24⏌
Ruby's Oyster | **Rye** 23⏌
Sweet Sue's | **Phoenicia** 24⏌
Tanzy's | **Hudson** 17⏌
Versailles | **Greenwich** 24⏌
Village Tea. | **New Paltz** 25⏌
Wobble Café | **Ossining** 21⏌

BRUNCH

Z Arch | **Brewster** 27⏌
Z Bedford Post/Barn | **Bedford** 23⏌
Beech Tree Grill | **Poughkp** 22⏌
Beehive | **Armonk** 21⏌
Z Bernard's | **Ridgefield** 27⏌
NEW Bistro Latino | **Tuck** ⏌
NEW Cafe Le Perche | **Hudson** ⏌
Calico | **Rhinebeck** 25⏌
Cathryn's | **Cold Spring** 23⏌
NEW Cedar St. | **Dobbs Ferry** ⏌
Z Chiboust | **Tarrytown** 24⏌
Z City Limits | **White Pl** 19⏌
Z Crabtree's | **Chappaqua** 25⏌
Z Equus | **Tarrytown** 25⏌
Fig & Olive | **Scarsdale** ⏌
Gates | **New Canaan** 19⏌
Harper's | **Dobbs Ferry** ⏌
Jaipore Indian | **Brewster** 23⏌
Juniper | **Hastings/Hud** ⏌
La Duchesse | **Mt. Tremper** 19⏌

Lanterna Tuscan | **Nyack** 24⏌
Le Canard | **Kingston** 23⏌
Z Le Provençal | **Mamaro** 23⏌
Local 111 | **Philmont** 23⏌
Maggie's Krooked | **Tanners** ⏌
Main Course | **New Paltz** 25⏌
Z McKinney/Doyle | **Pawling** 25⏌
Miss Lucy's | **Saugerties** 22⏌
Z Moderne Barn | **Armonk** 22⏌
Nina | **Middletown** 25⏌
Z Rest. X/Bully | **Congers** 27⏌
River Grill | **Newburgh** 20⏌
Roger Sherman | **New Canaan** 24⏌
Ruby's Oyster | **Rye** 23⏌
Tap House | **Tuck** 20⏌
NEW Tavern/Diamond | ⏌
   Saugerties
Tavern/Beekman | **Rhinebeck** 20⏌
Underhills | **Bronxville** 21⏌
Violette | **Woodstock** 20⏌
Watercolor Cafe | **Larch** 18⏌
Wobble Café | **Ossining** 21⏌
Z X2O Xaviars | **Yonkers** 27⏌

BUFFET

(Check availability)
Abis | **multi.** 19⏌
Bistro Z | **Tarrytown** 20⏌
Bollywood | **P'ville** 20⏌
NEW Cinnamon | **Rhinebeck** ⏌
Z Coromandel | **multi.** 25⏌
80 West | **White Pl** 19⏌
Garden Café | **Woodstock** 26⏌
India Hse. | **Montrose** 22⏌
Jaipore Indian | **Brewster** 23⏌
Malabar Hill | **Elmsford** 21⏌
Mohonk Mtn. Hse. | **New Paltz** 18⏌
Mount Fuji | **Hillburn** 19⏌
Mughal Palace | **Valhalla** 25⏌
Rani Mahal | **Mamaro** 23⏌
Red Hook Curry | **Red Hook** 21⏌
Royal Palace | **White Pl** 20⏌
Saffron | **Middletown** 19⏌
Schlesinger's | **New Windsor** 23⏌
NEW Siete Ocho Siete | ⏌
   New Roch
Z Spadaro | **New Roch** 26⏌
Spice Vill. | **Tuck** 22⏌
Sunset Cove | **Tarrytown** 16⏌

Swaddee Hse. | **Thornwood** 21
Tandoori Taste | **Port Chester** 21
Tanjore | **Fishkill** 25
NEW Texas de Brazil | **Yonkers** -
Thali | **Ridgefield** 24
Torches/Hudson | **Newburgh** 17

BUSINESS DINING

Alba's | **Port Chester** 23
Arrivederci | **Sherman** -
Z Artist's Palate | **Poughkp** 26
Z Bedford Post/Farm | **Bedford** 25
Benjamin Steak | **White Pl** 24
Bird & Bottle Inn | **Garrison** 22
Bistro Z | **Tarrytown** 20
Z BLT Steak | **White Pl** 23
Bull & Buddha | **Poughkp** 19
Caffé Azzurri | **Hartsdale** 22
Capital Grille | **Stamford** 25
Centro | **Greenwich** 20
Chez Jean-Pierre | **Stamford** 24
Chutney | **Irvington** 23
Crave | **Poughkp** 25
Cucina | **Woodstock** 25
NEW Darien Social | **Darien** -
Division St. Grill | **Peekskill** 20
Dolphin | **Yonkers** 21
80 West | **White Pl** 19
Elm St. Oyster | **Greenwich** 24
Z Equus | **Tarrytown** 25
Ferrante | **Stamford** 20
Z 42 | **White Pl** 22
Gabriele's | **Greenwich** -
Z Glenmere | **Chester** 24
Goose | **Darien** -
Graziella's | **White Pl** 19
Z Haiku | **multi.** 22
Half Moon | **Dobbs Ferry** 19
Harrys/Hartsdale | **Hartsdale** 20
Z Harvest/Hudson | 22
   Hastings/Hud
Z Il Barilotto | **Fishkill** 27
Il Castello | **Mamaro** 24
Il Portico | **Tappan** 23
Il Sogno | **Port Chester** 24
Inn/Stone Ridge | **Stone Ridge** 21
Z Jean-Louis | **Greenwich** 28
Kotobuki | **Stamford** 24

La Bocca | **White Pl** 23
La Bretagne | **Stamford** 24
Z La Panetière | **Rye** 27
Le Canard | **Kingston** 23
Z Le Château | **S Salem** 25
Z Lusardi's | **Larch** 24
Madonia | **Stamford** -
Marc Charles | **Armonk** 20
NEW Mario's Tratt. | **Kingston** -
NEW Mezon | **Danbury** -
Milonga | **N White Plains** 22
Z Moderne Barn | **Armonk** 22
Morton's | **Stamford** 24
Z Mulino's | **White Pl** 24
Osteria Applausi | **Old Greenwich** 24
Pinocchio | **Eastchester** 21
NEW Pranzi | **White Pl** -
Z Rest. X/Bully | **Congers** 27
River Grill | **Newburgh** 20
Ruth's Chris | **Tarrytown** 25
Sammy's | **Bronxville** 22
Z Sapore | **Fishkill** 26
Swoon | **Hudson** 24
Z Tarry Lodge | **Port Chester** 24
NEW Tavern/Diamond | -
   Saugerties
Z Thomas Henkelmann | 28
   Greenwich
Tramonto | **Hawthorne** 19
Trinity Grill | **Harrison** 20
TuttaBella | **Scarsdale** 23
Union | **Haverstraw** 24
Valbella | **Riverside** 25
Valley/Garrison | **Garrison** 23
Waters Edge | **Darien** 19
Willett House | **Port Chester** 24
Z X2O Xaviars | **Yonkers** 27
NEW ZaZa | **Stamford** -

BYO

Abis | **Greenwich** 19
Aroi Thai | **Rhinebeck** 22
Beach Hse. Café | 18
   Old Greenwich
Z Big W's | **Wingdale** 26
Brasitas | **Stamford** 25
Burgers/Shakes | **Greenwich** 22
Café Amarcord | **Beacon** 24
Cafe Giulia | **Lakeville** 22

Camillo's | **Montgomery**	18
Capital Grille | **Stamford**	25
Community Table | **Washington**	27
Conte's Fishmkt. | **Mt. Kisco**	22
Copacabana | **Port Chester**	21
⨿ Coromandel | **multi.**	25
⨿ Crabtree's | **Chappaqua**	25
DABA | **Hudson**	21
David Chen | **Armonk**	18
Division St. Grill | **Peekskill**	20
Docas | **Ossining**	21
Dolphin | **Yonkers**	21
NEW Don Tommaso's | **Yorktown Hts**	–
D Thai | **Thornwood**	–
Elephant | **Kingston**	24
Elia Taverna | **Bronxville**	23
Elm St. Oyster | **Greenwich**	24
Emilio Rist. | **Harrison**	25
Encore Bistro | **Larch**	23
⨿ Equus | **Tarrytown**	25
⨿ Escoffier | **Hyde Pk**	27
España | **Larch**	20
Gaby's Cafe | **Rhinebeck**	–
Hudson St. | **Cornwall/Hud**	–
Isamu | **Beacon**	25
Jean Claude's | **Warwick**	25
Julianna's | **Cortlandt Man**	24
Juniper | **Hastings/Hud**	–
Kira | **Armonk**	23
⨿ Le Château | **S Salem**	25
Litchfield Saltwater | **Litchfield**	20
Little Kabab | **Mt. Kisco**	–
Little Thai/Buddha | **multi.**	23
Local 111 | **Philmont**	23
NEW Local/Ice Cream | **Chappaqua**	–
Maggie's Krooked | **Tanners**	–
Masala Kraft | **Hartsdale**	22
Meli-Melo | **Greenwich**	25
Morgans Fish | **Rye**	21
Murasaki | **Nyack**	22
Napa & Co. | **Stamford**	24
Nino's | **Bedford Hills**	21
⨿ Ocean Hse. | **Croton/Hud**	27
Olé Molé | **Stamford**	19
Opus 465 | **Armonk**	18
Pagoda | **Scarsdale**	17

Pascal's | **Larch**	23
Passage to India | **Mt. Kisco**	22
Peekamoose | **Big Indian**	24
Penang Grill | **Greenwich**	22
Peppino's | **Katonah**	20
Peter Pratt's | **Yorktown**	25
Phoenix | **Mt. Tremper**	–
Piatto Grill | **Yorktown Hts**	20
Piero's | **Port Chester**	24
⨿ Plates | **Larch**	25
Q Rest. | **Port Chester**	22
⨿ Red Hat | **Irvington**	23
Red Hook Curry | **Red Hook**	21
Red Plum | **Mamaro**	21
NEW RéNapoli | **Old Greenwich**	–
Rigatoni | **Pelham**	21
River City Grille | **Irvington**	19
Rue/Crêpes | **Harrison**	19
Ship to Shore | **Kingston**	22
Shiraz | **Elmsford**	20
Solé Rist. | **New Canaan**	21
Temptations Cafe | **Nyack**	16
Ten Twenty Post | **Darien**	21
Thai Angels | **Mt. Kisco**	21
Thai Golden | **Carmel**	23
Tomatillo | **Dobbs Ferry**	22
Tombolino's | **Yonkers**	23
Tony's | **Woodridge**	–
Toscana | **Ridgefield**	22
Turkish Cuisine | **White Pl**	21
Turkish Meze | **Mamaro**	23
Twisted Soul | **Poughkp**	24
Ümami Café | **Croton/Hud**	21
Underhills | **Bronxville**	21
Valentina's | **Carmel**	–
Velo | **Nyack**	24
Village | **Litchfield**	20
Village Tea. | **New Paltz**	25
Vox | **N Salem**	21
West St. Grill | **Litchfield**	24
Willett House | **Port Chester**	24
Winvian | **Litchfield**	27
Wobble Café | **Ossining**	21
Woodland | **Lakeville**	22
⨿ Xaviars | **Piermont**	28
⨿ X2O Xaviars | **Yonkers**	27
⨿ Zephs' | **Peekskill**	25

CATERING

🔲 An American Bistro	**Tuck**	23
Aroma Thyme	**Ellenville**	23
Aux Délices	**multi.**	24
🔲 Bernard's	**Ridgefield**	27
Cafe Mirage	**Port Chester**	22
Cathryn's	**Cold Spring**	23
Cena 2000	**Newburgh**	23
🔲 Coromandel	**New Roch**	25
🔲 Crabtree's	**Chappaqua**	25
Damon Baehrel	**Earlton**	29
🔲 Eastchester Fish	**Scarsdale**	25
🔲 Equus	**Tarrytown**	25
🔲 Freelance Cafe	**Piermont**	28
Gadaleto's	**New Paltz**	21
🔲 Gigi Tratt.	**Rhinebeck**	24
Golden Rod	**New Roch**	18
🔲 Harvest/Hudson	**Hastings/Hud**	22
🔲 Il Barilotto	**Fishkill**	27
🔲 Il Cenàcolo	**Newburgh**	28
Il Tesoro	**Goshen**	25
Kira	**Armonk**	23
Koo	**Rye**	23
La Camelia	**Mt. Kisco**	23
La Fontanella	**Pelham**	24
Lanterna Tuscan	**Nyack**	24
Le Canard	**Kingston**	23
Main Course	**New Paltz**	25
Malabar Hill	**Elmsford**	21
🔲 Marcello's	**Suffern**	26
🔲 McKinney/Doyle	**Pawling**	25
Moscato	**Scarsdale**	23
Mughal Palace	**Valhalla**	25
New World	**Saugerties**	22
Nina	**Middletown**	25
Olé Molé	**Stamford**	19
Opus 465	**Armonk**	18
Pantry	**Wash Depot**	24
🔲 Plates	**Larch**	25
Portofino Rist.	**Staatsburg**	23
Q Rest.	**Port Chester**	22
🔲 Rest. X/Bully	**Congers**	27
River Grill	**Newburgh**	20
Riverview	**Cold Spring**	24
Santa Fe	**Tarrytown**	17
Ship to Shore	**Kingston**	22
🔲 Sonora	**Port Chester**	24

🔲 Sushi Mike's	**Dobbs Ferry**	26
Thali	**multi.**	24
Ümami Café	**Croton/Hud**	21
Underhills	**Bronxville**	21
Valley/Garrison	**Garrison**	23
Willett House	**Port Chester**	24
Would	**Highland**	22
🔲 Xaviars	**Piermont**	28

CHILD-FRIENDLY

(Alternatives to the usual fast-food places; * children's menu available)

Abatino's*	**N White Plains**	20
Abis*	**multi.**	19
American Pie*	**Sherman**	22
Armadillo B&G*	**Kingston**	25
Aroma Thyme*	**Ellenville**	23
Asiana Cafe	**Greenwich**	21
Baba Louie's*	**Hudson**	24
Bacio Tratt.	**Cross River**	23
🔲 Bagels & More	**Hartsdale**	21
Bailey's*	**Ridgefield**	21
Bear Cafe	**Woodstock**	24
Beehive*	**Armonk**	21
Bellizzi*	**multi.**	15
Bertucci's*	**multi.**	16
Blazer Pub	**Purdys**	22
Blue Dolphin	**Katonah**	23
Boxcar Cantina	**Greenwich**	21
Bread Alone	**multi.**	22
California Pizza*	**Scarsdale**	17
Centro*	**Greenwich**	20
Chat	**Larch**	18
🔲 Cheesecake Fac.*	**White Pl**	17
Chuck's Steak*	**multi.**	18
Ciao!	**Eastchester**	19
🔲 City Limits*	**multi.**	19
Corner Bakery	**Pawling**	23
Cosimo's Brick*	**multi.**	20
Cosimo's Tratt.*	**Poughkp**	19
Coyote Flaco*	**multi.**	23
David Chen	**Armonk**	18
DiNardo's*	**Pound Ridge**	19
Earth Foods	**Hudson**	21
East Harbor	**Yonkers**	21
Edo*	**Pelham**	20
Egg's Nest*	**High Falls**	19
Epstein's Deli*	**multi.**	19
Fifty Coins*	**Ridgefield**	16

Fuji Mtn.* | **Larch**	15
Gasho of Japan* | **Central Valley**	18
Gates* | **New Canaan**	19
Golden Rod | **New Roch**	18
Grandma's* | **Yorktown Hts**	15
Gus's Franklin Pk.* | **Harrison**	21
Hickory BBQ* | **Kingston**	18
Hunan Larchmont | **Larch**	17
Johnny's* | **Mt. Vernon**	25
Kit's Thai | **Stamford**	21
Legal Sea Foods* | **White Pl**	19
Lexington Sq. Café* | **Mt. Kisco**	21
Mango Café* | **Mt. Kisco**	18
Mary Ann's* | **Port Chester**	15
Meetinghouse* | **Bedford Vill**	20
Melting Pot* | **Darien**	17
Michael's Tavern* | **P'ville**	17
Modern Rest.* | **New Roch**	22
Mount Fuji* | **Hillburn**	19
New World* | **Saugerties**	22
Nino's | **S Salem**	20
Northern Spy* | **High Falls**	18
Okinawa* | **Mt. Kisco**	20
Olé Molé | **Stamford**	19
Orem's Diner* | **Wilton**	15
Painter's* | **Cornwall/Hud**	19
Pantry | **Wash Depot**	24
P.F. Chang's | **White Pl**	18
Portofino Pizza | **Goldens Br**	22
Q Rest.* | **Port Chester**	22
Ray's Cafe | **Larch**	19
River City Grille* | **Irvington**	19
Route 22* | **Armonk**	14
Rye Grill* | **Rye**	18
Santa Fe* | **Tivoli**	22
Sesame Seed | **Danbury**	21
Seven Woks | **Scarsdale**	18
Southport Brew.* | **Stamford**	16
Striped Bass* | **Tarrytown**	16
☒ Sushi Mike's | **Dobbs Ferry**	26
Sweet Sue's | **Phoenicia**	24
Temptations Cafe* | **Nyack**	16
Tequila Mock.* | **New Canaan**	18
Thai Garden | **Orangeburg**	22
Thali* | **multi.**	24
Tomatillo* | **Dobbs Ferry**	22
Town Dock Tavern* | **Rye**	19
Travelers* | **Ossining**	19

Turkish Meze* | **Mamaro**	23
Tuscan Oven | **Mt. Kisco**	20
Village Tea.* | **New Paltz**	25
Vinny's* | **Stamford**	20
Wobble Café* | **Ossining**	21

DANCING

Cafe Maya/Maya | **Wapp Falls**	22
Chat | **Larch**	18
Don Coqui | **New Roch**	23
Fez | **Stamford**	20
Mickey/Molly Spill. | **Eastchester**	15
Mohonk Mtn. Hse. | **New Paltz**	18
Mount Fuji | **Hillburn**	19
Schlesinger's | **New Windsor**	23
NEW Siete Ocho Siete | **New Roch**	-
Virgo's Sip N Soul Cafe | **Beacon**	-
ZaZa | **Scarsdale**	16

DELIVERY

Abatino's | **N White Plains**	20
Aux Délices | **multi.**	24
Bertucci's | **Darien**	16
Boatyard/Smokey Joe's | **Stamford**	19
Bobby Valentine | **Stamford**	15
Candlelight Inn | **Scarsdale**	22
Coyote Flaco | **multi.**	23
David Chen | **Armonk**	18
Epstein's Deli | **multi.**	19
Ginban Asian | **Mamaro**	23
Golden Rod | **New Roch**	18
☒ Haiku | **Cross River**	22
Imperial | **N White Plains**	17
Kit's Thai | **Stamford**	21
Kotobuki | **Stamford**	24
Kujaku | **Stamford**	18
☒ Lefteris Gyro | **Tarrytown**	21
Little Kabab | **Mt. Kisco**	-
Maggie's Krooked | **Tanners**	-
Modern Rest. | **New Roch**	22
Noda's Steak | **White Pl**	19
Pellicci's | **Stamford**	19
Polpo | **Greenwich**	24
Post Corner Pizza | **Darien**	20
Reality Bites | **Nyack**	20
Royal Palace | **White Pl**	20
NEW Salsa Fresca | **Bedford Hills**	-

EARLY-BIRD MENUS

Bull's Bridge | **Kent**	16
Casa Rina | **Thornwood**	18
Chuck's Steak | **Darien**	18
NEW Don Tommaso's | **Yorktown Hts**	-
Z Eastchester Fish | **Scarsdale**	25
Enzo's | **Mamaro**	20
Grande Centrale | **Congers**	19
Grandma's | **Yorktown Hts**	15
Le Canard | **Kingston**	23
Mt. Ivy Cafe | **Pomona**	18
Orissa | **Dobbs Ferry**	24
Pasta Cucina | **multi.**	18
Pas-Tina's | **Hartsdale**	19
Z Plates | **Larch**	25
Z Ship Lantern | **Milton**	26
Tony's | **Woodridge**	-
Zitoune | **Mamaro**	19

ENTERTAINMENT

(Call for days and times of performances)

Z Bernard's | varies | **Ridgefield**	27
Bobby Valentine | karaoke | **Stamford**	15
Café Mezzaluna | varies | **Saugerties**	23
Z Crabtree's | piano/vocals | **Chappaqua**	25
Division St. Grill | piano | **Peekskill**	20
Harrys/Hartsdale | cover bands | **Hartsdale**	20
Hudson Water | varies | **W Haverstraw**	18
Luc's Café | jazz | **Ridgefield**	24
New World | blues/rock | **Saugerties**	22
Opus 465 | bands | **Armonk**	18
Z Red Hat | jazz | **Irvington**	23
Rosendale Cafe | varies | **Rosendale**	15
Southport Brew. | varies | **Stamford**	16
Watercolor Cafe | live music | **Larch**	18
Whistling Willie's | varies | **Cold Spring**	19

FIREPLACES

Adrienne | **New Milford**	25
Alba's | **Port Chester**	23
Angelina's | **Tuck**	21
Z Arch | **Brewster**	27
Arrivederci | **Sherman**	-
NEW Bangall Whaling | **Stanfordville**	-
Bank St. Tavern | **New Milford**	18
Bear Cafe | **Woodstock**	24
Z Bedford Post/Barn | **Bedford**	23
Z Bedford Post/Farm | **Bedford**	25
Belvedere | **Staatsburg**	20
Benjamin Steak | **White Pl**	24
Z Bernard's | **Ridgefield**	27
Bird & Bottle Inn | **Garrison**	22
Z Blue Hill | **Poc Hills**	28
Boathouse | **Lakeville**	17
Boxcar Cantina | **Greenwich**	21
Briar's | **Briarcliff Manor**	17
Brothers Tratt. | **Beacon**	25
Bruynswyck Inn | **Wallkill**	-
Bull's Bridge | **Kent**	16
Bull's Head | **Campbell Hall**	18
Cabin | **Greenburgh**	15
NEW Cactus Rose | **Wilton**	-
NEW Cafe Le Perche | **Hudson**	-
Cafe Maya/Maya | **Fishkill**	22
Cafe Tamayo | **Saugerties**	25
Camillo's | **Montgomery**	18
Canterbury | **Cornwall/Hud**	23
Casa Rina | **Thornwood**	18
Catamount | **Mt. Tremper**	17
Z Caterina/Medici | **Hyde Pk**	27
NEW Cedar St. | **Dobbs Ferry**	-
Chaiwalla | **Salisbury**	25
Charlotte's | **Millbrook**	21
Chat | **Scarsdale**	18
Chateau Hathorn | **Warwick**	23
Chuck's Steak | **Danbury**	18
Coyote Flaco | **New Roch**	23
Z Crabtree's | **Chappaqua**	25
Cucina | **Woodstock**	25
Doc's Tratt. | **Kent**	19
Dolphin | **Yonkers**	21
Z Equus | **Tarrytown**	25
Fife 'n Drum | **Kent**	18
Frankie/Johnnie's | **Rye**	24
Friends & Family | **Accord**	22
Gabriele's | **Greenwich**	-
Ginger Man | **Greenwich**	18
Giulio's/Harvest | **Tappan**	-
Global Palate | **W Park**	26

Goose	**Darien**	–
G.W. Tavern	**Wash Depot**	20
Half Moon	**Dobbs Ferry**	19
☑ Harvest/Hudson	**Hastings/Hud**	22
Hickory BBQ	**Kingston**	18
Hoffman Hse.	**Kingston**	23
Hopkins Inn	**Warren**	19
Horse & Hound	**S Salem**	19
Hudson Hse. Inn	**Cold Spring**	22
Hudson's Ribs	**Fishkill**	19
Hudson Water	**W Haverstraw**	18
Inn/Stone Ridge	**Stone Ridge**	21
Iron Forge Inn	**Warwick**	24
Irving Farm	**Millerton**	19
La Camelia	**Mt. Kisco**	23
☑ La Crémaillère	**Bedford**	27
La Duchesse	**Mt. Tremper**	19
Landmark Inn	**Warwick**	20
Last Chance	**Tanners**	22
Le Bouchon	**Cold Spring**	21
☑ Le Château	**S Salem**	25
L'Escale	**Greenwich**	23
Litchfield Saltwater	**Litchfield**	20
Little Pub	**Ridgefield**	23
Lodge	**Wingdale**	–
Long Ridge Tav.	**Stamford**	14
Louie's/Ave.	**Pearl River**	21
☑ Lusardi's	**Larch**	24
Madonia	**Stamford**	–
Mamma Assunta	**Tuck**	20
Mayflower Inn	**Washington**	24
Mickey/Molly Spill.	**Eastchester**	15
Mill House Panda	**Poughkp**	19
Mohonk Mtn. Hse.	**New Paltz**	18
Northern Spy	**High Falls**	18
Olde Stone Mill	**Tuck**	17
Old '76 House	**Tappan**	18
Oliva Cafe	**New Preston**	24
☑ Ondine	**Danbury**	26
☑ 121 Rest.	**N Salem**	22
Painter's	**Cornwall/Hud**	19
Pasta Cucina	**Suffern**	18
Peekamoose	**Big Indian**	24
Peter Pratt's	**Yorktown**	25
Plumbush Inn	**Cold Spring**	21
Pond Rest.	**Ancramdale**	14
Porter Hse.	**White Pl**	19

Raccoon Saloon	**Marlboro**	21
NEW Rambler's Rest	**Monroe**	–
☑ Rest. X/Bully	**Congers**	27
Ristorante Lucia	**Bedford**	18
River Club	**Nyack**	14
NEW Rock and Rye	**New Paltz**	–
Roger Sherman	**New Canaan**	24
Rye Grill	**Rye**	18
☑ Serevan	**Amenia**	27
Shadows	**Poughkp**	17
☑ Ship Lantern	**Milton**	26
☑ St. Andrew's	**Hyde Pk**	25
NEW Stony Brae	**Cragsmoor**	–
Swiss Hütte	**Hillsdale**	21
Tap House	**Tuck**	20
NEW Tavern/Diamond	**Saugerties**	–
Tavern/Highlands	**Garrison**	22
Tavern/Beekman	**Rhinebeck**	20
NEW Thai Elephant	**Patterson**	–
☑ Thomas Henkelmann	**Greenwich**	28
Tombolino's	**Yonkers**	23
Town Dock Tavern	**Rye**	19
Traditions 118	**Somers**	21
Travelers	**Ossining**	19
Valbella	**Riverside**	25
Vico	**Hudson**	19
Violette	**Woodstock**	20
Ward's Bridge	**Montgomery**	19
White Horse	**New Preston**	19
Winvian	**Litchfield**	27
Would	**Highland**	22

GREEN/LOCAL/ ORGANIC

Agriturismo	**Pine Plains**	23
☑ American Bounty	**Hyde Pk**	26
Another Fork	**Milan**	22
Aroma Thyme	**Ellenville**	23
☑ Artist's Palate	**Poughkp**	26
☑ Back Yard	**Montgomery**	26
☑ Bedford Post/Barn	**Bedford**	23
☑ Bedford Post/Farm	**Bedford**	25
☑ Blue Hill	**Poc Hills**	28
Boxcar Cantina	**Greenwich**	21
Bread Alone	**multi.**	22
Cafe Mio	**Gardiner**	–
Café of Love	**Mt. Kisco**	22

Catskill Rose | **Mt. Tremper** -

NEW China White | **multi.** -

Z Crabtree's | **Chappaqua** 25

Damon Baehrel | **Earlton** 29

Earth Foods | **Hudson** 21

Elephant | **Kingston** 24

NEW Elm | **New Canaan** -

NEW Farm to Table | **Fishkill** -

Z Freelance Cafe | **Piermont** 28

Garden Café | **Woodstock** 26

Harper's | **Dobbs Ferry** -

Harvest Café | **New Paltz** 23

Z Harvest Supper | **New Canaan** 27

Haven | **P'ville** 24

Homespun | **Beacon** 28

NEW Hudson | **Briarcliff Manor** -

NEW Hudson Hil's | **Cold Spring** -

Hudson St. | **Cornwall/Hud** -

Z Iron Horse Grill | **P'ville** 27

Julianna's | **Cortlandt Man** 24

Local | **Rhinebeck** -

Local 111 | **Philmont** 23

NEW Local/Ice Cream | -
  Chappaqua

Luna 61 | **Tivoli** 20

Maggie's Krooked | **Tanners** -

Manna Dew | **Millerton** 22

Miss Lucy's | **Saugerties** 22

Napa & Co. | **Stamford** 24

New World | **Saugerties** 22

Northern Spy | **High Falls** 18

Oriole 9 | **Woodstock** 20

Peter Pratt's | **Yorktown** 25

Phoenix | **Mt. Tremper** -

NEW Polpettina | **Eastchester** -

Pony Express | **P'ville** 22

Poppy's | **Beacon** 24

Red Devon | **Bangall** 23

NEW Rock and Rye | **New Paltz** -

Sweet Grass | **Tarrytown** 19

Sweet Sue's | **Phoenicia** 24

Swoon | **Hudson** 24

Tappo | **Stamford** -

Tavern/Highlands | **Garrison** 22

NEW Tavern/Gunk | **Ellenville** -

Z Terrapin | **Rhinebeck** 24

Z Thomas Henkelmann | 28
  Greenwich

Tomatillo | **Dobbs Ferry** 22

Valley/Garrison | **Garrison** 23

Village Tea. | **New Paltz** 25

West St. Grill | **Litchfield** 24

Winvian | **Litchfield** 27

Woody's All Natural | **Cornwall** 18

Would | **Highland** 22

Z Xaviars | **Piermont** 28

HISTORIC PLACES

(Year opened; * building)

1668 | Old '76 House* | **Tappan** 18

1679 | Hoffman Hse.* | **Kingston** 23

1700 | Canterbury* | **Cornwall/Hud** 23

1749 | Horse & Hound* | **S Salem** 19

1750 | La Crémaillère* | **Bedford** 27

1750 | Long Ridge Tav.* | **Stamford** 14

1759 | Rock and Rye* | **New Paltz** -

1760 | Iron Forge Inn* | **Warwick** 24

1760 | Pastorale* | **Lakeville** 23

1760 | Peter Pratt's* | **Yorktown** 25

1761 | Bird & Bottle Inn* | **Garrison** 22

1762 | Bull's Bridge* | **Kent** 16

1762 | Schlesinger's* | 23
  New Windsor

1766 | Tavern/Beekman* | 20
  Rhinebeck

1774 | Adrienne* | **New Milford** 25

1775 | Winvian* | **Litchfield** 27

1778 | Landmark Inn* | **Warwick** 20

1782 | Stissing Hse.* | **Pine Plains** 20

1783 | Roger Sherman* | 24
  New Canaan

1786 | Bull's Head* | **Campbell Hall** 18

1788 | Tuthill House* | **Gardiner** -

1790 | Bedford Post/Barn* | 23
  Bedford

1790 | Bedford Post/Farm* | 25
  Bedford

1790 | Crabtree's* | **Chappaqua** 25

1790 | La Camelia* | **Mt. Kisco** 23

1792 | La Piccola Casa* | **Mamaro** 21

1799 | Thomas Henkelmann* | 28
  Greenwich

1800 | Dutch Ale* | **Saugerties** -

1803 | Olde Stone Mill* | **Tuck** 17

1814 | Union* | **Haverstraw** 24

1824 | Terrapin* | **Rhinebeck** 24

1827 | Le Bouchon* | **Cold Spring** 21

1830 | Artist's Palate* | **Poughkp**	26
1830 | MOD* | **Hudson**	-
1832 | Hudson Hse. Inn* | **Cold Spring**	22
1838 | China Rose* | **Rhinecliff**	21
1839 | Vinum Cafe* | **Washingtonville**	-
1847 | Valhalla Crossing* | **Valhalla**	16
1850 | G.W. Tavern* | **Wash Depot**	20
1850 | La Duchesse* | **Mt. Tremper**	19
1850 | La Panetière* | **Rye**	27
1850 | Local* | **Rhinebeck**	-
1850 | Peekamoose* | **Big Indian**	24
1850 | Swiss Hütte* | **Hillsdale**	21
1850 | Violette* | **Woodstock**	20
1854 | Rhinecliff Hotel Bar* | **Rhinecliff**	19
1855 | Hudson Hse. Nyack* | **Nyack**	23
1860 | Frank Guido's* | **Kingston**	21
1860 | Liberty Public* | **Rhinebeck**	-
1860 | Northern Spy* | **High Falls**	18
1860 | Vanderbilt House Restaurant* | **Philmont**	-
1863 | Le Chambord Restaurant* | **Hopewell Jct**	-
1864 | Cafe Tamayo* | **Saugerties**	25
1867 | Plumbush Inn* | **Cold Spring**	21
1869 | Mohonk Mtn. Hse.* | **New Paltz**	18
1870 | Bruynswyck Inn* | **Wallkill**	-
1870 | Il Barilotto* | **Fishkill**	27
1870 | La Stazione* | **New Paltz**	21
1870 | Ship to Shore* | **Kingston**	22
1871 | Emilio Rist.* | **Harrison**	25
1872 | Schoolhouse* | **Wilton**	27
1875 | Bistro Brie* | **Windham**	21
1876 | Travelers* | **Ossining**	19
1880 | Giulio's/Harvest* | **Tappan**	-
1880 | Mayflower Inn* | **Washington**	24
1880 | Vico* | **Hudson**	19
1881 | Q Rest.* | **Port Chester**	22
1882 | Harney/Sons* | **Millerton**	21
1883 | Village Tea.* | **New Paltz**	25
1888 | Club Car* | **Mamaro**	-
1889 | Velo* | **Nyack**	24
1890 | Bangkok Spice* | **Shrub Oak**	23
1890 | Via Vanti!* | **Mt. Kisco**	23

1890 | Village* | **Litchfield**	20
1891 | Vintage 1891* | **Larch**	-
1892 | Nanuet Hotel* | **Nanuet**	21
1892 | Zuppa* | **Yonkers**	23
1897 | Mercato* | **Red Hook**	25
1898 | Woody's Parkside* | **Sparkill**	19
1899 | Lakeview Hse.* | **Newburgh**	21
1900 | Belvedere* | **Staatsburg**	20
1900 | Brasserie 292* | **Poughkp**	-
1900 | Camillo's* | **Montgomery**	18
1900 | Division St. Grill* | **Peekskill**	20
1900 | Koo* | **Rye**	23
1900 | Marco* | **Lake Mahopac**	21
1900 | Painter's* | **Cornwall/Hud**	19
1900 | Piero's* | **Port Chester**	24
1900 | Polpo* | **Greenwich**	24
1900 | Rye Roadhse.* | **Rye**	18
1900 | West St. Grill* | **Litchfield**	24
1900 | X2O Xaviars* | **Yonkers**	27
1902 | Last Chance* | **Tanners**	22
1902 | Plates* | **Larch**	25
1903 | Louie's/Ave.* | **Pearl River**	21
1903 | Willett House* | **Port Chester**	24
1904 | Iron Horse Grill* | **P'ville**	27
1905 | Pete's Saloon* | **Elmsford**	18
1907 | Le Château* | **S Salem**	25
1908 | Le Gamin* | **Hudson**	19
1910 | Julianna's* | **Cortlandt Man**	24
1910 | Red Hat* | **Irvington**	23
1911 | Glenmere* | **Chester**	24
1915 | Arch* | **Brewster**	27
1917 | Cobble Stone* | **Purchase**	15
1917 | Morello* | **Greenwich**	22
1919 | Walter's | **Mamaro**	22
1920 | Modern Rest.* | **New Roch**	22
1921 | Orem's Diner | **Wilton**	15
1925 | Ship Lantern | **Milton**	26
1927 | Reka's* | **White Pl**	19
1930 | Birdsall Hse.* | **Peekskill**	24
1930 | Route 22* | **Armonk**	14
1930 | Would* | **Highland**	22
1931 | Gus's Franklin Pk. | **Harrison**	21
1931 | Roma | **Tuck**	18
1932 | Lodge* | **Wingdale**	-
1932 | Sam's/Gedney | **White Pl**	19
1933 | Larchmont Tav. | **Larch**	17

1934 | Blazer Pub | **Purdys**	22
1935 | Colony Grill | **Stamford**	24
1935 | Post Rd. Ale* | **New Roch**	-
1939 | Clamp's | **New Milford**	-
1940 | Blue Dolphin | **Katonah**	23
1940 | River City Grille* | **Irvington**	19
1940 | Stonehenge | **Ridgefield**	22
1942 | Johnny's | **Mt. Vernon**	25
1946 | Hopkins Inn | **Warren**	19
1947 | La Manda's | **White Pl**	19
1947 | Mickey/Molly Spill.* | **Eastchester**	15
1947 | Pellicci's | **Stamford**	19
1948 | Ümami Café* | **Croton/Hud**	21
1949 | Sam's | **Dobbs Ferry**	18
1950 | Marianacci's | **Port Chester**	21
1950 | Solano's | **Mt. Vernon**	-
1952 | Epstein's Deli | **Yonkers**	19
1955 | Candlelight Inn | **Scarsdale**	22
1955 | Made In Asia* | **Armonk**	21
1958 | Martindale Chief | **Craryville**	11
1960 | Chef Antonio | **Mamaro**	20
1960 | Trevi Ristorante* | **W Harrison**	23
1960 | When Pigs Fly* | **Mabbettsville**	21

HOTEL DINING

Bedford Post

✓ Bedford Post/Barn | **Bedford**	23
✓ Bedford Post/Farm | **Bedford**	25

Beekman Arms Hotel

Tavern/Beekman | **Rhinebeck**	20

Belvedere Mansion

Belvedere | **Staatsburg**	20

Bird & Bottle Inn

Bird & Bottle Inn | **Garrison**	22

Buttermilk Falls Inn & Spa

Henry's/Buttermilk | **Milton**	-

Crabtree's Kittle House Inn

✓ Crabtree's | **Chappaqua**	25

Delamar Hotel

L'Escale | **Greenwich**	23

Diamond Mills Hotel

NEW Tavern/Diamond | **Saugerties**	-

DoubleTree Hotel

Bistro Z | **Tarrytown**	20

Emerson Resort & Spa

Catamount | **Mt. Tremper**	17
Phoenix | **Mt. Tremper**	-

Garrison

Valley/Garrison | **Garrison**	23

Glenmere Mansion

✓ Glenmere | **Chester**	24

Homestead Inn

✓ Thomas Henkelmann | **Greenwich**	28

Hopkins Inn

Hopkins Inn | **Warren**	19

Inn at Applewood

Would | **Highland**	22

Inn at Ca'Mea

Ca'Mea | **Hudson**	22

Inn at Stone Ridge

Inn/Stone Ridge | **Stone Ridge**	21

La Duchesse Anne

La Duchesse | **Mt. Tremper**	19

La Quinta Hotel

Marc Charles | **Armonk**	20

Le Chambord

Le Chambord Restaurant | **Hopewell Jct**	-

Madalin Hotel

Madalin's Table | **Tivoli**	19

Marriott Residence Inn

Aberdeen | **White Pl**	23

Mayflower Inn & Spa

Mayflower Inn | **Washington**	24

Mohonk Mountain Hse.

Mohonk Mtn. Hse. | **New Paltz**	18

Plumbush Inn

Plumbush Inn | **Cold Spring**	21

Radisson Plaza

NEW NoMa Social | **New Roch**	-

Renaissance Hotel

80 West | **White Pl**	19

Rhinecliff

Rhinecliff Hotel Bar | **Rhinecliff**	19

Ridgefield Motor Inn

Thali | **Ridgefield**	24

Ritz-Carlton Westchester

Bellota/42 | **White Pl**	-
✓ BLT Steak | **White Pl**	23
✓ 42 | **White Pl**	22

Roger Sherman Inn
  Roger Sherman | **New Canaan** 24

Simmons' Way Village Inn
  2 No. 9 | **Millerton** 27

Stonehenge Inn
  Stonehenge | **Ridgefield** 22

Swiss Hütte Country Inn
  Swiss Hütte | **Hillsdale** 21

Vanderbilt House Hotel
  NEW Vanderbilt House _|
    Restaurant | **Philmont**

Vernon Hills Shopping Ctr.
  Fig & Olive | **Scarsdale** _|

Westchester Marriott
  Ruth's Chris | **Tarrytown** 25

Winvian Resort
  Winvian | **Litchfield** 27

LATE DINING

(Weekday closing hour)

Barcelona | 12:45 AM | **Stamford** 24
Bartaco | varies | **multi.** _|
Bobby Valentine | 12:30 AM | **Stamford** 15
Brazen Fox | 2 AM | **White Pl** 17
Candlelight Inn | 3 AM | **Scarsdale** 22
Cobble Stone | 12 AM | **Purchase** 15
Colony Grill | 12 AM | **Stamford** 24
NEW Craftsman Ale | 12 AM | **Harrison** _|
Daily Planet | 12 AM | **LaGrangeville** 17
Don Coqui | varies | **New Roch** 23
Eveready Diner | 2 AM | **Hyde Pk** 20
NEW Karma Lounge | 2 AM | **Poughkp** _|
Lazy Boy Saloon | varies | **White Pl** 19
Le Jardin du Roi | 12 AM | **Chappaqua** 21
Little Mex. Cafe | 12 AM | **New Roch** 21
Mackenzie's | 12 AM | **Old Greenwich** 16
Mickey/Molly Spill. | varies | **Mt. Vernon** 15
Nautilus | 24 hrs. | **Mamaro** 16
Orem's Diner | 12 AM | **Wilton** 15
Piper's Kilt | 12:30 AM | **Eastchester** 22
Ron Blacks | 2 AM | **White Pl** 16

NEW Siete Ocho Siete | varies | _|
  New Roch
NEW Taste | varies | **Buchanan** _|
NEW Thornwood Ale | 2 AM | _|
  Thornwood
Vinny's | 2 AM | **Stamford** 20
Watercolor Cafe | 12 AM | **Larch** 18
NEW Yard House | varies | _|
  Yonkers

MEET FOR A DRINK

Anthony's Pizza | **White Pl** 22
Antoine McGuire | **Haverstraw** 24
Armadillo B&G | **Kingston** 25
Aroma Thyme | **Ellenville** 23
Asian Tempt. | **White Pl** 20
@ the Corner | **Litchfield** 20
Baang Cafe | **Riverside** 23
Bank St. Tavern | **New Milford** 18
Bartaco | **multi.** _|
Bayou | **Mt. Vernon** 19
Beech Tree Grill | **Poughkp** 22
Bellota/42 | **White Pl** _|
Benjamin Steak | **White Pl** 24
2 Birdsall Hse. | **Peekskill** 24
NEW Bistro Latino | **Tuck** _|
Bistro Z | **Tarrytown** 20
2 BLT Steak | **White Pl** 23
2 Blue Hill | **Poc Hills** 28
Boathouse | **Lakeville** 17
Bobby Valentine | **Stamford** 15
Boitson's | **Kingston** _|
Boxcar Cantina | **Greenwich** 21
NEW Brasserie 292 | **Poughkp** _|
Brazen Fox | **White Pl** 17
Bridge View | **Sleepy Hollow** 22
Bull & Buddha | **Poughkp** 19
NEW Burrata | **Eastchester** _|
Byrne & Hanrahan | **Yonkers** _|
Bywater | **Rosendale** 23
NEW Cactus Rose | **Wilton** _|
Café of Love | **Mt. Kisco** 22
Caffé Azzurri | **Hartsdale** 22
Candlelight Inn | **Scarsdale** 22
Chat | **multi.** 18
NEW Craftsman Ale | **Harrison** _|
Crew | **Poughkp** 22
Croton Creek | **Crot Falls** 20

NEW Darien Social | **Darien**	⌐¹
Dolphin | **Yonkers**	21
Don Coqui | **New Roch**	23
Egg's Nest | **High Falls**	19
Elephant | **Kingston**	24
Eleven 11 | **Fishkill**	22
Emma's Ale House | **White Pl**	18
Euro Asian | **Port Chester**	17
F.A.B. | **Mt. Kisco**	19
Fez | **Stamford**	20
Fife 'n Drum | **Kent**	18
Fifty Coins | **Ridgefield**	16
Fig & Olive | **Scarsdale**	⌐¹
Z 42 | **White Pl**	22
Frankie/Johnnie's | **Rye**	24
Friends & Family | **Accord**	22
Full Moon | **White Pl**	24
Gabriele's | **Greenwich**	⌐¹
Gilded Otter | **New Paltz**	16
Ginger Man | **Greenwich**	18
Goose | **Darien**	⌐¹
Graziella's | **White Pl**	19
NEW Growlers | **Tuck**	⌐¹
Gusano Loco | **Mamaro**	21
Z Haiku | **multi.**	22
Half Moon | **Dobbs Ferry**	19
Harrys/Hartsdale | **Hartsdale**	20
Z Harvest/Hudson | **Hastings/Hud**	22
Haven | **P'ville**	24
Hoffman Hse. | **Kingston**	23
Horse & Hound | **S Salem**	19
Hudson Grille | **White Pl**	20
Hudson Hse. Nyack | **Nyack**	23
NEW Impulse Hibachi | **White Pl**	⌐¹
NEW Karma Lounge | **Poughkp**	⌐¹
Kona Grill | **Stamford**	17
Kraft Bistro | **Bronxville**	21
Lazy Boy Saloon | **White Pl**	19
Le Canard | **Kingston**	23
Lexington Sq. Café | **Mt. Kisco**	21
Little Pub | **Ridgefield**	23
Local | **Rhinebeck**	⌐¹
Lolita | **Greenwich**	22
Long Ridge Tav. | **Stamford**	14
Mackenzie's | **Old Greenwich**	16
Madalin's Table | **Tivoli**	19

Mango Café | **Mt. Kisco**	18
Marc Charles | **Armonk**	20
Mediterraneo | **Greenwich**	21
Melting Pot | **Darien**	17
NEW Mezon | **Danbury**	⌐¹
Michael's Tavern | **P'ville**	17
Mickey/Molly Spill. | **multi.**	15
Milonga | **N White Plains**	22
Z Moderne Barn | **Armonk**	22
Mountain Brauhaus | **Gardiner**	24
Z Mulino's | **White Pl**	24
Napa & Co. | **Stamford**	24
Neo World | **Mt. Kisco**	23
Nino's | **Bedford Hills**	21
Northern Spy | **High Falls**	18
Z 121 Rest. | **N Salem**	22
Palmer's Crossing | **Larch**	21
Peekskill Brew | **Peekskill**	19
Pine Social | **New Canaan**	23
(P.M.) Wine Bar | **Hudson**	⌐¹
Porter Hse. | **White Pl**	19
Pumpernickel | **Ardsley**	15
Raccoon Saloon | **Marlboro**	21
Rainwater | **Hastings/Hud**	16
NEW Rambler's Rest | **multi.**	⌐¹
Red Onion | **Saugerties**	23
Red Plum | **Mamaro**	21
Z Rest. North | **Armonk**	26
Z Rest. X/Bully | **Congers**	27
Rhinecliff Hotel Bar | **Rhinecliff**	19
NEW Rizzuto's | **Stamford**	20
NEW Rock and Rye | **New Paltz**	⌐¹
Ron Blacks | **White Pl**	16
Rye Grill | **Rye**	18
Rye Roadhse. | **Rye**	18
Sammy's | **Bronxville**	22
Santa Fe | **Tivoli**	22
Seasons American | **Somers**	18
NEW Siete Ocho Siete | **New Roch**	⌐¹
NEW Sofrito | **White Pl**	⌐¹
Z Sonora | **Port Chester**	24
Southwest Cafe | **Ridgefield**	22
Tap House | **Tuck**	20
Tappo | **Stamford**	⌐¹
Z Tarry Lodge | **Port Chester**	24
Tavern/Beekman | **Rhinebeck**	20

NEW Tavern/Gunk | **Ellenville**	-
Temptation Tea | **Mt. Kisco**	22
Tengda | **Darien**	22
Tequila Mock. | **New Canaan**	18
NEW Texas de Brazil | **Yonkers**	-
NEW Thornwood Ale | **Thornwood**	-
NEW Toad Holly | **Tillson**	-
Traditions 118 | **Somers**	21
Tramonto | **Hawthorne**	19
Tuthill House | **Gardiner**	-
12 Grapes | **Peekskill**	21
Union | **Haverstraw**	24
Valhalla Crossing | **Valhalla**	16
Vega | **Hartsdale**	21
Via Vanti! | **Mt. Kisco**	23
Village Social | **Mt. Kisco**	-
Vinny's | **Stamford**	20
NEW Vintage 1891 | **Larch**	-
Virgo's Sip N Soul Cafe | **Beacon**	-
Vox | **N Salem**	21
Westchester Burger | **White Pl**	20
Wherehouse | **Newburgh**	-
Whistling Willie's | **Cold Spring**	19
White Wolf | **Napanoch**	-
NEW Yard House | **Yonkers**	-
NEW ZaZa | **Stamford**	-
Zuppa | **Yonkers**	23

OFFBEAT

Azuma Sushi | **Hartsdale**	25
Bartaco | **Port Chester**	-
Z Birdsall Hse. | **Peekskill**	24
Boatyard/Smokey Joe's | **Stamford**	19
Bridge View | **Sleepy Hollow**	22
Café Mezzaluna | **Saugerties**	23
Cafe Mirage | **Port Chester**	22
Chaiwalla | **Salisbury**	25
Clamp's | **New Milford**	-
Conte's Fishmkt. | **Mt. Kisco**	22
Country Bistro | **Salisbury**	-
NEW Craftsman Ale | **Harrison**	-
Culinary Creations | **Pine Bush**	-
Damon Baehrel | **Earlton**	29
Earth Foods | **Hudson**	21
Egg's Nest | **High Falls**	19
Fez | **Stamford**	20
NEW Growlers | **Tuck**	-

Gunk Haus | **Highland**	24
Gusano Loco | **Mamaro**	21
Z Haiku | **multi.**	22
Infinity Hall/Bistro | **Norfolk**	20
Kit's Thai | **Stamford**	21
Lalibela | **Mt. Kisco**	-
Last Chance | **Tanners**	22
Little Kabab | **Mt. Kisco**	-
Lubins-N-Links | **Tarrytown**	24
Lucky's | **Stamford**	18
Max's Memphis | **Red Hook**	21
Melting Pot | **multi.**	17
NEW Mint Premium | **Tarrytown**	-
Neo World | **Mt. Kisco**	23
New World | **Saugerties**	22
Oriental Hse. | **Pine Bush**	-
Painter's | **Cornwall/Hud**	19
Pantry | **Wash Depot**	24
Pasta Vera | **Greenwich**	20
Ray's Cafe | **Larch**	19
Reality Bites | **Nyack**	20
Rosendale Cafe | **Rosendale**	15
Rue/Crêpes | **Harrison**	19
Rye Roadhse. | **Rye**	18
Salsa | **New Milford**	25
Sesame Seed | **Danbury**	21
Shiraz | **Elmsford**	20
Solano's | **Mt. Vernon**	-
Taiim Falafel | **Hastings/Hud**	-
Tanzy's | **Hudson**	17
Temptation Tea | **Mt. Kisco**	22
Thali | **multi.**	24
Tratt. Vivolo | **Harrison**	25
Twisted Soul | **Poughkp**	24
Virgo's Sip N Soul Cafe | **Beacon**	-
When Pigs Fly | **Mabbettsville**	21
Wherehouse | **Newburgh**	-
Wobble Café | **Ossining**	21
Would | **Highland**	22
Yobo | **Newburgh**	21
Z Zephs' | **Peekskill**	25

OUTDOOR DINING

(G=garden; P=patio; S=sidewalk; T=terrace; W=waterside)

Adrienne | P | **New Milford**	25
Z Arch | P | **Brewster**	27
Armadillo B&G | P | **Kingston**	25
Bartaco | P | **Port Chester**	-

Bear Cafe | G, W | **Woodstock** 24
Bistro Rollin | S | **Pelham** 23
Z Blue Hill | P | **Poc Hills** 28
Bull's Head | G, T | **Campbell Hall** 18
Bywater | G, W | **Rosendale** 23
NEW Cactus Rose | P | **Wilton** -
NEW Cafe Le Perche | G | **Hudson** -
Café/Green | P, T | **Danbury** 22
Caffé Azzurri | P | **Hartsdale** 22
Canterbury | P, W | **Cornwall/Hud** 23
Catamount | P, T, W | **Mt. Tremper** 17
Z Caterina/Medici | T | **Hyde Pk** 27
Cathryn's | G | **Cold Spring** 23
Catskill Rose | G, P | **Mt. Tremper** -
Cena 2000 | P, W | **Newburgh** 23
Chat | T | **Scarsdale** 18
Chez Jean-Pierre | S | **Stamford** 24
Z Crabtree's | G | **Chappaqua** 25
Dolphin | P, W | **Yonkers** 21
Encore Bistro | S | **Larch** 23
Z Equus | T | **Tarrytown** 25
Z Gigi Tratt. | P | **Rhinebeck** 24
Z Glenmere | T | **Chester** 24
G.W. Tavern | T, W | **Wash Depot** 20
Half Moon | T, W | **Dobbs Ferry** 19
Z Harvest/Hudson | G, P, W | 22
   Hastings/Hud
Hoffman Hse. | G, P | **Kingston** 23
Hopkins Inn | T | **Warren** 19
Hudson Hse. Inn | P, W | 22
   Cold Spring
Hudson Water | T | **W Haverstraw** 18
Il Bacio Tratt. | S | **Bronxville** 20
Il Sorriso | P | **Irvington** 21
Inn/Stone Ridge | T | **Stone Ridge** 21
Z Iron Horse Grill | P | **P'ville** 27
NEW Karma Lounge | T | -
   Poughkp
La Camelia | P | **Mt. Kisco** 23
Lazy Boy Saloon | S | **White Pl** 19
Le Bouchon | G | **Cold Spring** 21
Le Fontane | G | **Katonah** 22
Z Lefteris Gyro | S | **Tarrytown** 21
Le Jardin du Roi | G | **Chappaqua** 21
L'Escale | T, W | **Greenwich** 23
NEW Liberty Public | P | **Rhinebeck** -
Lodge | P | **Wingdale** -
Mayflower Inn | P | **Washington** 24

Mediterraneo | P | **Greenwich** 21
Niko's Greek | P | **White Pl** 20
Nina | P | **Middletown** 25
Northern Spy | P | **High Falls** 18
Oliva Cafe | T | **New Preston** 24
Z 121 Rest. | P, T | **N Salem** 22
Opus 465 | P | **Armonk** 18
Pastorale | T | **Lakeville** 23
Raccoon Saloon | T, W | **Marlboro** 21
Red Dot | G | **Hudson** 17
Z Red Hat | P, W | **Irvington** 23
River Grill | P, W | **Newburgh** 20
Riverview | P | **Cold Spring** 24
Roasted Peppers | S | **Mamaro** 21
NEW Rock and Rye | P | **New Paltz** -
Roger Sherman | P | **New Canaan** 24
Santa Fe | S | **Tivoli** 22
Z Schoolhouse | P, W | **Wilton** 27
Seaside Johnnie's | T, W | **Rye** 12
Shadows | P, W | **Poughkp** 17
Stissing Hse. | T | **Pine Plains** 20
NEW Stony Brae | P | **Cragsmoor** -
Striped Bass | P, W | **Tarrytown** 16
Sunset Cove | P, W | **Tarrytown** 16
Z Tarry Lodge | T | **Port Chester** 24
NEW Tavern/Diamond | P | -
   Saugerties
NEW Tavern/Gunk | P | **Ellenville** -
Z Terrapin | P, S | **Rhinebeck** 24
Terra Rist. | P | **Greenwich** 23
NEW Thai Elephant | T | **Patterson** -
Torches/Hudson | P, W | 17
   Newburgh
Ümami Café | T | **Croton/Hud** 21
Underhills | S | **Bronxville** 21
Valley/Garrison | T, W | **Garrison** 23
NEW Vanderbilt House -
   Restaurant | T, W | **Philmont**
Vox | G, P, T | **N Salem** 21
West St. Grill | S | **Litchfield** 24
Woody's All Natural | P | **Cornwall** 18
Would | P | **Highland** 22

PEOPLE-WATCHING

Asian Tempt. | **White Pl** 20
Baang Cafe | **Riverside** 23
Bartaco | **multi.** -
Bear Cafe | **Woodstock** 24
Z Bedford Post/Barn | **Bedford** 23

Bedford Post/Farm | **Bedford** 25
Beech Tree Grill | **Poughkp** 22
Bellota/42 | **White Pl** —
Benjamin Steak | **White Pl** 24
BLT Steak | **White Pl** 23
Boathouse | **Lakeville** 17
Brazen Fox | **White Pl** 17
Bull & Buddha | **Poughkp** 19
Chef Luis | **New Canaan** 25
NEW China White | **Greenwich** —
Community Table | **Washington** 27
NEW Darien Social | **Darien** —
Dolphin | **Yonkers** 21
Don Coqui | **New Roch** 23
NEW Elm | **New Canaan** —
Euro Asian | **Port Chester** 17
Ferrante | **Stamford** 20
Fez | **Stamford** 20
Fife 'n Drum | **Kent** 18
42 | **White Pl** 22
Frankie/Johnnie's | **Rye** 24
Freelance Cafe | **Piermont** 28
Gabriele's | **Greenwich** —
Gigi Tratt. | **Rhinebeck** 24
Ginban Asian | **Mamaro** 23
Ginger Man | **Greenwich** 18
G.W. Tavern | **Wash Depot** 20
Haiku | **multi.** 22
Half Moon | **Dobbs Ferry** 19
Harrys/Hartsdale | **Hartsdale** 20
Harvest/Hudson | **Hastings/Hud** 22
Hudson Grille | **White Pl** 20
Il Cenàcolo | **Newburgh** 28
Jean-Louis | **Greenwich** 28
Koo | **Rye** 23
Le Canard | **Kingston** 23
Lexington Sq. Café | **Mt. Kisco** 21
Lolita | **Greenwich** 22
Lusardi's | **Larch** 24
Madalin's Table | **Tivoli** 19
Mayflower Inn | **Washington** 24
Mediterraneo | **P'ville** 20
Mickey/Molly Spill. | **Mamaro** 15
Moderne Barn | **Armonk** 22
Mulino's | **White Pl** 24
New World | **Saugerties** 22
North Star | **Pound Ridge** 20

Oliva Cafe | **New Preston** 24
Pastorale | **Lakeville** 23
Pine Social | **New Canaan** 23
(P.M.) Wine Bar | **Hudson** —
Polpo | **Greenwich** 24
Porter Hse. | **White Pl** 19
Rebeccas | **Greenwich** 26
Red Dot | **Hudson** 17
Rest. X/Bully | **Congers** 27
Ron Blacks | **White Pl** 16
Ruby's Oyster | **Rye** 23
NEW Sofrito | **White Pl** —
Sonora | **Port Chester** 24
Swoon | **Hudson** 24
Tappo | **Stamford** —
Tarry Lodge | **Port Chester** 24
Temptation Tea | **Mt. Kisco** 22
NEW Texas de Brazil | **Yonkers** —
NEW Thornwood Ale | **Thornwood** —
Torches/Hudson | **Newburgh** 17
12 Grapes | **Peekskill** 21
Underhills | **Bronxville** 21
NEW Vintage 1891 | **Larch** —
Wasabi/Grill | **New City** 26
West St. Grill | **Litchfield** 24
Winvian | **Litchfield** 27
NEW Yard House | **Yonkers** —
NEW ZaZa | **Stamford** —
Zuppa | **Yonkers** 23

POWER SCENES

Alba's | **Port Chester** 23
Baang Cafe | **Riverside** 23
Bear Cafe | **Woodstock** 24
Bedford Post/Farm | **Bedford** 25
Bellota/42 | **White Pl** —
Benjamin Steak | **White Pl** 24
BLT Steak | **White Pl** 23
Boathouse | **Lakeville** 17
Capital Grille | **Stamford** 25
Crabtree's | **Chappaqua** 25
Dolphin | **Yonkers** 21
Equus | **Tarrytown** 25
Ferrante | **Stamford** 20
42 | **White Pl** 22
Gabriele's | **Greenwich** —
Graziella's | **White Pl** 19
Il Portico | **Tappan** 23

Z Jean-Louis | **Greenwich**	28
Koo | **Rye**	23
Z Lusardi's | **Larch**	24
Mayflower Inn | **Washington**	24
Z Moderne Barn | **Armonk**	22
Morton's | **multi.**	24
Moscato | **Scarsdale**	23
Z Mulino's | **White Pl**	24
Polpo | **Greenwich**	24
NEW Pranzi | **White Pl**	-
Ruth's Chris | **Tarrytown**	25
Z Sapore | **Fishkill**	26
NEW Sofrito | **White Pl**	-
Z Thomas Henkelmann | **Greenwich**	28
Valbella | **Riverside**	25
Z Wasabi/Grill | **New City**	26
West St. Grill | **Litchfield**	24
Willett House | **Port Chester**	24
Zuppa | **Yonkers**	23

PRIVATE ROOMS

(Restaurants charge less at off times; call for capacity)

Z Bedford Post/Farm | **Bedford**	25
Z Bernard's | **Ridgefield**	27
Z Blue Hill | **Poc Hills**	28
Centro | **Greenwich**	20
Eclisse | **Stamford**	21
Z Equus | **Tarrytown**	25
Z 42 | **White Pl**	22
Ginger Man | **Greenwich**	18
Goose | **Darien**	-
Graziella's | **White Pl**	19
Kujaku | **Stamford**	18
Z La Panetière | **Rye**	27
Mayflower Inn | **Washington**	24
Morello | **Greenwich**	22
Olde Stone Mill | **Tuck**	17
Plum Tree | **New Canaan**	20
Polpo | **Greenwich**	24
Primavera | **Crot Falls**	24
Roger Sherman | **New Canaan**	24
Ruby's Oyster | **Rye**	23
Stonehenge | **Ridgefield**	22
Tengda | **Greenwich**	22
Z Terrapin | **Rhinebeck**	24
Thali | **New Canaan**	24
Z Thomas Henkelmann | **Greenwich**	28

PRIX FIXE MENUS

(Call for prices and times)

Z Arch | **Brewster**	27
Bear Cafe | **Woodstock**	24
Z Bernard's | **Ridgefield**	27
Z Blue Hill | **Poc Hills**	28
Cafe Tamayo | **Saugerties**	25
Caffé Azzurri | **Hartsdale**	22
Z Cookery | **Dobbs Ferry**	26
Z Crabtree's | **Chappaqua**	25
Emilio Rist. | **Harrison**	25
Z Equus | **Tarrytown**	25
Halstead Ave. | **Harrison**	20
Z Harvest/Hudson | **Hastings/Hud**	22
Hudson Hse. Inn | **Cold Spring**	22
Z Iron Horse Grill | **P'ville**	27
Jackie's Bistro | **Eastchester**	22
Z Jean-Louis | **Greenwich**	28
Kraft Bistro | **Bronxville**	21
Z La Crémaillère | **Bedford**	27
Z La Panetière | **Rye**	27
Le Canard | **Kingston**	23
Z Ondine | **Danbury**	26
Pascal's | **Larch**	23
Pas-Tina's | **Hartsdale**	19
Quinta Steak | **Pearl River**	21
Z Rest. X/Bully | **Congers**	27
Z Schoolhouse | **Wilton**	27
Z Sonora | **Port Chester**	24
Tavern/Beekman | **Rhinebeck**	20
Turkish Meze | **Mamaro**	23
Village Tea. | **New Paltz**	25
Z Xaviars | **Piermont**	28
Z X2O Xaviars | **Yonkers**	27

ROMANTIC PLACES

Adrienne | **New Milford**	25
Z Arch | **Brewster**	27
Bambou | **Greenwich**	21
Z Bedford Post/Farm | **Bedford**	25
Bellota/42 | **White Pl**	-
Belvedere | **Staatsburg**	20
Z Bernard's | **Ridgefield**	27
Bird & Bottle Inn | **Garrison**	22
Bistro Bonne Nuit | **New Canaan**	25
NEW Bistro Latino | **Tuck**	-
Bistro Rollin | **Pelham**	23
Z Blue Hill | **Poc Hills**	28

Z Buffet/Gare | **Hastings/Hud** 28
Bull's Head | **Campbell Hall** 18
Café d'Azur | **Darien** -
Café of Love | **Mt. Kisco** 22
Caffé Azzurri | **Hartsdale** 22
Canterbury | **Cornwall/Hud** 23
Caravela | **Tarrytown** 22
Z Caterina/Medici | **Hyde Pk** 27
Chat | **Scarsdale** 18
Chez Jean-Pierre | **Stamford** 24
Cienega | **New Roch** -
Z Crabtree's | **Chappaqua** 25
Crave | **Poughkp** 25
Division St. Grill | **Peekskill** 20
Emilio Rist. | **Harrison** 25
Encore Bistro | **Larch** 23
Z Equus | **Tarrytown** 25
Z Escoffler | **Hyde Pk** 27
Finalmente | **Sleepy Hollow** 24
Frankie/Johnnie's | **Rye** 24
Gaudio's | **Yorktown Hts** 18
Giulio's/Harvest | **Tappan** -
Z Glenmere | **Chester** 24
Z Harvest Supper | **New Canaan** 27
Henry's/Buttermilk | **Milton** -
Hopkins Inn | **Warren** 19
Il Portico | **Tappan** 23
Il Sorriso | **Irvington** 21
Inn/Stone Ridge | **Stone Ridge** 21
Z Iron Horse Grill | **P'ville** 27
Jackie's Bistro | **Eastchester** 22
Z Jean-Louis | **Greenwich** 28
Julianna's | **Cortlandt Man** 24
NEW La Bella Havana | **Yonkers** -
La Bretagne | **Stamford** 24
La Camelia | **Mt. Kisco** 23
Z La Crémaillère | **Bedford** 27
La Duchesse | **Mt. Tremper** 19
La Fontanella | **Pelham** 24
Z La Panetière | **Rye** 27
La Piccola Casa | **Mamaro** 21
Le Canard | **Kingston** 23
Le Chambord Restaurant |
Hopewell Jct -
Z Le Château | **S Salem** 25
Z Le Provençal | **Mamaro** 23
Lodge | **Wingdale** -
Mamma Assunta | **Tuck** 20

Massa' | **Scarsdale** -
Mayflower Inn | **Washington** 24
Melting Pot | **White Pl** 17
Z Mima | **Irvington** 25
Moscato | **Scarsdale** 23
Z Mulino's | **White Pl** 24
Napa & Co. | **Stamford** 24
Nessa | **Port Chester** 21
Z No. 9 | **Millerton** 27
Oliva Cafe | **New Preston** 24
Z Ondine | **Danbury** 26
Z 121 Rest. | **N Salem** 22
Opus 465 | **Armonk** 18
Orissa | **Dobbs Ferry** 24
Pascal's | **Larch** 23
Pastorale | **Lakeville** 23
Peter Pratt's | **Yorktown** 25
Plumbush Inn | **Cold Spring** 21
Posto 22 | **New Roch** 21
Z Rest. X/Bully | **Congers** 27
Roger Sherman | **New Canaan** 24
Rosa's La Scarbitta | **Mamaro** -
Sazan | **Ardsley** 24
Shiraz | **Elmsford** 20
Z Sonora | **Port Chester** 24
Stonehenge | **Ridgefield** 22
Tavern/Beekman | **Rhinebeck** 20
Z Thomas Henkelmann | 28
Greenwich
Tratt. Vivolo | **Harrison** 25
Travelers | **Ossining** 19
Trinity Grill | **Harrison** 20
Two Spear St. | **Nyack** 22
NEW Vintage 1891 | **Larch** -
White Horse | **New Preston** 19
Winvian | **Litchfield** 27
Z Xaviars | **Piermont** 28
Z Zephs' | **Peekskill** 25
Zitoune | **Mamaro** 19

SENIOR APPEAL

American Pie | **Sherman** 22
Arrivederci | **Sherman** -
Z Bedford Post/Farm | **Bedford** 25
Bruynswyck Inn | **Wallkill** -
Z Buffet/Gare | **Hastings/Hud** 28
Bull's Bridge | **Kent** 16
Bull's Head | **Campbell Hall** 18

Cabin | **Greenburgh**	15
Cafe Giulia | **Lakeville**	22
Cafe Portofino | **Piermont**	23
Camillo's | **Montgomery**	18
Canterbury | **Cornwall/Hud**	23
Charlotte's | **Millbrook**	21
❷ Crabtree's | **Chappaqua**	25
Division St. Grill | **Peekskill**	20
Encore Bistro | **Larch**	23
Epstein's Deli | **multi.**	19
❷ Equus | **Tarrytown**	25
Eveready Diner | **Brewster**	20
Fife 'n Drum | **Kent**	18
Graziella's | **White Pl**	19
❷ Harvest Supper | **New Canaan**	27
Hoffman Hse. | **Kingston**	23
Il Castello | **Mamaro**	24
Il Sorriso | **Irvington**	21
Inn/Stone Ridge | **Stone Ridge**	21
❷ Iron Horse Grill | **P'ville**	27
Jackie's Bistro | **Eastchester**	22
Kisco Kosher | **White Pl**	17
La Camelia | **Mt. Kisco**	23
❷ La Crémaillère | **Bedford**	27
Lakeview Hse. | **Newburgh**	21
❷ La Panetière | **Rye**	27
Le Chambord Restaurant | **Hopewell Jct**	-
❷ Le Château | **S Salem**	25
Le Petit Bistro | **Rhinebeck**	25
❷ Le Provençal | **Mamaro**	23
Little Pub | **Ridgefield**	23
Lodge | **Wingdale**	-
Long Ridge Tav. | **Stamford**	14
Louie's/Ave. | **Pearl River**	21
❷ Marcello's | **Suffern**	26
Melting Pot | **Darien**	17
Milonga | **N White Plains**	22
Mohonk Mtn. Hse. | **New Paltz**	18
Mt. Ivy Cafe | **Pomona**	18
❷ Mulino's | **White Pl**	24
NEW Mythos | **Thornwood**	-
Nino's | **S Salem**	20
Nino's | **Bedford Hills**	21
Pantry | **Wash Depot**	24
Pascal's | **Larch**	23
Pellicci's | **Stamford**	19
Plumbush Inn | **Cold Spring**	21

Portofino Pizza | **Goldens Br**	22
Portofino Rist. | **Staatsburg**	23
Risotto | **Thornwood**	21
Roger Sherman | **New Canaan**	24
Rue/Crêpes | **Harrison**	19
Ruth's Chris | **Tarrytown**	25
Scarsdale Metro | **Scarsdale**	17
❷ Ship Lantern | **Milton**	26
Stonehenge | **Ridgefield**	22
Swiss Hütte | **Hillsdale**	21
T&J Villaggio | **Port Chester**	21
NEW Taste | **Buchanan**	-
Tavern/Beekman | **Rhinebeck**	20
❷ Tawa | **Stamford**	27
❷ Thomas Henkelmann | **Greenwich**	28
Tony's | **Woodridge**	-
Travelers | **Ossining**	19
Underhills | **Bronxville**	21
Valentino's | **Yonkers**	24
Waters Edge | **Darien**	19
West St. Grill | **Litchfield**	24
White Horse | **New Preston**	19
Winvian | **Litchfield**	27
Woodland | **Lakeville**	22

SINGLES SCENES

Antoine McGuire | **Haverstraw**	24
Armadillo B&G | **Kingston**	25
Asian Tempt. | **White Pl**	20
Baang Cafe | **Riverside**	23
Bartaco | **multi.**	-
Bayou | **Mt. Vernon**	19
Beech Tree Grill | **Poughkp**	22
Bellota/42 | **White Pl**	-
Boathouse | **Lakeville**	17
Bobby Valentine | **Stamford**	15
Boitson's | **Kingston**	-
NEW Brasserie 292 | **Poughkp**	-
Bull & Buddha | **Poughkp**	19
Bywater | **Rosendale**	23
China Rose | **Rhinecliff**	21
Cobble Stone | **Purchase**	15
Cosimo's Tratt. | **Poughkp**	19
Elephant | **Kingston**	24
Eleven 11 | **Fishkill**	22
Euro Asian | **Port Chester**	17
Frankie/Johnnie's | **Rye**	24

NEW Growlers	**Tuck**	–
☑ Haiku	**multi.**	22
Hudson Grille	**White Pl**	20
Hudson Hse. Nyack	**Nyack**	23
NEW Karma Lounge	**Poughkp**	–
Kona Grill	**Stamford**	17
Lazy Boy Saloon	**White Pl**	19
Lexington Sq. Café	**Mt. Kisco**	21
Lolita	**Greenwich**	22
Long Ridge Tav.	**Stamford**	14
Mackenzie's	**Old Greenwich**	16
Madalin's Table	**Tivoli**	19
Mary Ann's	**Port Chester**	15
Max's Memphis	**Red Hook**	21
Mediterraneo	**Greenwich**	21
Melting Pot	**White Pl**	17
Mexican Radio	**Hudson**	18
Michael's Tavern	**P'ville**	17
Mickey/Molly Spill.	**Mamaro**	15
☑ 121 Rest.	**N Salem**	22
(P.M.) Wine Bar	**Hudson**	–
Porter Hse.	**White Pl**	19
Rainwater	**Hastings/Hud**	16
Ron Blacks	**White Pl**	16
Rye Grill	**Rye**	18
Sam's	**Dobbs Ferry**	18
Santa Fe	**Tarrytown**	17
NEW Sofrito	**White Pl**	–
Southport Brew.	**Stamford**	16
Tengda	**Katonah**	22
Tequila Sunrise	**Larch**	17
Terra Rist.	**Greenwich**	23
Torches/Hudson	**Newburgh**	17
Underhills	**Bronxville**	21
Village Social	**Mt. Kisco**	–
NEW Vintage 1891	**Larch**	–
Virgo's Sip N Soul Cafe	**Beacon**	–
Wherehouse	**Newburgh**	–
Whistling Willie's	**Cold Spring**	19
NEW Yard House	**Yonkers**	–
Zuppa	**Yonkers**	23

Bangkok Spice	**Shrub Oak**	23
Café Amarcord	**Beacon**	24
Cafe Giulia	**Lakeville**	22
Café Mezzaluna	**Saugerties**	23
Chaiwalla	**Salisbury**	25
Chateau Hathorn	**Warwick**	23
Community Table	**Washington**	27
Da Giorgio	**New Roch**	25
Damon Baehrel	**Earlton**	29
Full Moon	**White Pl**	24
Global Palate	**W Park**	26
Greens	**Copake**	23
Gunk Haus	**Highland**	24
Hoffman Hse.	**Kingston**	23
Hokkaido	**New Paltz**	27
Isamu	**Beacon**	25
Jean Claude's	**multi.**	25
Karamba	**White Pl**	22
Last Chance	**Tanners**	22
Louie & Johnnies'	**Yonkers**	22
Lubins-N-Links	**Tarrytown**	24
Lucky Buddha	**Thornwood**	24
Magoya	**Chester**	23
Me-Oh-My	**Red Hook**	25
Murasaki	**Nyack**	22
Osteria Applausi	**Old Greenwich**	24
Pine Social	**New Canaan**	23
Route 100	**Yonkers**	22
Saigon Café	**Poughkp**	23
Salsa	**New Milford**	25
Tavern/Highlands	**Garrison**	22
Thai Garden	**Orangeburg**	22
Thai Golden	**Carmel**	23
3 Boys From Italy	**White Pl**	23
Tony's	**Woodridge**	–
Trevi Ristorante	**W Harrison**	23
TuttaBella	**Scarsdale**	23
Twisted Soul	**Poughkp**	24
Tyrynda	**Sleepy Hollow**	23
Valley/Garrison	**Garrison**	23
Winvian	**Litchfield**	27

SLEEPERS
(Good food, but little known)

Agriturismo	**Pine Plains**	23
Alvin/Friends	**New Roch**	26
Arrosto	**Port Chester**	23
Avocado	**Cornwall**	22

TRENDY

Agriturismo	**Pine Plains**	23
Arrosto	**Port Chester**	23
☑ Artist's Palate	**Poughkp**	26
Asian Tempt.	**White Pl**	20
Baang Cafe	**Riverside**	23

Bambou | **Greenwich**	21
Bartaco | **Port Chester**	–
Bear Cafe | **Woodstock**	24
Z Bedford Post/Barn | **Bedford**	23
Bellota/42 | **White Pl**	–
Z Birdsall Hse. | **Peekskill**	24
NEW Bistro Latino | **Tuck**	–
Z BLT Steak | **White Pl**	23
Blue Asian | **Mt. Kisco**	19
Z Blue Hill | **Poc Hills**	28
Boitson's | **Kingston**	–
NEW Brasserie 292 | **Poughkp**	–
Bull & Buddha | **Poughkp**	19
NEW Burrata | **Eastchester**	–
Café Barcel | **Nyack**	25
NEW China White | **Greenwich**	–
Cienega | **New Roch**	–
Community Table | **Washington**	27
Z Cookery | **Dobbs Ferry**	26
Cucina | **Woodstock**	25
NEW Darien Social | **Darien**	–
Dolphin | **Yonkers**	21
NEW Elm | **New Canaan**	–
Elm St. Oyster | **Greenwich**	24
Eos Greek | **Stamford**	24
Fez | **Stamford**	20
Z 42 | **White Pl**	22
Z Freelance Cafe | **Piermont**	28
Full Moon | **White Pl**	24
Z Gigi Tratt. | **Rhinebeck**	24
Ginban Asian | **Mamaro**	23
NEW Growlers | **Tuck**	–
Z Haiku | **multi.**	22
Z Harvest Supper | **New Canaan**	27
NEW Karma Lounge | **Poughkp**	–
Koo | **Rye**	23
Kotobuki | **Stamford**	24
Lanterna Tuscan | **Nyack**	24
La Puerta Azul | **Salt Pt**	23
NEW Liberty Public | **Rhinebeck**	–
Local 111 | **Philmont**	23
Lolita | **Greenwich**	22
Madalin's Table | **Tivoli**	19
Mediterraneo | **Greenwich**	21
Z Moderne Barn | **Armonk**	22
Morgans Fish | **Rye**	21
Napa & Co. | **Stamford**	24
Neo World | **Mt. Kisco**	23

New World | **Saugerties**	22
Nina | **Middletown**	25
Oliva Cafe | **New Preston**	24
Orissa | **Dobbs Ferry**	24
NEW Panzur | **Tivoli**	–
NEW Park 143 | **Bronxville**	–
Pastorale | **Lakeville**	23
(P.M.) Wine Bar | **Hudson**	–
NEW Polpettina | **Eastchester**	–
Z Rebeccas | **Greenwich**	26
Red Dot | **Hudson**	17
Z Red Hat | **Irvington**	23
Red Onion | **Saugerties**	23
Red Plum | **Mamaro**	21
Z Rest. North | **Armonk**	26
Z Rest. X/Bully | **Congers**	27
Z Rosie's Bistro | **Bronxville**	23
Ruby's Oyster | **Rye**	23
NEW Sofrito | **White Pl**	–
Solé Rist. | **New Canaan**	21
Z Sonora | **Port Chester**	24
Spoon | **Chappaqua**	20
Swoon | **Hudson**	24
Tappo | **Stamford**	–
Z Tarry Lodge | **Port Chester**	24
Temptation Tea | **Mt. Kisco**	22
Tengda | **multi.**	22
Z Terrapin | **Rhinebeck**	24
Z Thomas Henkelmann | **Greenwich**	28
12 Grapes | **Peekskill**	21
Ümami Café | **Croton/Hud**	21
Underhills | **Bronxville**	21
Union | **Haverstraw**	24
Village Social | **Mt. Kisco**	–
NEW Vintage 1891 | **Larch**	–
Z Wasabi/Grill | **New City**	26
Watermoon | **Rye**	23
West St. Grill | **Litchfield**	24
Z X2O Xaviars | **Yonkers**	27
NEW ZaZa | **Stamford**	–
Z Zephs' | **Peekskill**	25
Zitoune | **Mamaro**	19

VIEWS

Abruzzi Tratt. | **Patterson**	21
Z Arch | **Brewster**	27
NEW Bangall Whaling | **Stanfordville**	–

Bear Cafe | **Woodstock** — 24

Belvedere | **Staatsburg** — 20

Z Blue Hill | **Poc Hills** — 28

Bridge View | **Sleepy Hollow** — 22

Bruynswyck Inn | **Wallkill** — ⌐

Bull's Bridge | **Kent** — 16

Bull's Head | **Campbell Hall** — 18

Café/Green | **Danbury** — 22

Canterbury | **Cornwall/Hud** — 23

Cena 2000 | **Newburgh** — 23

Charlotte's | **Millbrook** — 21

China Rose | **Rhinecliff** — 21

Dolphin | **Yonkers** — 21

80 West | **White Pl** — 19

Z Equus | **Tarrytown** — 25

Z 42 | **White Pl** — 22

Z Glenmere | **Chester** — 24

G.W. Tavern | **Wash Depot** — 20

Half Moon | **Dobbs Ferry** — 19

Harvest Café | **New Paltz** — 23

Z Harvest/Hudson | **Hastings/Hud** — 22

Hopkins Inn | **Warren** — 19

Hudson Hse. Inn | **Cold Spring** — 22

Hudson Water | **W Haverstraw** — 18

Il Sorriso | **Irvington** — 21

Lakeview Hse. | **Newburgh** — 21

Le Chambord Restaurant | **Hopewell Jct** — ⌐

Z Le Château | **S Salem** — 25

L'Escale | **Greenwich** — 23

Maggie's Krooked | **Tanners** — ⌐

Mohonk Mtn. Hse. | **New Paltz** — 18

Mount Fuji | **Hillburn** — 19

Olde Stone Mill | **Tuck** — 17

Peekamoose | **Big Indian** — 24

Phoenix | **Mt. Tremper** — ⌐

Raccoon Saloon | **Marlboro** — 21

Rani Mahal | **Mamaro** — 23

Z Red Hat | **Irvington** — 23

Reka's | **White Pl** — 19

Rhinecliff Hotel Bar | **Rhinecliff** — 19

River Club | **Nyack** — 14

River Grill | **Newburgh** — 20

Riverview | **Cold Spring** — 24

Seaside Johnnie's | **Rye** — 12

Shadows | **Poughkp** — 17

Ship to Shore | **Kingston** — 22

NEW Siete Ocho Siete | **New Roch** — ⌐

Z St. Andrew's | **Hyde Pk** — 25

Stonehenge | **Ridgefield** — 22

Striped Bass | **Tarrytown** — 16

Sunset Cove | **Tarrytown** — 16

Swiss Hütte | **Hillsdale** — 21

NEW Tavern/Diamond | **Saugerties** — ⌐

Tavern/Highlands | **Garrison** — 22

NEW Tavern/Gunk | **Ellenville** — ⌐

Thai Golden | **Carmel** — 23

Z Thomas Henkelmann | **Greenwich** — 28

Torches/Hudson | **Newburgh** — 17

Tratt. Vivolo | **Harrison** — 25

Trevi Ristorante | **W Harrison** — 23

Tuthill House | **Gardiner** — ⌐

Two Spear St. | **Nyack** — 22

Valley/Garrison | **Garrison** — 23

NEW Vanderbilt House Restaurant | **Philmont** — ⌐

Village | **Litchfield** — 20

Virgo's Sip N Soul Cafe | **Beacon** — ⌐

Vox | **N Salem** — 21

White Horse | **New Preston** — 19

Winvian | **Litchfield** — 27

Woodland | **Lakeville** — 22

Woody's Parkside | **Sparkill** — 19

Would | **Highland** — 22

Z X2O Xaviars | **Yonkers** — 27

WINNING WINE LISTS

Alba's | **Port Chester** — 23

Aroma Thyme | **Ellenville** — 23

Bear Cafe | **Woodstock** — 24

Benjamin Steak | **White Pl** — 24

Z Bernard's | **Ridgefield** — 27

Z BLT Steak | **White Pl** — 23

Z Blue Hill | **Poc Hills** — 28

Z Buffet/Gare | **Hastings/Hud** — 28

Cafe Tamayo | **Saugerties** — 25

Capital Grille | **Stamford** — 25

Z Caterina/Medici | **Hyde Pk** — 27

Cathryn's | **Cold Spring** — 23

Cava Wine | **New Canaan** — 22

Chez Jean-Pierre | **Stamford** — 24

Cosimo's Brick | **Newburgh** — 20

Z Crabtree's | **Chappaqua**	25
Elm St. Oyster | **Greenwich**	24
Emilio Rist. | **Harrison**	25
Enzo's | **Mamaro**	20
Z Equus | **Tarrytown**	25
Z Escoffier | **Hyde Pk**	27
Flames Steak | **Briarcliff Manor**	22
Z 42 | **White Pl**	22
Frankie/Johnnie's | **Rye**	24
Z Freelance Cafe | **Piermont**	28
Gabriele's | **Greenwich**	-
Z Glenmere | **Chester**	24
Gnarly Vine | **New Roch**	17
Harrys/Hartsdale | **Hartsdale**	20
Z Harvest/Hudson | **Hastings/Hud**	22
Hudson Hse. Inn | **Cold Spring**	22
Hudson's Ribs | **Fishkill**	19
Z Il Barilotto | **Fishkill**	27
Z Il Cenàcolo | **Newburgh**	28
Il Sorriso | **Irvington**	21
Z Jean-Louis | **Greenwich**	28
La Bretagne | **Stamford**	24
La Camelia | **Mt. Kisco**	23
Z La Crémaillère | **Bedford**	27
Z La Panetière | **Rye**	27
Le Chambord Restaurant | **Hopewell Jct**	-
Le Fontane | **Katonah**	22
Litchfield Saltwater | **Litchfield**	20
Z Luca Rist. | **Wilton**	26
Z Lusardi's | **Larch**	24
Marco | **Lake Mahopac**	21
Melting Pot | **Darien**	17
Meritage | **Scarsdale**	23
NEW Mezon | **Danbury**	-
Z Mima | **Irvington**	25
Z Moderne Barn | **Armonk**	22
Morton's | **Stamford**	24
Napa & Co. | **Stamford**	24
Nessa | **Port Chester**	21
Northern Spy | **High Falls**	18
Z Ondine | **Danbury**	26
Peter Pratt's | **Yorktown**	25
Z Plates | **Larch**	25
(P.M.) Wine Bar | **Hudson**	-
NEW Pranzi | **White Pl**	-
Z Rebeccas | **Greenwich**	26
Z Rest. North | **Armonk**	26
Ruth's Chris | **Tarrytown**	25
Z Sapore | **Fishkill**	26
Swoon | **Hudson**	24
Tappo | **Stamford**	-
Z Tarry Lodge | **Port Chester**	24
Terra Rustica | **Briarcliff Manor**	19
Z Thomas Henkelmann | **Greenwich**	28
Tuscan Oven | **Mt. Kisco**	20
TuttaBella | **Scarsdale**	23
Underhills | **Bronxville**	21
Valbella | **Riverside**	25
Valley/Garrison | **Garrison**	23
Velo | **Nyack**	24
NEW Vintage 1891 | **Larch**	-
Vinum Cafe | **Washingtonville**	-
West St. Grill | **Litchfield**	24
Willett House | **Port Chester**	24
Winvian | **Litchfield**	27
Would | **Highland**	22
Z Xaviars | **Piermont**	28
NEW ZaZa | **Stamford**	-

THE BERKSHIRES
RESTAURANT
DIRECTORY

TOP FOOD

27 Old Inn/Green | *American*
Blantyre | *American/French*
25 Wheatleigh | *American/French*
Nudel | *American*
Tratt. Rustica* | *Italian*

TOP DECOR

29 Blantyre | *American/French*
Wheatleigh | *American/French*
26 Old Inn/Green | *American*
25 Cranwell Resort | *American*
24 Old Mill | *American*

Aegean Breeze *Greek*
`19` `16` `19` `$39`

Great Barrington | 327 Stockbridge Rd. (bet. Cooper & Crissey Rds.) |
413-528-4001 | www.aegean-breeze.com

It's "not quite Santorini", but this "comfortable" Great Barrington
Greek is "a reliable choice" for "tasty taverna food"; white stucco
decor with blue accents creates a "relaxing" backdrop for "friendly,
informal service", and while a few find the menu "pricey", "terrific"
daily specials offer "reasonable" value.

Allium *American*
`18` `19` `17` `$46`

Great Barrington | 42-44 Railroad St. (Main St.) | 413-528-2118 |
www.alliumberkshires.com

Fans of this "upscale" Great Barrington sib of Williamstown's Mezze
praise the "ambitious" New American "comfort food for locavores"
and "hip" digs; the less enthused complain that lately the "limited
menu" "misses the mark", tabs are "a bit expensive" and service
"varies from ok to clueless"; even so, it remains a "happening place."

Alpamayo *Peruvian*
`-` `-` `-` `M`

Lee | 60 Main St. (Franklin St.) | 413-243-6000 |
www.alpamayorestaurant.com

Lee diners looking for something different find it at this two-year-old
Peruvian where baked-corn-kernel nibbles precede the likes of paella, ceviche and whole rotisserie chicken, all served in generous
portions; chocolate-hued walls, red-tiled floors and white tablecloths dress up the cafe setting, and the tabs are affordable.

Alta *Mediterranean*
`21` `18` `22` `$44`

Lenox | 34 Church St. (bet. Housatonic & Walker Sts.) | 413-637-0003 |
www.altawinebar.com

"Locals and visitors alike" head to this "congenial" Lenox eatery and
wine bar for "delicious" Mediterranean fare and "top-notch" *vini* at
"upper-moderate" prices; service is "lovely", while the "porch on a
breezy summer night" suits "those of a certain age" who find the
"pretty" but "generally crowded" interior on the "noisy" side.

Aroma Bar & Grill *Indian*
`22` `13` `19` `$27`

Great Barrington | 485 Main St. (South St.) | 413-528-3116 |
www.aromabarandgrill.com

"What a surprise!" declare Great Barrington denizens of this "rare
find" "run by a lovely family", which prepares its "authentic" Indian
fare "as spicy as you like"; "well-chosen wines" and "affordable"
rates are pluses, and there's always takeout for those who don't care
for the "informal" setting.

---

* Indicates a tie with restaurant above

Baba Louie's Sourdough Pizza *Pizza*   24 | 13 | 18 | $23

Great Barrington | 286 Main St. (bet. Elm & Railroad Sts.) | 413-528-8100
Pittsfield | 34 Depot St. (McKay St.) | 413-499-2400
www.babalouiespizza.com

"Superb" pizza with "paper-thin" sourdough crusts and "creative, sophisticated" toppings lead to "lines out the door" at this Great Barrington spot and its offshoots, where "scrumptious" salads, soups and sandwiches round out the "bargain" menu; staffers "aim to please", and although it's "cramped", there's much more "elbow room" at the "attractive" Pittsfield sibling and the Hudson branch.

Barrington Brewery &   14 | 14 | 17 | $24
Restaurant *American*

Great Barrington | 420 Stockbridge Rd./Rte. 7 (Crissey Rd.) | 413-528-8282 | www.barringtonbrewery.net

"It's all about the beer" at this "bustling" Great Barrington micro-brewery, but there's "something for everyone" in the way of food too, namely "plentiful" portions of "homey" American eats with "no pretense"; "quick service", "modest" tabs and a "casual" if "chaotic" vibe in a "rustic, barnlike" setting make it "fun" for "families."

Bistro Zinc *French*   21 | 22 | 19 | $48

Lenox | 56 Church St. (bet. Housatonic & Tucker Sts.) | 413-637-8800 | www.bistrozinc.com

"Sophisticated" Gallic fare pairs with "polished" decor at this Lenox bistro where patrons can sit in the "sleek" dining room or "be part of the buzz" at the bar; although a few are annoyed by "Manhattan prices" and the "attitude problem" of many of "the people you're supposed to be tipping" (others are "friendly and accommodating"), it's nevertheless a "go-to" "for a special night out", so "reserve early."

Bizen *Japanese*   24 | 18 | 19 | $40

Great Barrington | 17 Railroad St. (Main St.) | 413-528-4343

"Sparklingly fresh, creative" sushi and a "huge menu" of "memorable" grilled fare "worth" the price keep this "popular" Great Barrington Japanese "always packed"; the "can-be-spotty" service is made up for by "engaging" chef Michael Marcus (BTW, that's his "wonderful pottery on view"), while those who consider the "noisy", "close quarters" "less than Zen" find "the tatami rooms a boon", especially when splurging on the prix fixe kaiseki.

ⓩ Blantyre Restaurant *American/French*   27 | 29 | 28 | $163

Lenox | Blantyre | 16 Blantyre Rd. (Walker St.) | 413-637-3556 | www.blantyre.com

With a "romantic, intimate" setting that conjures "Gilded Age" "luxury" and staffers who give patrons the "royal treatment", this "outstanding" prix fixe–only French–New American dining room in a Lenox inn earns The Berkshires' No. 1 scores for Decor and Service; the fare "makes you swoon" as much as the "megabucks" needed to pay for it, yet "it's worth every penny" for an experience that's "special in every sense"; P.S. it's "formal", so jacket and tie required at dinner, and no children under 12.

	FOOD	DECOR	SERVICE	COST

Bombay ⓂIndian
22 | 14 | 18 | $30

Lee | Quality Inn | 435 Laurel St./Rte. 20 (Lake Rd.) | 413-243-6731 | www.fineindiandining.com

Indian fare that's "sizzling with flavor" and "prepared to your liking" draws Lee curryphiles to this "comfortable" spot where a lunch buffet (in high season) that "can't be beat for value" is upstaged only by the "extraordinary" Sunday brunch; "service is willing", and if you sit overlooking Lake Laurel, it takes your mind off the "drab" decor.

NEW Brick House Pub Food
- | - | - | M

Housatonic | 425 Park St. (Front St.) | 413-274-0020 | www.brickhousema.com

After a change of hands, this long-standing North Housatonic saloon reopened with a midpriced menu of posh pub grub (think burgers with lime aïoli and truffle fries) made with local, organic ingredients and matched by a rotating selection of craft beers; a makeover of the bar left more room for live music, while a planned renovation will dress up the dining room and add a wraparound porch.

Brix Wine Bar ⊠Ⓜ French
23 | 20 | 22 | $42

Pittsfield | 40 West St. (bet. McKay & North Sts.) | 413-236-9463 | www.brixwinebar.com

"What's not to like?" asks the "younger crowd" who hie to this "hip" Pittsfield bistro for its "excellent" French bistro fare, "well-chosen wines", "reasonable prices" and "chic", "brick-lined" setting; "personable" service and an "*intime*" vibe help to make it "perfect for a date", as long as you don't mind a little "noise" (and a no-rez policy).

Brulées ⊠Ⓜ American/European
▽ 21 | 23 | 22 | $33

Pittsfield | 41 North St. (bet. East & School Sts.) | 413-443-0500 | www.brulees.com

"Everyone's excited" about this "promising" midpriced Pittsfield relative newcomer offering a "good variety" of "great" American-European eats, ranging from its signature pan-seared scallops to steaks, seafood and pastas, plus vittles for vegetarians and young 'uns; the roomy, "comfortably elegant" digs include a lounge, which hosts live music on weekends.

Cafe Adam Ⓜ European
23 | 17 | 20 | $43

Great Barrington | 325 Stockbridge Rd. (bet. Cooper & Crissey Rds.) | 413-528-7786 | www.cafeadam.org

"Skillful" chef-owner Adam Zieminski turns out a "small" but "fabulous" menu of "inspired" "European bistro cuisine" at this Great Barrington outpost; a "soothing" environment with a "nice porch" for when it's warm, "welcoming" staffers, "fair prices" and a "wonderful" "wine list that has real value" all factor into the "satisfying" experience.

Café Lucia ⊠Ⓜ Italian
23 | 20 | 22 | $51

Lenox | 80 Church St. (bet. Franklin & Housatonic Sts.) | 413-637-2640 | www.cafelucialenox.com

"Sophisticated", "wonderful" Italian cooking ("you'll swoon for the osso buco") plus a staff that "aims to please" make this Lenox venue in an "elegant" 1840s farmhouse an "'in' spot", despite somewhat "elevated tariffs"; surveyors seeking "lots of energy" choose to sit inside, while those who find it too "cramped" and "noisy" (especially when they "pack them in during Tanglewood") ask for the "lovely deck"; P.S. closed in winter.

Castle Street Cafe *American/French*   20 | 18 | 20 | $41

Great Barrington | 10 Castle St. (Main St.) | 413-528-5244 | www.castlestreetcafe.com

"An old standby and deservedly so", this "reliable" Great Barrington American-French "charmer" draws "repeat customers" for "bargain" "quick bites" in the bar or "solid" bistro "standards" at more expensive tabs in the dining room; the service is "warm", the wine list is "moderately priced" and "great" live jazz on weekends gives the "homey" digs a "festive" feel, so no wonder it's "still going strong."

Chez Nous Ⓜ *French*   24 | 20 | 24 | $48

Lee | 150 Main St. (Academy St.) | 413-243-6397 | www.cheznousbistro.com

"Wonderful all around" declare Lee locals of this "delightful" destination where chef Franck Tessier's "fantastic" French bistro fare is matched by spouse Rachel Portnoy's "scrumptious desserts", not to mention her "charming" greetings; an "impressive", "well-priced wine list" adds to the "good value", while "marvelous service" "without hauteur" and a setting in a "historic house" with "quiet, romantic corners" add to the "appeal."

Coyote Flaco Ⓜ *Mexican*   23 | 18 | 22 | $34

Williamstown | 505 Cold Spring Rd. (Bee Hill Rd.) | 413-458-4240 | www.mycoyoteflaco.com

See review in Westchester Directory.

Cranwell Resort, Spa &   21 | 25 | 22 | $51
Golf Club *American*

Lenox | 55 Lee Rd./Rte. 20 (Rte. 7) | 413-881-1621 | www.cranwell.com

"Swellegant" sums up this "beautiful" Tudor-esque mansion resort in Lenox, where "people come from all over" for "well-prepared" New American fare served in an "unrushed" fashion in the "grand" Wyndhurst or Music Room restaurants; those who don't want to "go broke" eat at the more "moderate" Sloane's Tavern, dispensing "publike" provisions, while calorie counters hit the Spa Cafe for lunch.

Dakota Steakhouse *Steak*   17 | 17 | 18 | $36

Pittsfield | 1035 South St. (Dan Fox Dr.) | 413-499-7900 | www.steakseafood.com

"You get a lot for your money" at this Pittsfield steakhouse famed for its "pig-out Sunday buffet" brunch, "well-stocked salad bar" and "generous" if "pedestrian" "proteins, be they seafood or land-based"; the "Western motif" complete with "stuffed animals" may be "tired" and service can be "lackluster", but it nevertheless "hits the spot", especially for "families", as it's quite "child-friendly."

FOOD | DECOR | SERVICE | COST

Dream Away Lodge 🖪 *American*   17 | 21 | 19 | $34

Becket | 1342 County Rd. (Stanley Rd.) | 413-623-8725 |
www.thedreamawaylodge.com

"A true original", this "oddball" New American "in the middle of no-where" in Becket puts the "kitsch in kitchen" with an affordable, "un-usual menu" running from burgers to tagines served by a "pleasant" crew; even those who consider the eats "average" admit the "hoote-nanny atmosphere" (a 19th-century farm-cum-"old cathouse"-cum-speakeasy) "makes up for it", as does the nightly live music.

Elizabeth's 🖪🖪🗭 *Eclectic*   24 | 13 | 23 | $35

Pittsfield | 1264 East St. (Newell St.) | 413-448-8244

"Utterly delicious" pastas, "legendary salads" and one "tantalizing" fish and meat dish per night comprise the roster at this "off-the-beaten-track" Pittsfield Eclectic "institution" with a "devoted fan base"; a "dinerlike" setting prompts the question "what decor?", but tabs are "a true bargain" and chef-owner Tom Ellis is a "trip" who'll accept "an IOU" if you haven't got "good old cash or a check."

Fin *Japanese*   23 | 19 | 19 | $44

Lenox | 27 Housatonic St. (Church St.) | 413-637-9171 |
www.finsushi.com

Even though it's "far from the ocean", this "easygoing" Lenox Japanese stocks sushi "so fresh it wiggles", along with some "cre-ative specials" among the cooked fare; such "big quality" helps off-set the "small", "noisy" digs dominated by a red lacquered bar, while takeout's an option when it's "hard to get into."

NEW Fiori *Italian*   – | – | – | E

Great Barrington | 47 Railroad St. (Main St.) | 413-528-0351 |
www.fiorirestaurant.com

Local lads Alexander and Matthew Feldman are behind this Great Barrington Northern Italian turning out handmade pastas, risottos and wood-grilled meats, with a $30 prix fixe offsetting slightly pricey tabs; the easygoing setting features a busy bar (serving small plates), fre-quent live music and dancing, plus a patio for fair weather.

Firefly *American*   17 | 17 | 17 | $38

Lenox | 71 Church St. (Housatonic St.) | 413-637-2700 |
www.fireflylenox.com

"Berkshires casual" is the style of this Lenox New American where "locals meet" in the "cozy" dining rooms or on the "pleasant" porch when it's warm; some say the midpriced fare is "imagina-tive" and "well prepared" while others claim it's "mediocre" – but there's consensus on the "erratic service" and the appeal of the "late-night bar."

Flavours of Malaysia 🖪 *Asian*   21 | 12 | 20 | $29

Pittsfield | 75 North St. (McKay St.) | 413-443-3188 |
www.flavoursintheberkshires.com

An "elaborate" assortment of dishes from China, Malaysia, India and Thailand come "cooked to order" and as "spicy" as you like at

FOOD DECOR SERVICE COST

this "wonderful" Pittsfield Asian; though "remodeling" wouldn't hurt and the live bands on weekends "change the atmosphere", the "accommodating" staff and "outstanding value" help make it "deserving of the crowds it attracts."

Frankie's Ristorante Italiano *Italian* | 18 | 18 | 20 | $41 |

Lenox | 80 Main St. (Cliftwood St.) | 413-637-4455 | www.frankiesitaliano.com

"Enjoyable" "red-sauce preparations" "entice" "families" to this "welcoming" Lenox Italian restaurant where a "young", "on-the-ball" staff serves in dining rooms warmed up with "old photos on the walls"; true, it's "not high end", but it's "not stuffy" either, just a "good spot" for those "on a budget"; P.S. the "porch in summer is a plus."

Gramercy Bistro *American/Eclectic* | 23 | 21 | 22 | $43 |

North Adams | MASS MoCA | 87 Marshall St. (bet. River St. & Rte. 2) | 413-663-5300 | www.gramercybistro.com

Located in MASS MoCa, this "standout" chef-owned North Adams bistro feeds "famished" museumgoers a "diverse menu" of "stellar" seasonal American-Eclectic fare; "reasonable pricing", an "attentive" crew, "comfortable" modern surroundings and a summertime patio all add to the "pleasure."

Gypsy Joynt *American* ∇ | 16 | 13 | 16 | $17 |

Great Barrington | 293 Main St. (Railroad St.) | 413-644-8811 | www.gypsyjoyntcafe.com

Now installed in Napa's old space, this Great Barrington American "hangout" continues to dish up organic, affordable fare; some say the eats are "just ok", but "friendly service" and "great music" on weekends add up to a "funky good time"; P.S. many of the "delightfully random" adornments (flags, beads, posters and such) made the move – still, the Decor score is most likely outdated.

Haven *American/Bakery* | 23 | 15 | 16 | $21 |

Lenox | 8 Franklin St. (Main St.) | 413-637-8948 | www.havencafebakery.com

The "elite meet to eat" "wonderful", "high-end" breakfasts and "flavorful, hearty" lunches (plus "indulgent" "homestyle" dinners in season) at this "low-key" American cafe and bakery in "trendy" Downtown Lenox; "gourmet coffees, teas" and "cocktails based on Berkshire mountains spirits" are also available in the "spacious, unassuming" room – and "oh yeah, they have wireless" too.

NEW Hops & Vines ⑤Ⓜ *American* | - | - | - | M |

Williamstown | 16 Water St. (Main St.) | 413-884-1372 | www.hopsandvinesma.com

Aptly named, this new Williamstown two-for-one takes its beverages as seriously as its French-accented New American cooking, offering cocktails, craft beers and boutique wines to match the moderately priced dishes; one half of the venue is a hopping beer hall with picnic-style tables and TVs, while the other half is a dressier, quieter brasserie, with wine hues and brick walls.

| | FOOD | DECOR | SERVICE | COST |

The Hub 🖾 *American* ▽ 23 | 21 | 22 | $36

North Adams | 55 Main St. (State St.) | 413-662-2500 |
www.thehubrestaurant.com

Often "packed", this North Adams American "upscale diner" "lives up
to its name" as a "hangout" that's "tough to beat" for "comfort food";
"professional" servers patrol the storefront setting where the eats
are "priced right" and the house wines are a similarly "good value."

John Andrews *American* 24 | 22 | 23 | $54

South Egremont | 224 Hillsdale Rd. (Blunt Rd.) | 413-528-3469 |
www.jarestaurant.com

A "nicely dressed, soft-spoken clientele" gathers at this "fine-dining
rendezvous" "in the woods" of South Egremont to "sit back and enjoy" "superior" New American cooking served by an "informed,
friendly" staff in "delightful", "romantic" surroundings; naturally,
such a "celebratory" experience commands an "expensive" tab, although the budget-conscious claim "even the bar menu is a class
act", and "more reasonable" to boot.

John Harvard's Brew House *Pub Food* 16 | 17 | 17 | $25

Hancock | Country Inn at Jiminy Peak | 37 Corey Rd., 3rd fl.
(Brodie Mountain Rd.) | 413-738-5500 | www.johnharvards.com

"Terrific beer" is all you need to know about this "casual" Hancock
outpost of the brewpub chain dispensing a "wide selection" of "craft-
brewed" suds to wash down "ok" American "comfort food"; though it
can "feel like a frat house" ("expect a drinking crowd"), it's perfectly
"adequate" as an "after-work hangout" with "reasonable prices."

Jonathan's Bistro *American* 20 | 17 | 19 | $37

Lenox | Lenox Commons | 55 Pittsfield Rd. (bet. Dugway Rd. & Main St.) |
413-637-8022

"A pleasant surprise hidden in a shopping center", this "casual"
Lenox New American turns out "something for all appetites",
ranging from "tasty sandwiches" to "original" entrees; although a
few find the fare "uneven", most say it's "on the mark" and laud
the "lovely wine list", "good prices", "comfortable" digs and patio
for summer dining.

𝗡𝗘𝗪 Kemble Inn *American* - | - | - | E

Lenox | 2 Kemble St. (Walker St.) | 413-637-4113 | www.kembleinn.com

Set in a restored Gilded Age mansion in Lenox, this New American
addition prepares somewhat pricey prix fixes for dinner, plus à la
carte breakfasts and lunches in season only; whether you choose
the stylish slate-blue-and-tan dining room, the candlelit piano
lounge or the warm-weather veranda, reservations are a must;
P.S. open weekends only in winter.

La Terrazza *American/Italian* ▽ 23 | 24 | 20 | $55

Lenox | Gateways Inn | 51 Walker St. (bet. Church & Kemble Sts.) |
413-637-2532 | www.gatewaysinn.com

You "walk into what looks like someone's house" at this Italian-
American eatery in Lenox's "lovely" Gateways Inn (it was the

Procter mansion, back in the day); cream-colored walls and soft music in the dining room create an "elegant" backdrop for somewhat pricey but "outstanding homemade pastas" and such, while the "excellent wine and spirits" include an extravagant selection of single-malt scotch.

Lucia's Latin Kitchen *Pan-Latin*

| - | - | - | I |

Pittsfield | 239 Onota St. (Locust St.) | 413-442-4440 |
www.luciaslatinkitchen.com

Homestyle Ecuadorian cuisine is the specialty of this bargain-priced Pan-Latin in a tiny, super-casual shack in Pittsfield; there's no liquor, but patrons can slake their thirst with fruity drinks while watching Lucia herself at work in the open kitchen.

Marketplace Café *American*

| - | - | - | I |

NEW **Pittsfield** | 53 North St. (West St.) | 413-358-4777 |
www.ourmarketplacecafe.com

Marketplace Kitchen *American*

Sheffield | 18 Elm Ct. (Main St.) | 413-248-5040 |
www.marketplacekitchen.com

"Breakfast wraps that will fortify you until dusk", plus "terrific soups" and flatbread pizzas are among the American eats on offer at this Sheffield spin-off of Marketplace, the specialty foods shop nearby; the "diner"-style digs are cheery and the rates "inexpensive", especially on Tuesday nights when "home-cooked meals" that feed a family of four cost only $25; P.S. the Pittsfield offshoot is new.

Mezze Bistro + Bar *American*

| 22 | 22 | 22 | $51 |

Williamstown | 777 Cold Spring Rd./Rte. 7 (Taconic Trail) | 413-458-0123 |
www.mezzebistro.com

Ensconced in an "inviting", "airy" 19th-century farmhouse (reflecting its farm-to-table philosophy), this "exciting" Williamstown New American eatery dispenses "sophisticated" cuisine via a team of staffers who "know the right pace"; even those surveyors who complain of "inflated" prices agree it's "the place to impress your out-of-town friends."

Mill on the Floss Ⓜ *French*

| 23 | 23 | 24 | $51 |

New Ashford | 342 New Ashford Rd./Rte. 7 (Kelly Ln.) | 413-458-9123 |
www.millonthefloss.com

It's "a little old-fashioned" and "that's a good thing" declare the "discerning clientele" of this "long-established" New Ashford French "classic" where "everything is superb", from the "quality" "country fare" and "personal" service to the "glorious" 18th-century farmhouse setting; sure, it's "special" (read: pricey), but there's a nightly three-course prix fixe that's "the bargain of the century."

Mission Bar & Tapas ❶ *Spanish*

| 23 | 19 | 22 | $30 |

Pittsfield | 438 North St. (Maplewood Ave.) | no phone |
www.missionbarandtapas.com

A "slice of SoHo in Downtown Pittsfield", this "trendy" Spanish "hangout" has "mastered" a menu of "tasty" tapas to match its "wonderful" Iberian wines – and for pretty "low prices" too; a staff that "aims to please" works the "funky", low-lit room where musicians and a "kitchen open until midnight" mean it stays "lively" until "late."

Morgan House Restaurant *New England* 15 | 16 | 17 | $39

Lee | Morgan Hse. | 33 Main St. (Park Pl.) | 413-243-3661 | www.morganhouseinn.com

"Comforting in an old country inn kind of way", this "friendly" spot in Lee has "been around for years", dishing up moderately priced, "traditional" New England fare in an early-19th-century onetime stagecoach stop; some complain the eats are "ordinary" and the vibe "touristy", but the "good bar crowd" might disagree.

☑ Nudel ⓜ *American* 25 | 15 | 21 | $41

Lenox | 37 Church St. (bet. Housatonic & Walker Sts.) | 413-551-7183 | www.nudelrestaurant.com

"Wow", "this man can cook!" exclaim those taking a "culinary romp" at chef Bjorn Somlo's "vibrant" New American enlivening "sleepy" Lenox with an "excellent", "ever-changing", midpriced menu of "ingenious cuisine" highlighting pastas (aka nudels) and "whatever's fresh" that day; the "no-reservations scenario" makes it "tough to get into" the "cubbyhole" of a space, so "show up early" or expect "a big wait."

☑ Old Inn on the Green 27 | 26 | 26 | $63
Restaurant ⓜ *American*

New Marlborough | Old Inn on the Green |
134 Hartsville New Marlborough Rd./Rte. 57 (Rte. 272) |
413-229-7924 | www.oldinn.com

"You need a compass to find" this "idyllic" New Marlborough "treasure" set in a "romantic" 1760s inn, but once there you'll be "blown away" by chef-owner Peter Platt's "prodigious menu" of "fabulous" New American cuisine, voted No. 1 for Food in the Berkshires; a "superb wine list", "professional staff" and "lovely" rooms "lit only by candles and fireplaces" are part of the package, and while it'll "empty your pocketbook", "it's worth it" for such a "magical experience"; P.S. the $35 prix fixe offered on some nights is a "fantastic" "steal."

Old Mill ⓜ *American* 24 | 24 | 25 | $47

South Egremont | 53 Main St. (Baldwin Hill Rd. S.) | 413-528-1421 | www.oldmillberkshires.com

It's "pure country charm" at this "quaint" South Egremont veteran turning out "first-rate" American fare via the "best-trained staff" in a "pretty" 1797 old mill with "crooked floors" and "a gorgeous fireplace"; one "drawback" is no reservations for fewer than five, but there's a "cozy bar to warm your cockles while you wait", or you can eat there from a lighter menu – it's "easier on the budget" and you "get the best of both worlds."

Once Upon a Table *American/Continental* 21 | 15 | 19 | $38

Stockbridge | The Mews | 36 Main St./Rte. 102 (bet. Elm St. & Rte. 7) | 413-298-3870 | www.onceuponatablebistro.com

"Blessed with a loyal following", this "delightful" Stockbridge American-Continental "hidden away" in a mews beside the Red Lion

Inn dispenses "well-prepared" dishes deemed "worth the squeeze" in the "intimate" (make that *very* small") setting; "quick service" means it's "good for lunch", while you "can take your time" at dinner, "if you can get in."

Perigee *Eclectic/New England*   19 | 18 | 20 | $46

Lee | 1575 Pleasant St. (bet. Church & Willow Sts.) | 413-394-4047 | www.perigee-restaurant.com

This "casual", "off-the-beaten-path" spot in Lee offers Eclectic–New England fare (trademarked as Berkshire cuisine) that some say is "consistently good" and others find sometimes "too elaborate", with tabs a tad "high for the area"; still, everyone agrees on the "appealing" two-story setting and "wonderful owner" who heads up an "accommodating" staff.

Pho Saigon *Vietnamese*   22 | 12 | 18 | $22

Lee | 5 Railroad St. (Main St.) | 413-243-6288

"Who'd have thought you'd find authentic Vietnamese in Lee?" ask astonished newcomers to this "tiny place" run by a "friendly, talkative owner" turning out "homestyle" pho and other dishes, plus "excellent pad Thai" to boot; yes, it's "low on decor, but high on taste and value", and it "hits the spot" after a "night of partying."

Prime Italian Steakhouse & Bar 🗷Ⓜ *Italian/Steak*   ▽ 21 | 22 | 22 | $48

Lenox | 15 Franklin St. (Main St.) | 413-637-2998 | www.primelenox.com

"A good bet" for "red meat and red wine" plus "old favorite dishes" like chef-owner Gennaro Gallo's homemade gnocchi, this Lenox Southern Italian steakhouse beloved of the "business" set makes everyone "feel welcome"; indeed, it's "pricey", but unsurprisingly so given the upscale touches that abound in both the fare and the "hip decor" with a backlit bar.

🆕 Public Eat + Drink *American*   - | - | - | M

North Adams | 34 Holden St. (Center St.) | 413-664-4444 | www.publiceatanddrink.com

Jazzed-up American comfort food is the specialty of this laid-back North Adams newcomer with pared-down digs sporting a long bar and industrial-chic accents like exposed ducts and brick walls; regional craft brews and signature cocktails are highlights of the drinks selection, while weekly trivia nights and live music provide entertainment.

Red Lion Inn Restaurant *New England*   18 | 22 | 21 | $46

Stockbridge | Red Lion Inn | 30 Main St./Rte. 102 (bet. Main & Water Sts.) | 413-298-5545 | www.redlioninn.com

Stockbridge's "grande dame", this 1773 inn simply "screams Norman Rockwell" while dispensing "safe" New England "classics" in the "fine, old", "formal" dining room, "rustic" Widow Bingham's Tavern or "casual" Lion's Den pub, where tariffs are "lower"; "service is top-notch", and even though grumps grumble it's "only for tourists", it's practically "mandatory" to "go once."

	FOOD	DECOR	SERVICE	COST

Rouge ⓜ *French* | 22 | 18 | 17 | $49 |

West Stockbridge | 3 Center St. (Main St./Rte. 41) | 413-232-4111 | www.rougerestaurant.com

Chef William Merelle's "mouthwatering" French cuisine coupled with spouse Maggie's "warm hospitality" make this West Stockbridge bistro a "popular" "go-to" for the "elite and hoi polloi" alike; a relatively recent expansion doubled the rouge-accented space, although it still gets "jammed" in the "lively" bar where the less "expensive", "interesting tapas menu" is "a treat", leaving only "loud" decibels and sometimes "lackadaisical service" as issues.

Route 7 Grill ⓜ *BBQ* | 18 | 13 | 19 | $36 |

Great Barrington | 999 S. Main St. (bet. Brookside & Lime Kiln Rds.) | 413-528-3235 | www.route7grill.com

"Awfully good babyback ribs" are among the "well-priced", "finger-licking" fare at this Great Barrington BBQ specialist focusing on "locally raised meats and produce"; "Texans" and others less enthused declare it "just ok", but most enjoy the "nice buzz" in the "family-friendly" space, made cheery by its "raging fire" and "horseshoe bar."

Shiro Sushi & Hibachi *Japanese* | 20 | 16 | 18 | $34 |

Great Barrington | 105 Stockbridge Rd. (bet. Blue Hill Rd. & Brooke Ln.) | 413-528-1898

Shiro Lounge *Japanese*

Pittsfield | 48 North St. (School St.) | 413-236-8111
www.berkshiro.com

Sushi is "difficult to find in the Berkshires", but "the art is alive" at this Japanese duo purveying "artistic" fare; true, the digs have all "the ambiance of a tire shop", but the staff is "pleasant" and the prices moderate, plus the "hilarious" hibachi chefs grilling "bountiful" meals at the Great Barrington original "make it fun for the whole family."

Siam Square Thai Cuisine *Thai* | 19 | 16 | 20 | $25 |

Great Barrington | 290 Main St. (Railroad St.) | 413-644-9119 | www.siamsquares.com

"The only game in town" for Thai, this "casual", somewhat "quiet" Great Barrington spot draws many "regulars" with its "wide array" of "terrific" fare featuring the occasional "kick"; it's "a good value" and the dishes come "served quickly and with a smile", making it "one of the best pre-movie" options around.

Spice Dragon *American/Asian* | 22 | 23 | 20 | $40 |
(fka Jae's Spice)

Pittsfield | 297 North St. (bet. Summer & Union Sts.) | 413-443-1234 | www.eatatspicedragon.com

Don't worry if the "adventurous menu" of midpriced "designer" Pan-Asian fare at this "beautiful" Pittsfield "gem" (formerly called Jae's Spice) "seems daunting", because "you can't go wrong" – there are even "tasty" "American choices" "for the non-chopstick crowd"; although it's "warehouse-sized", the space has a "warm atmosphere", with the "bonus" of being "close to the Barrington Stage" theater and a "nice staff" to ensure you "make the curtain."

	FOOD	DECOR	SERVICE	COST

Stagecoach Tavern ⛄Ⓜ *American* ▽ 17 | 23 | 20 | $40

Sheffield | Race Brook Lodge | 864 S. Undermountain Rd./Rte. 41
(Berkshire School Rd.) | 413-229-8585 | www.stagecoachtavern.net
It's so "atmospheric", "you can imagine tying your horse outside"
this "inviting" 1829 tavern in Sheffield, where a seasonal menu of
"dependable" American fare comes served in "cozy", "candlelit"
rooms with fireplaces, making it "perfect on a snowy night"; the
"sweet" staff adds to the "convivial" vibe, while moderate tabs are
another reason it's "worth going."

Sullivan Station Restaurant Ⓜ *New England* 15 | 18 | 20 | $30

Lee | 109 Railroad St. (Elm St.) | 413-243-2082 |
www.sullivanstationrestaurant.com
"A Lee standby", this restored "historic" onetime train depot is all
"old-fashioned charm", from its "large portions" of affordable,
"plain" New England eats to its "homey" digs with "decor featuring
locomotive pictures and railroad nostalgia"; "lunch is always good"
and just the ticket if you're with kids, especially when the Berkshire
Scenic Railway toots by.

NEW Sushi House *Asian* - | - | - | M

North Adams | 45 Main St. (Marshall St.) | 413-664-9388
Sushi finally arrives in North Adams courtesy of this Pan-Asian newcomer that also offers Chinese, Korean, Thai and cooked Japanese
dishes on its reasonably priced menu; red lacquered chairs, black-
and-white paintings and lanterns over the bar dress up the otherwise plain brick-storefront setting, which fills up fast because it's
quite small (takeout is always an option).

Sushi Thai Garden *Japanese/Thai* ▽ 20 | 15 | 21 | $30

Williamstown | 27 Spring St. (Rte. 2) | 413-458-0004 |
www.sushithaigarden-ma.com
The "Thai food is hearty and hot" and the sushi "surprisingly good"
at this "dependable" Williamstown spot; although the "tables are
close together", the decor in the "casual" brick storefront setting is
"fine", while "bargain" rates, "attentive service" and overall menu
"variety" make it a "good place to go with a group of friends."

Trattoria Il Vesuvio *Italian* 19 | 17 | 20 | $41

Lenox | 242 Pittsfield Rd. (bet. Lime Kiln & New Lenox Rds.) |
413-637-4904 | www.trattoria-vesuvio.com
Fans of this "reliable" Lenox Italian claim the menu of "traditional"
red sauce may "not change much", but it's as "comforting as a warm
blanket on a cold day", plus the "homemade bread is great"; the converted hundred-year-old stable is "cavernous" but cozy, thanks to
the wood-fired brick oven and "family-owned" feeling.

Trattoria Rustica *Italian* 25 | 21 | 21 | $48

Pittsfield | 27 McKay St. (West St.) | 413-499-1192 |
www.trattoria-rustica.com
This "charming" Southern Italian is "worth a detour" to Pittsfield declare devotees of chef-owner Davide Manzo's "delicious", "sophisti-

cated" cooking; the lantern-lit, brick-and-stone setting creates a "romantic" vibe in winter, while courtyard dining is "wonderful" when it's warm, so even though it's a little "expensive", it's a "special place."

Truc Orient Express *Vietnamese*   22 | 19 | 20 | $32

West Stockbridge | 3 Harris St. (Main St./Rte. 40) | 413-232-4204 | www.trucorientexpress.com

"A Berkshires legend", this "amazing", over-30-year-old West Stockbridge Vietnamese offers its "splendid", "artfully presented" fare for "great prices"; the owners provide a "quiet", "welcoming" mood in "easygoing" digs, which are adorned with art from their homeland and augmented with an "extraordinary" attached gift shop.

Viva Ⓜ *Spanish*   23 | 19 | 21 | $38

Glendale | 14 Glendale Rd. (Mohawk Lake Rd.) | 413-298-4433 | www.vivaberkshires.com

"Excellent paella" and "wonderful tapas" are representative of the "confident Spanish cooking" that draws Glendale denizens to this "out-of-the-way" spot near the Norman Rockwell museum; an "unobtrusive" staff serves in the "spacious", colorful room where a Picasso-like mural adds to the "fun" environment.

Ⓩ Wheatleigh Restaurant *American/French*   25 | 29 | 27 | $93

Lenox | Wheatleigh | 11 Hawthorne Rd. (Hawthorne St.) | 413-637-0610 | www.wheatleigh.com

"Gatsby would have been proud" of Lenox's "magnificent" Italianate mansion, where it's "class all the way", from rooms exuding "elegance by the cartload" to the "fabulous" New American–French fare and "pampering" staff; a few fret about "prohibitive" tabs, but most suggest you "take out a second mortgage" and "splurge", because "life doesn't get much better than this"; P.S. jackets suggested.

Xicohtencatl *Mexican*   21 | 19 | 20 | $33

Great Barrington | 50 Stockbridge Rd. (State Rd./Rte. 23) | 413-528-2002 | www.xicohmexican.com

"No average Mexican", this Great Barrington spot dispenses "inspired", "flavorful" eats via a "crowd-pleasing staff" that can "discuss the subtleties"; "lively decor", a "huge margarita list" and "moderate prices" add to the "fun", while the patio is "mellow."

THE BERKSHIRES
INDEXES

Cuisines 244
Locations 246
Special Features 248

Cuisines

Includes names, locations and Food ratings.

AMERICAN

Allium | **Great Barr**	18
Barrington Brew | **Great Barr**	14
☑ Blantyre | **Lenox**	27
Brulées | **Pittsfield**	21
Castle St. | **Great Barr**	20
Cranwell Resort | **Lenox**	21
Dream Away | **Becket**	17
Firefly | **Lenox**	17
Gramercy | **N Adams**	23
Gypsy Joynt | **Great Barr**	16
Haven | **Lenox**	23
NEW Hops/Vines | **Williamstown**	–
Hub | **N Adams**	23
John Andrews | **S Egremont**	24
Jonathan's | **Lenox**	20
NEW Kemble Inn | **Lenox**	–
La Terrazza | **Lenox**	23
Marketplace | **multi.**	–
Mezze Bistro | **Williamstown**	22
☑ Nudel | **Lenox**	25
☑ Old Inn/Green | **New Marl**	27
Old Mill | **S Egremont**	24
Once Upon | **Stockbridge**	21
NEW Public Eat/Drink | **N Adams**	–
Spice Dragon | **Pittsfield**	22
Stagecoach Tav. | **Sheffield**	17
☑ Wheatleigh | **Lenox**	25

ASIAN

Flavours/Malaysia | **Pittsfield**	21
Spice Dragon | **Pittsfield**	22

BAKERIES

Haven | **Lenox**	23

BARBECUE

Rte. 7 Grill | **Great Barr**	18

CONTINENTAL

Once Upon | **Stockbridge**	21

ECLECTIC

Elizabeth's | **Pittsfield**	24
Gramercy | **N Adams**	23
Perigee | **Lee**	19

EUROPEAN

Brulées | **Pittsfield**	21
Cafe Adam | **Great Barr**	23

FRENCH

☑ Blantyre | **Lenox**	27
Mill on Floss | **New Ashford**	23
☑ Wheatleigh | **Lenox**	25

FRENCH (BISTRO)

Bistro Zinc | **Lenox**	21
Brix Wine | **Pittsfield**	23
Castle St. | **Great Barr**	20
Chez Nous | **Lee**	24
Rouge | **W Stockbridge**	22

GREEK

Aegean Breeze | **Great Barr**	19

INDIAN

Aroma B&G | **Great Barr**	22
Bombay | **Lee**	22

ITALIAN

(N=Northern; S=Southern)

Café Lucia | **Lenox**	23
NEW Fiori | N | **Great Barr**	–
Frankie's Rist. | **Lenox**	18
La Terrazza | **Lenox**	23
Prime Italian | S | **Lenox**	21
Tratt. Il Vesuvio | **Lenox**	19
Tratt. Rustica | S | **Pittsfield**	25

JAPANESE

(* sushi specialist)

Bizen* | **Great Barr**	24
Fin* | **Lenox**	23
Shiro* | **multi.**	20

NEW Sushi House* | N Adams ‒

Sushi Thai Gdn.* | Williamstown 20

MEDITERRANEAN

Alta | Lenox 21

MEXICAN

Coyote Flaco | Williamstown 23

Xicohtencatl | Great Barr 21

NEW ENGLAND

Morgan House | Lee 15

Perigee | Lee 19

Red Lion Inn | Stockbridge 18

Sullivan Station | Lee 15

PAN-LATIN

Lucia's Latin Kitchen | Pittsfield ‒

PERUVIAN

Alpamayo | Lee ‒

PIZZA

Baba Louie's | multi. 24

PUB FOOD

NEW Brick House | Housatonic ‒

John Harvard's | Hancock 16

SPANISH

(* tapas specialist)

Mission Bar* | Pittsfield 23

Viva* | Glendale 23

STEAKHOUSES

Dakota Steak | Pittsfield 17

Prime Italian | Lenox 21

THAI

Siam Sq. Thai | Great Barr 19

Sushi Thai Gdn. | Williamstown 20

VIETNAMESE

Pho Saigon | Lee 22

Truc Orient | W Stockbridge 22

Locations

Includes names, cuisines and Food ratings.

BECKET

Dream Away | *Amer.* — 17

GLENDALE

Viva | *Spanish* — 23

GREAT BARRINGTON

Aegean Breeze | *Greek* — 19
Allium | *Amer.* — 18
Aroma B&G | *Indian* — 22
Baba Louie's | *Pizza* — 24
Barrington Brew | *Amer.* — 14
Bizen | *Japanese* — 24
Cafe Adam | *Euro.* — 23
Castle St. | *Amer./French* — 20
NEW Fiori | *Italian* — -
Gypsy Joynt | *Amer.* — 16
Rte. 7 Grill | *BBQ* — 18
Shiro | *Japanese* — 20
Siam Sq. Thai | *Thai* — 19
Xicohtencatl | *Mex.* — 21

HANCOCK

John Harvard's | *Pub* — 16

HOUSATONIC

NEW Brick House | *Pub* — -

LEE

Alpamayo | *Peruvian* — -
Bombay | *Indian* — 22
Chez Nous | *French* — 24
Morgan House | *New Eng.* — 15
Perigee | *Eclectic/New Eng.* — 19
Pho Saigon | *Viet.* — 22
Sullivan Station | *New Eng.* — 15

LENOX

Alta | *Med.* — 21
Bistro Zinc | *French* — 21
Z Blantyre | *Amer./French* — 27
Café Lucia | *Italian* — 23

Cranwell Resort | *Amer.* — 21
Fin | *Japanese* — 23
Firefly | *Amer.* — 17
Frankie's Rist. | *Italian* — 18
Haven | *Amer./Bakery* — 23
Jonathan's | *Amer.* — 20
NEW Kemble Inn | *Amer.* — -
La Terrazza | *Amer./Italian* — 23
Z Nudel | *Amer.* — 25
Prime Italian | *Italian/Steak* — 21
Tratt. Il Vesuvio | *Italian* — 19
Z Wheatleigh | *Amer./French* — 25

NEW ASHFORD

Mill on Floss | *French* — 23

NEW MARLBOROUGH

Z Old Inn/Green | *Amer.* — 27

NORTH ADAMS

Gramercy | *Amer./Eclectic* — 23
Hub | *Amer.* — 23
NEW Public Eat/Drink | *Amer.* — -
NEW Sushi House | *Asian* — -

SOUTH EGREMONT

John Andrews | *Amer.* — 24
Old Mill | *Amer.* — 24

PITTSFIELD

Baba Louie's | *Pizza* — 24
Brix Wine | *French* — 23
Brulées | *Amer./Euro.* — 21
Dakota Steak | *Steak* — 17
Elizabeth's | *Eclectic* — 24
Flavours/Malaysia | *Asian* — 21
Lucia's Latin Kitchen | *Pan-Latin* — -
Marketplace | *Amer.* — -
Mission Bar | *Spanish* — 23
Shiro | *Japanese* — 20
Spice Dragon | *Amer./Asian* — 22
Tratt. Rustica | *Italian* — 25

SHEFFIELD

Marketplace | *Amer.* ___

Stagecoach Tav. | *Amer.* 17

STOCKBRIDGE

Once Upon | *Amer./Continental* 21

Red Lion Inn | *New Eng.* 18

WEST STOCKBRIDGE

Rouge | *French* 22

Truc Orient | *Viet.* 22

WILLIAMSTOWN

Coyote Flaco | *Mex.* 23

NEW Hops/Vines | *Amer.* ___

Mezze Bistro | *Amer.* 22

Sushi Thai Gdn. | *Japanese/Thai* 20

LOCATIONS

Special Features

Listings cover the best in each category and include names, locations and Food ratings. Multi-location restaurants' features may vary by branch.

ADDITIONS

(Properties added since the last edition of the book)

Alpamayo | **Lee**	-|
Brick House | **Housatonic**	-|
Fiori | **Great Barr**	-|
Hops/Vines | **Williamstown**	-|
Kemble Inn | **Lenox**	-|
Lucia's Latin Kitchen | **Pittsfield**	-|
Public Eat/Drink | **N Adams**	-|
Sushi House | **N Adams**	-|

BRUNCH

Bombay | **Lee**	22|
Cafe Adam | **Great Barr**	23|
Dakota Steak | **Pittsfield**	17|
☑ Wheatleigh | **Lenox**	25|
Xicohtencatl | **Great Barr**	21|

BUSINESS DINING

Allium | **Great Barr**	18|
Cranwell Resort | **Lenox**	21|
NEW Fiori | **Great Barr**	-|
La Terrazza | **Lenox**	23|
Spice Dragon | **Pittsfield**	22|

CATERING

Bizen | **Great Barr**	24|
Bombay | **Lee**	22|
Castle St. | **Great Barr**	20|
John Andrews | **S Egremont**	24|
Mezze Bistro | **Williamstown**	22|

CHILD-FRIENDLY

(Alternatives to the usual fast-food places; * children's menu available)

Aegean Breeze | **Great Barr**	19|
Baba Louie's | **Great Barr**	24|
Barrington Brew* | **Great Barr**	14|
Bistro Zinc* | **Lenox**	21|
Café Lucia | **Lenox**	23|
Castle St. | **Great Barr**	20|
Coyote Flaco* | **Williamstown**	23|

Dakota Steak* | **Pittsfield**	17|
Elizabeth's | **Pittsfield**	24|
Marketplace | **Sheffield**	-|
Morgan House | **Lee**	15|
Old Mill | **S Egremont**	24|
Once Upon | **Stockbridge**	21|
Red Lion Inn* | **Stockbridge**	18|
Rouge | **W Stockbridge**	22|
Rte. 7 Grill* | **Great Barr**	18|
Shiro | **Great Barr**	20|
Siam Sq. Thai | **Great Barr**	19|
Sullivan Station* | **Lee**	15|
Sushi Thai Gdn. | **Williamstown**	20|
Tratt. Il Vesuvio* | **Lenox**	19|
Xicohtencatl* | **Great Barr**	21|

DINING ALONE

(Other than hotels and places with counter service)

Alta | **Lenox**	21|
Baba Louie's | **multi.**	24|
NEW Brick House | **Housatonic**	-|
Cafe Adam | **Great Barr**	23|
Castle St. | **Great Barr**	20|
Coyote Flaco | **Williamstown**	23|
Fin | **Lenox**	23|
Gypsy Joynt | **Great Barr**	16|
NEW Hops/Vines | **Williamstown**	-|
Marketplace | **Sheffield**	-|
Mission Bar | **Pittsfield**	23|
Once Upon | **Stockbridge**	21|
Pho Saigon | **Lee**	22|
Rte. 7 Grill | **Great Barr**	18|
Sullivan Station | **Lee**	15|

ENTERTAINMENT

(Call for days and times of performances)

☑ Blantyre | piano | **Lenox**	27|
NEW Brick House | live music |	-|
Housatonic	

Castle St. | jazz/piano | **Great Barr** 20

Dream Away | live music | **Becket** 17

Gypsy Joynt | live music | 16
Great Barr

Mission Bar | folk/indie rock | 23
Pittsfield

🆕 Public Eat/Drink | games; ⏤
trivia | **N Adams**

Red Lion Inn | varies | 18
Stockbridge

FIREPLACES

Aegean Breeze | **Great Barr** 19

Barrington Brew | **Great Barr** 14

☒ Blantyre | **Lenox** 27

Cranwell Resort | **Lenox** 21

Dakota Steak | **Pittsfield** 17

Dream Away | **Becket** 17

John Andrews | **S Egremont** 24

La Terrazza | **Lenox** 23

Mezze Bistro | **Williamstown** 22

Mill on Floss | **New Ashford** 23

Morgan House | **Lee** 15

☒ Old Inn/Green | **New Marl** 27

Old Mill | **S Egremont** 24

Red Lion Inn | **Stockbridge** 18

Rte. 7 Grill | **Great Barr** 18

Stagecoach Tav. | **Sheffield** 17

Truc Orient | **W Stockbridge** 22

☒ Wheatleigh | **Lenox** 25

HISTORIC PLACES

(Year opened; * building)

1760 | Old Inn/Green* | 27
New Marl

1773 | Red Lion Inn* | **Stockbridge** 18

1797 | Old Mill* | **S Egremont** 24

1810 | Dream Away* | **Becket** 17

1817 | Morgan House* | **Lee** 15

1829 | Stagecoach Tav.* | **Sheffield** 17

1840 | Café Lucia* | **Lenox** 23

1840 | Spice Dragon* | **Pittsfield** 22

1841 | Chez Nous* | **Lee** 24

1893 | Sullivan Station* | **Lee** 15

1893 | Wheatleigh* | **Lenox** 25

1894 | Cranwell Resort* | **Lenox** 21

1896 | Kemble Inn* | **Lenox** ⏤

1900 | Tratt. Il Vesuvio* | **Lenox** 19

1924 | Brix Wine* | **Pittsfield** 23

HOTEL DINING

Blantyre
☒ Blantyre | **Lenox** 27

Gateways Inn
La Terrazza | **Lenox** 23

Morgan Hse.
Morgan House | **Lee** 15

Old Inn on the Green
☒ Old Inn/Green | **New Marl** 27

Quality Inn
Bombay | **Lee** 22

Race Brook Lodge
Stagecoach Tav. | **Sheffield** 17

Red Lion Inn
Red Lion Inn | **Stockbridge** 18

Wheatleigh
☒ Wheatleigh | **Lenox** 25

MEET FOR A DRINK

Alta | **Lenox** 21

Bistro Zinc | **Lenox** 21

🆕 Brick House | **Housatonic** ⏤

Brix Wine | **Pittsfield** 23

Brulées | **Pittsfield** 21

Castle St. | **Great Barr** 20

Chez Nous | **Lee** 24

Gramercy | **N Adams** 23

🆕 Hops/Vines | ⏤
Williamstown

Mission Bar | **Pittsfield** 23

Old Mill | **S Egremont** 24

Prime Italian | **Lenox** 21

Red Lion Inn | **Stockbridge** 18

Spice Dragon | **Pittsfield** 22

Stagecoach Tav. | **Sheffield** 17

MICROBREWERIES

Barrington Brew | **Great Barr** 14

OFFBEAT

Barrington Brew | **Great Barr**	14
Elizabeth's | **Pittsfield**	24
Gypsy Joynt | **Great Barr**	16
Lucia's Latin Kitchen | **Pittsfield**	–

OUTDOOR DINING

(G=garden; P=patio)

Aegean Breeze | P | **Great Barr**	19
Alta | P | **Lenox**	21
Barrington Brew | G | **Great Barr**	14
Cafe Adam | P | **Great Barr**	23
Café Lucia | G, P | **Lenox**	23
NEW Fiori | P | **Great Barr**	–
Firefly | P | **Lenox**	17
Frankie's Rist. | P | **Lenox**	18
Gramercy | P | **N Adams**	23
John Andrews | P | **S Egremont**	24
Jonathan's | P | **Lenox**	20
NEW Kemble Inn | P | **Lenox**	–
Z Old Inn/Green | P | **New Marl**	27
Red Lion Inn | P | **Stockbridge**	18
Rouge | P | **W Stockbridge**	22
Shiro | P | **Great Barr**	20
Sullivan Station | P | **Lee**	15
Tratt. Il Vesuvio | P | **Lenox**	19
Tratt. Rustica | P | **Pittsfield**	25
Xicohtencatl | P | **Great Barr**	21

PEOPLE-WATCHING

Allium | **Great Barr**	18
Alta | **Lenox**	21
Bistro Zinc | **Lenox**	21
NEW Fiori | **Great Barr**	–
Mezze Bistro | **Williamstown**	22

PRIVATE ROOMS

(Restaurants charge less at off times; call for capacity)

Bizen | **Great Barr**	24
Z Blantyre | **Lenox**	27
Castle St. | **Great Barr**	20
Cranwell Resort | **Lenox**	21
Dakota Steak | **Pittsfield**	17
Mill on Floss | **New Ashford**	23
Red Lion Inn | **Stockbridge**	18

Rouge | **W Stockbridge**	22
Stagecoach Tav. | **Sheffield**	17
Z Wheatleigh | **Lenox**	25

PRIX FIXE MENUS

(Call for prices and times)

Bizen | **Great Barr**	24
Z Blantyre | **Lenox**	27
NEW Fiori | **Great Barr**	–
NEW Kemble Inn | **Lenox**	–
Z Old Inn/Green | **New Marl**	27
Z Wheatleigh | **Lenox**	25

QUIET CONVERSATION

Z Blantyre | **Lenox**	27
Cranwell Resort | **Lenox**	21
Gramercy | **N Adams**	23
John Andrews | **S Egremont**	24
NEW Kemble Inn | **Lenox**	–
La Terrazza | **Lenox**	23
Mill on Floss | **New Ashford**	23
Stagecoach Tav. | **Sheffield**	17
Z Wheatleigh | **Lenox**	25

ROMANTIC PLACES

Z Blantyre | **Lenox**	27
Chez Nous | **Lee**	24
Cranwell Resort | **Lenox**	21
John Andrews | **S Egremont**	24
NEW Kemble Inn | **Lenox**	–
Mill on Floss | **New Ashford**	23
Z Old Inn/Green | **New Marl**	27
Tratt. Rustica | **Pittsfield**	25
Z Wheatleigh | **Lenox**	25

SENIOR APPEAL

Aegean Breeze | **Great Barr**	19
Cranwell Resort | **Lenox**	21
La Terrazza | **Lenox**	23
Morgan House | **Lee**	15
Red Lion Inn | **Stockbridge**	18

SINGLES SCENES

Alta | **Lenox**	21
NEW Brick House | **Housatonic**	–

Brix Wine | **Pittsfield** 23

Castle St. | **Great Barr** 20

Prime Italian | **Lenox** 21

Spice Dragon | **Pittsfield** 22

Sushi Thai Gdn. | **Williamstown** 20

SLEEPERS

(Good food, but little known)

Aroma B&G | **Great Barr** 22

Fin | **Lenox** 23

Gramercy | **N Adams** 23

Haven | **Lenox** 23

Hub | **N Adams** 23

La Terrazza | **Lenox** 23

Mill on Floss | **New Ashford** 23

Mission Bar | **Pittsfield** 23

Pho Saigon | **Lee** 22

Tratt. Rustica | **Pittsfield** 25

Truc Orient | **W Stockbridge** 22

Viva | **Glendale** 23

TAKEOUT

Aegean Breeze | **Great Barr** 19

Baba Louie's | **Great Barr** 24

Barrington Brew | **Great Barr** 14

Bistro Zinc | **Lenox** 21

Bizen | **Great Barr** 24

Café Lucia | **Lenox** 23

Castle St. | **Great Barr** 20

Dakota Steak | **Pittsfield** 17

John Andrews | **S Egremont** 24

Marketplace | **Sheffield** -

Morgan House | **Lee** 15

Once Upon | **Stockbridge** 21

Rouge | **W Stockbridge** 22

Shiro | **Great Barr** 20

Siam Sq. Thai | **Great Barr** 19

Stagecoach Tav. | **Sheffield** 17

NEW Sushi House | **N Adams** -

Sushi Thai Gdn. | **Williamstown** 20

Truc Orient | **W Stockbridge** 22

TEEN APPEAL

Baba Louie's | **multi.** 24

Barrington Brew | **Great Barr** 14

Coyote Flaco | **Williamstown** 23

Dakota Steak | **Pittsfield** 17

TRENDY

Allium | **Great Barr** 18

Bistro Zinc | **Lenox** 21

Bizen | **Great Barr** 24

Brix Wine | **Pittsfield** 23

Cafe Adam | **Great Barr** 23

Castle St. | **Great Barr** 20

Fin | **Lenox** 23

NEW Fiori | **Great Barr** -

NEW Hops/Vines | **Williamstown** -

John Andrews | **S Egremont** 24

Mission Bar | **Pittsfield** 23

Prime Italian | **Lenox** 21

NEW Public Eat/Drink | **N Adams** -

Rouge | **W Stockbridge** 22

Spice Dragon | **Pittsfield** 22

Xicohtencatl | **Great Barr** 21

VIEWS

Bombay | **Lee** 22

Cranwell Resort | **Lenox** 21

NEW Kemble Inn | **Lenox** -

Z Wheatleigh | **Lenox** 25

WINNING WINE LISTS

Alta | **Lenox** 21

Brix Wine | **Pittsfield** 23

Cafe Adam | **Great Barr** 23

Castle St. | **Great Barr** 20

Chez Nous | **Lee** 24

Gramercy | **N Adams** 23

John Andrews | **S Egremont** 24

Jonathan's | **Lenox** 20

La Terrazza | **Lenox** 23

Mezze Bistro | **Williamstown** 22

Mission Bar | **Pittsfield** 23

Z Old Inn/Green | **New Marl** 27

THE BERKSHIRES

SPECIAL FEATURES

Wine Vintage Chart

This chart is based on a 30-point scale. The ratings (by U. of South Carolina law professor **Howard Stravitz**) reflect vintage quality and the wine's readiness to drink. A dash means the wine is past its peak or too young to rate. Loire ratings are for dry whites.

Whites	95	96	97	98	99	00	01	02	03	04	05	06	07	08	09	10
France:																
Alsace	24	23	23	25	23	25	26	22	21	22	23	21	26	26	23	26
Burgundy	27	26	22	21	24	24	23	27	23	26	26	25	26	25	25	-
Loire Valley	-	-	-	-	-	-	-	25	20	22	27	23	24	24	24	25
Champagne	26	27	24	25	25	25	21	26	21	-	-	-	-	-	-	-
Sauternes	21	23	25	23	24	24	29	24	26	21	26	25	27	24	27	-
California:																
Chardonnay	-	-	-	-	22	21	24	25	22	26	29	24	27	23	27	-
Sauvignon Blanc	-	-	-	-	-	-	-	-	-	25	24	27	25	24	25	-
Austria:																
Grüner V./Riesl.	22	-	25	22	26	22	23	25	25	24	23	26	25	24	25	-
Germany:	22	26	22	25	24	-	29	25	26	27	28	26	26	26	26	-

Reds	95	96	97	98	99	00	01	02	03	04	05	06	07	08	09	
France:																
Bordeaux	25	25	24	25	24	29	26	24	26	25	28	24	24	25	27	-
Burgundy	26	27	25	24	27	22	23	25	25	23	28	24	24	25	27	-
Rhône	26	22	23	27	26	27	26	-	26	25	27	25	26	23	27	-
Beaujolais	-	-	-	-	-	-	-	-	-	-	27	25	24	23	28	25
California:																
Cab./Merlot	27	24	28	23	25	-	27	26	25	24	26	24	27	26	25	-
Pinot Noir	-	-	-	-	-	-	26	25	24	25	26	24	27	24	26	-
Zinfandel	-	-	-	-	-	-	25	24	26	24	23	21	26	23	25	-
Oregon:																
Pinot Noir	-	-	-	-	-	-	-	26	24	25	24	25	24	27	24	-
Italy:																
Tuscany	25	24	29	24	27	24	27	-	24	27	25	26	25	24	-	-
Piedmont	21	27	26	25	26	28	27	-	24	27	26	26	27	26	-	-
Spain:																
Rioja	26	24	25	22	25	24	28	-	23	27	26	24	24	25	26	-
Ribera del Duero/Priorat	25	26	24	25	25	24	27	-	24	27	26	24	25	27	-	-
Australia:																
Shiraz/Cab.	23	25	24	26	24	24	26	26	25	25	26	21	23	26	24	-
Chile:	-	-	-	-	24	22	25	23	24	24	27	25	24	26	24	-
Argentina:																
Malbec	-	-	-	-	-	-	-	-	-	25	26	27	26	26	25	-

Vote at zagat.com

ZAGAT
Westchester
Hudson Valley Map

Most Popular Restaurants

Map coordinates follow each name. Places in the Westchester area lie in sections A-H (see adjacent map); those in the Hudson Valley lie in sections I-P

1. X20 Xaviars (G-2)
2. Blue Hill/Stone Barns (D-4)
3. Tarry Lodge (F-6)
4. Xaviars/Piermont (E-3)
5. Harvest/Hudson (F-3)
6. Red Hat on River (E-3)
7. Rest. X/Bully Boy (D-3)
8. Crabtree's Kittle Hse. (C-5)
9. La Panetière (F-6)
10. Buffet de la Gare (F-3)
11. Cookery (F-3)
12. Iron Horse Grill (D-4)
13. Freelance Cafe (E-3)
14. BLT Steak (E-4)
15. Haiku† (G-4)
16. Lefteris Gyro† (C-5, E-4)
17. Cheesecake Factory (D-2, E-5)
18. Lusardi's (G-5)
19. Eastchester Fish (F-4)
20. La Crémaillère (D-6)
21. City Limits† (E-4)
22. Equus (E-4)
23. American Bounty (N-4)
24. Moderne Barn (D-5)
25. Mulino's (E-5)
26. Ocean Hse. (C-3)
27. Sonora (F-6)
28. Terrapin (L-5)
29. Gigi Tratt. (L-5)
30. Aroma Osteria (O-5)
31. An American Bistro (F-4)
32. Serevan (M-7)
33. Sushi Mike's (E-3)
34. Rosie's Bistro (G-4)
35. 121 Rest. (A-7)
36. Wasabi/Grill* (D-2, D-3)
37. Escoffier (N-4)
38. Frank Pepe Pizzeria† (F-4)
39. Le Château (B-7)
40. Le Provençal* (F-5)
41. Ruth's Chris (E-4)
42. Caterina de Medici (N-4)
43. Hudson Hse. Nyack (D-3)
44. Il Cenàcolo (P-4)
45. Artist's Palate (N-4)
46. Aberdeen (E-5)
47. Zephs' (B-3)
48. Bedford Post/Farm (C-6)
49. Le Petit Bistro (M-4)
50. Il Barilotto (P-5)

---

* Indicates tie with above   † Indicates multiple branches